COLLECTED PLAYS
VOLUME ONE

John Mortimer

COLLECTED PLAYS
VOLUME ONE

A VOYAGE ROUND MY FATHER

COLLABORATORS

THE DOCK BRIEF

WHAT SHALL WE TELL CAROLINE?

LUNCH HOUR

OBERON BOOKS
LONDON

Contents

A VOYAGE ROUND MY FATHER

.

Characters

FATHER
SON
MOTHER
IRIS
RINGER LEAN
HEADMASTER
HAM
JAPHET
REIGATE
MISS COX
MISS BAKER
MR BOUSTEAD
MR THONG
JUDGE
DORIS
SPARKS
DIRECTOR
FIRST ATS
SECOND ATS
ELIZABETH
GEORGE
MISS FERGUSON
MR MORROW
WITNESS
GIRL
FIRST BOY
SECOND BOY
DOCTOR

A Voyage Round My Father was first presented at Greenwich Theatre in 1970. This version was presented by Michael Codron Ltd. on 4 August 1971 at the Haymarket Theatre, London, with the following cast:

FATHER, Alec Guinness

SON, Jeremy Brett

MOTHER, Leueen MacGrath

ELIZABETH, Nicola Pagett

SON, as a boy, Jason Kemp

HEADMASTER/GEORGE, Jack May

HAM/BOUSTEAD/
SPARKS/MR MORROW, Mark Kingston

MATRON/MISS COX/
DORIS/SOCIAL WORKER, Phyllida Law

MRS REIGATE/MISS BAKER/
FIRST ATS/WITNESS, Rhoda Lewis

RINGER/THONG/DIRECTOR, Andrew Sachs

JAPHET/JUDGE/
CAMERAMAN/ DOCTOR, Richard Fraser

SECOND ATS, Tilly Tremayne

REIGATE, Jeremy Burring

IRIS, Melanie Wallace

CHILDREN,
Jason Kemp, Jeremy Burring, Melanie Wallace

USHERS/
FILM TECHNICIANS, Richard Manuel, Keith Watson

Director, Ronald Eyre

Set design, Voytek

ACT ONE

There is a trellis up centre wider at the top than the base, sweeping from the floor until it is out of sight in the flies; a bench, a ladder and a table with three chairs. Otherwise the stage is bare.

As the curtain rises, the SON (grown up) is sitting at the table reading his diary. The FATHER enters.

FATHER: Roses – not much of a show of roses.

SON: (*Grown up.*) Not bad.

FATHER: Onions – hardly a bumper crop would you say?

SON: (*Grown up.*) I suppose not.

> (*The FATHER, a man in his sixties, wearing a darned tweed suit, and carrying a clouded malacca walking-stick is, with blind eyes, inspecting his garden.*)

FATHER: Earwigs at the dahlias. You remember, when you were a boy, you remember our great slaughter of earwigs?

SON: I remember.

FATHER: You see the dahlias?

SON: Yes.

FATHER: Describe them for me. Paint me the picture

SON: Well, they're red – and yellow. And blowsy…

FATHER: (*Puzzled.*) Blowsy?

SON: They look sort of middle-aged – over-ripe.

FATHER: Earwig traps in place, are they?

SON: Yes. They're in place.

FATHER: When you were a boy, we often bagged a hundred earwigs in a single foray! Do you remember?

SON: I remember.

> (*The SON moves away from the FATHER and speaks to the audience.*)
> My father wasn't always blind. The three of us lived in a small house surrounded, as if for protection, by an enormous garden…
> (*The MOTHER enters.*)

FATHER: Where's the boy got to?

MOTHER: Disappeared apparently.

FATHER: He's running wild.

SON: He was driven to the station, where he caught a train to London and the Law Courts, to his work as a barrister in a great hearse-like motor which he would no more have thought of replacing every year than he would have accepted a different kind of suit or a new gardening hat. As soon as possible he returned to the safety of the dahlias, and the ritual of the evening earwig hunt. Visitors were rare and, if spotted, my father would move deeper into the foliage until the danger was past. Those were the days when my father could see – before I went away to school. When it was always a hot afternoon and a girl called Iris taught me to whistle.

(*The SON, as a boy, and a small girl called IRIS run on.*)

IRIS: Stick out your lips. Stick them out far. Go on. Farther. Much farther. Now blow. Not too hard. Blow gently. Gently. Don't laugh. Take it serious. Blow!

(*There is the sound of a whistle.*)

SON: What was that?

IRIS: What do you mean – what was that?

SON: Someone whistled.

IRIS: It was you.

SON: Me?

IRIS: It was you whistling!

SON: I can do it! I know how to do it!

IRIS: Well, you've learnt something...

FATHER: The boy's running wild again.

MOTHER: Oh, I don't think so.

FATHER: Oh, yes, he is. And a good thing, too. When I was a boy in Africa, they sent me off – all by myself – to a small hotel up country to run wild for three months. I took my birthday cake with me and kept it under my bed. I well remember – (*He laughs.*) – when my birthday came round I took the cake out, sat on my bed, and ate it. That was my celebration!

MOTHER: He'll soon be going away to school...

FATHER: What did you say?

MOTHER: He'll be going away to school. We can't expect him to stay here – for ever...

(*The FATHER gets a step-ladder and starts to walk up it, singing to himself.*)

FATHER: (*Singing.*) 'She was as bee-eautiful as a butterfly
And as proud as a queen
Was pretty little Polly Perkins of Paddington Green.
I'm a broken-hearted milkman,
In grief I'm arrayed,
Through the keeping of the company
Of a young servant maid.'

SON: (*Grown up.*) One day he bought a step-ladder for pruning the apple trees. He hit his head on the branch of a tree and the retinas left the balls of his eyes.
(*Sudden, total black-out in which we hear the SON's voice.*)
That's the way I looked to my father from childhood upwards. That's how my wife and his grandchildren looked. My father was blind but we never mentioned it.
(*The lights fade up slowly to reveal the FATHER and MOTHER sitting round a breakfast table. The FATHER is clearly totally blind, the MOTHER is helping him cut up his toast.*)
(*Grown up.*) He had a great disinclination to mention anything unpleasant. What was that? Courage, cowardice, indifference or caring too completely? Why didn't he blaspheme, beat his head against the pitch black sitting-room walls? Why didn't he curse God? He had a great capacity for rage – but never at the universe.
(*The SON (grown up) goes.*
The family eat in silence until the FATHER suddenly bursts out.)

FATHER: My egg! It's bloody runny! It's in a nauseating condition! What do you want to do? Choke me to death? (*Shouts.*) Have you all gone *mad?* Am I totally surrounded by *cretins?*
(*Another silence while they go on eating.*)
(*Singing.*) 'In six months she married,
That hard-hearted girl,
But it wasn't to a Viscount,
It wasn't to an Earl
It wasn't to a Baronite,

But a shade or two WUS!
'Twas to the bow-legged conductor
Of a twopenny bus!'

MOTHER: Marmalade?

FATHER: Thank you.

(*Silence.*)

The evolution of the horse was certainly a most tortuous process. None of your six-day nonsense! Six days' labour wouldn't evolve one primitive earthworm. Is the boy still here?

MOTHER: Please, dear. Don't be tactless.

FATHER: I thought he'd gone away to school.

MOTHER: *Pas devant le garçon.*

FATHER: What?

MOTHER: He doesn't like it mentioned.

FATHER: Well, either he's going away or he's not. I'm entitled to know. If he's here this evening he can help me out with the earwigs.

MOTHER: Mr Lean's going to drive him. *A trois heures et demi.*

FATHER: Half past three, eh?

MOTHER: Yes, dear. Mr Lean's going to drive him.

FATHER: (*To SON.*) You'll learn to construct an equilateral triangle and the Latin word for parsley. Totally useless information...

MOTHER: We really ought not to discourage the boy. (*To SON.*) You'll find the French very useful.

FATHER: What on earth for?

MOTHER: Going to France.

FATHER: What's he want to go to France for? There's plenty to do in the garden. The coffee's frozen! (*He drinks.*) It's like arctic mud!

MOTHER: Shall I make you some fresh?

FATHER: No. I like it. All education's perfectly useless. But it fills in the *time?* The boy can't sit around here all day until he gets old enough for marriage. He can't sit around – doing the crossword.

MOTHER: (*Laughing.*) Married! Plenty of time to think of that when he's learned to keep his bedroom tidy. The headmaster seemed rather charming.

FATHER: No-one ever got a word of sense out of a schoolmaster! If they *knew* anything they'd be out doing it. (*To the SON.*) That'll be your misfortune for the next few years. To be constantly rubbing up against second-rate minds.

MOTHER: At the start of each term apparently the new boys are given a little speech of welcome.

FATHER: Ignore that! Particularly if they offer you advice on the subject of life. At a pinch you may take their word on equilateral hexagons – but remember! Life's a closed book to schoolmasters.

MOTHER: We'll label your trunk this afternoon.

FATHER: You won't expect any advice from me, I hope? All advice's perfectly useless...

MOTHER: I've still got to mark your hockey stick.

FATHER: You're alone in the world, remember. No-one can tell you what to do about it.

(*The SON, as a boy, starts to cry.*)

What's the matter with the boy?

MOTHER: (*Apparently incredulous.*) He's not crying!

FATHER: (*Coming out with some advice at last.*) Say the word 'rats'. No-one can cry when they're saying the word 'rats'. It has to do with the muscles of the face.

SON: (*Trying to stop himself crying.*) Rats.

(*The FATHER, MOTHER and SON (as a boy) go.*)

(*Grown up.*) Mr Ringer Lean was an ex-jockey who drove my father's antique Morris Oxford. He treated it as though it were a nervous stallion.

(*RINGER LEAN enters, carrying a school trunk on his shoulder.*)

RINGER: Car's gone lame. Going don't suit her. Shit scared are you? Being sent away...

(*The SON (as a boy) comes on to the stage. He is wearing school uniform, carrying a suitcase and looking extremely depressed.*)

SON: (*Grown up.*) I was to be prepared for life. Complete with football boots, gym shoes, house shoes, shirts grey, shirts white, Bulldog Drummond, mint humbugs, boxing gloves, sponge bags, and my seating plans for all the London theatres.

(*The SON (as a boy) puts down the trunk and rests on it.*)

RINGER: They sent me away when I was your age. Newmarket Heath. Bound as a stable lad. Bloody terrified I was, at your age...

SON: Were you?

RINGER: Yes. They shouldn't send you away. You're going to develop too tall for a jockey.

SON: I don't think they want me to be a jockey...

RINGER: Broke a few bones, I did, when they sent me away. Ribs fractured. Collar-bone smashed. Pelvis pounded to pieces. Bad mounts. Bad Governors. Hey! When a Governor gets after you, you know what?...

SON: What?

RINGER: Get up the hay loft, and pull the ladder up after you. Because they can't climb. Oh, yes. Recall that. Governors can't climb. Often I've hid up the hay loft one, two, three hours sometimes. Till the Governor got a winner, and change of heart. I've slept up there often. All right if the rats don't nip you.

SON: Thanks.

RINGER: Only bit of advice I got to give you – never avoid a mount. There was this lad at our stable – he avoided a half-broken two-year-old. Nasty tempered one with a duff eye. Well, this lad was shit scared to ride it, you know what he did?

SON: No...

RINGER: Nobbled himself with a blunt razor blade. Severed a tendon and then gangrene. Poor lad had to kiss his leg good-bye.

SON: It's not really a stable...

RINGER: So never try and nobble yourself. That's my advice. Or sterilize the blade. Hold it in a flame. Kills the germs on it!

SON: It's more a school than a stable...

RINGER: Oh well, wherever there's lads, I expect it's much the same...

SON: (*Grown up.*) My father had warned me – but this was far worse than I'd expected.
(*The lights change.*
The staff and HEADMASTER enter.)
HEADMASTER: Now, new boys. Stand up now. Let me look at you. Some day, some long distant day, you will be one-yearers, and then two-yearers, and then three-yearers. You will go away, and you will write letters, and I shall try hard to remember you. Then you'll be old boys. Old Cliffhangers. O.C.'s you shall become, and the fruit of your loins shall attend the School by the Water. Leave the room the boy who laughed. The fruit of your loins shall return and stand here, even as you stand here. And we shall teach them. We shall give them sound advice. So that hungry generations of boys shall learn not to eat peas with their knives, or butter their hair, or clean their finger-nails with bus tickets. You shall be taught to wash, to bowl straight and wipe your dirty noses. When you are in the sixth form you shall see something of golf. You will look on the staff as your friends. At all times you will call us by nicknames. I am Noah. My wife is Mrs Noah. You are the animals. My son Lance is Shem. Mr Pearce and Mr Box are Ham and Japhet. Matey is Matey. Mr Bingo Ollard is Mr Bingo Ollard. These mysteries have I expounded to you, oh litter of runts.
(*The lights change as the HEADMASTER, MATEY, and JAPHET leave. Two boys move the bench into position. The SON (as a boy) brings on a blackboard. HAM starts drawing a right-angled triangle on it.*)
SON: (*Grown up, to the audience.*) The masters who taught us still suffered from shell shock and battle fatigue. Some had shrapnel lodged in their bodies and the classroom would turn, only too easily, into another Paschendale.
(*The SON (as a boy) and another boy of his own age, named REIGATE, sit on the bench in front of HAM's blackboard, watching him complete his drawing of Pythagoras' theorem.*)
HAM: The square on the longest side of a right-angled bloody triangle is – is what, boy?

SON: (*Standing up.*) I don't know…

HAM: (*Suddenly yelling.*) Straff you, boy. Bomb and howitzer and straff the living daylights out of you. God bomb you to hell! (*He throws books at the SON.*) Get your tin hat on. It's coming over now! It's equal to the square… What square, you unfortunate cretin? On the other two sides. Right-angled bloody triangle! Straff you, boy! Bomb and howitzer you! God bomb you to hell! All right. All right. War's over… Armistice day. Demob. I suppose you want compensation?

(*The boys pick up the books.*)

SON: If you like, sir.

HAM: How many books did I throw?

SON: Six, sir. Not counting the duster.

HAM: Threepence a book and say a penny the duster. Is that fair?

SON: I'd say so, sir.

HAM: Is that one-and-six?

SON: I think it's one and sevenpence, sir.

(*Grown up.*) From Ham I learnt the healing power of money…

(*FATHER enters as HAM and the boys go, HAM taking the blackboard.*)

FATHER: I am writing to you from outside the President's Court at the start of a Divorce Case. Like all divorce cases, this one is concerned with sex, which you will find to be a subject filled with comic relief. Pears Dupray, K.C., who is agin me in this case is not a foeman worthy of my steel. He will no doubt fumble his cross-examination and may even fail to prove my adultery – although God knows – I have had inclination and opportunity to spare.

(*JAPHET, strumming a ukelele, appears up stage.*)

JAPHET: 'Hallelujah I'm a bum
Hallelujah Bum again
Hallelujah give us a hand out…
To revive us again…'

FATHER: Like you, I shall today be rubbing up against a second-rate mind…

SON: (*Grown up.*) Japhet, the second master, did his
    unsuccessful best to impart polish.

JAPHET: (*Sings.*) 'Hallelujah – I'm a bum…'
    Do you know what a bum is?

SON: Yes, sir.

JAPHET: Good.
    'Hallelujah. Bum again –
    Hallelujah, give us a hand out…'
    Now look. Nobody is going to laugh if you just use two
    simple chords. You see. Like this – and this. That's all.
    Just two simple chords. Always. For every tune. You take
    my tip, and look as if you know what you're doing.
    Nobody's going to laugh. Oh, by the way, you don't tie
    that tie of yours properly. Remind me to teach you to tie
    your tie, will you? Yes, you take my advice and sing in
    the back of your nose – so it sounds as if you've crossed
    the States by railroad. (*He starts to sing through his nose to
    the ukelele.*)
    'Oh, why don't you work
    Like other men do?
    How the heck can I work
    If there's no work to do…?
    Hallelujah. I'm a bum!'
    You see. Just two simple chords, and don't get ambitious.

SON: No, I won't, sir.

JAPHET: And do remember about that tie. It's really very
    easy, you know. Right over left, over left over right, over
    all, up the back and down the front, and that way you get
    the big knot. The way *He* wears it.

SON: He?

JAPHET: The King, of course.

SON: Oh, yes, sir – of course.

JAPHET: The King and I – we've got a lot in common.

SON: Yes, sir.

JAPHET: Same tie – same trouble.

SON: What trouble's that, sir?

JAPHET: Woman trouble. Deep, deep trouble. Just like the
    jolly old King…

(*JAPHET exits with his ukelele. The SON takes a letter out of his pocket and reads it.*)

SON: (*Grown up.*) I knew what he was talking about. He was talking about Lydia, a pale little red-headed girl who smelt vaguely of moth balls and who made our beds. The King and Japhet were both tussling with the problems from which my father made his living.

FATHER: You will be pleased to hear that I won Jimpson v. Jimpson, the wife being found guilty of infidelity in the front of a Daimler parked in Hampstead Garden Suburb. A vital part of the evidence consisted of footprints on the dashboard...

(*REIGATE comes in, bored, his hands in his pockets, and wanders near the SON. The SON, reading the letter, does not notice him.*)

The co-respondent was condemned in costs. My final speech lasted two hours and I made several jokes. At home we have been pricking out Korean chrysanthemums and making marmalade. Unusually large plague of earwigs this summer. Ever your loving father...

REIGATE: (*To the SON.*) Do you get many letters from home?

(*The FATHER and MOTHER get up and the MOTHER leads the FATHER out.*

The SON puts the letter hurriedly back in the envelope.)

SON: Hullo, Reigate. Once a week, I expect.

REIGATE: Keep the envelopes.

SON: For the stamps?

REIGATE: To put the fish in, on Sunday nights. The fish is disgusting. Put it in envelopes and post it down the bogs.

SON: Why in envelopes?

REIGATE: Well, you just can't put bits of fish, not straight in your pocket. (*He pauses.*) Is your mother slim?

SON: Fairly slim.

(*Pause.*)

REIGATE: Is your father good at golf?

SON: Pretty good.

REIGATE: My mother's slim as a bluebell.

SON: Well, mine's quite slim too, really. She goes to cocktail parties.

REIGATE: As slim as a bluebell! With yellow eyes.

SON: Yellow?

REIGATE: Like a panther.

SON: Oh, I see.

REIGATE: Very small feet. High heels, of course. Does your mother wear high heels?

SON: Whenever she goes to cocktail parties. She wears them then.

REIGATE: My mother wears high heels. *Even at breakfast.* Of course she's slim as a bluebell...

SON: (*Grown up.*) But November the eleventh brought embarrassing revelations. We were able to see those from whose loins, as Noah would say, we had actually sprung. (*The SON (as a boy) and REIGATE part and move to opposite sides of the stage. On his side, the SON is met by the MOTHER and the FATHER, come down for the Armistice Day service. REIGATE is met by his mother, a short, dumpy woman in a hat. HAM, JAPHET, and the MATRON enter. The MATRON has a tray of poppies, the other grown-ups have umbrellas. Finally the HEADMASTER enters.*)

HEADMASTER: Let us pray...

(*The parents and the boys form a congregation. MRS REIGATE closes her eyes in an attitude of devotion. The FATHER blows his nose loudly. REIGATE stares across at him. The SON (as a boy) looks at his FATHER in an agony of embarrassment, and then continues a close, and somewhat surprised study of REIGATE's mother.*)

Oh Lord, inasmuch as we are paraded now on Lower School Field on this, the Armistice Day, November the eleventh, nineteen hundred and thirty-six, help us to remember those O.C.'s who fell upon alien soil in the late Great Match. Grant us their spirit, we beseech Thee, that we may go 'over the top' to our Common Entrance and our Football Fixtures, armed with the 'cold steel' of Thy Holy Word. Give us, if Thy will be done, the Great Opportunity to shed our Blood for our Country and our

Beloved School, and fill us with that feeling of Sportsmanship which led our fathers to fix bayonets and play until the last whistle blew. We will now sing the concluding hymn on your hymn sheets: 'God of our Fathers, known of old.'

(*REIGATE's mother is singing in a rich patriotic contralto. The FATHER is singing, and his mouth seems to be moving in a different time from the rest the congregation. Gradually what he is singing becomes painfully clear over and above the reverberation of the hymn.*)

FATHER: (*Singing.*) '...bee-eautiful as a butterfly

And as proud as a queen

Was pretty little Polly Perkins

Of Paddington Green.'

(*Both the FATHER's song and the hymn come to an end at the same time.*)

ALL: Amen.

(*The HEADMASTER is saying good-bye, shaking parents' hands.*)

HEADMASTER: How do you do, Mrs Reigate? How very nice to see you again.

(*The HEADMASTER and the parents go.*)

SON: (*Grown up.*) Our parents, it was obvious, needed a quick coating of romance.

(*As a boy.*) She didn't look much like a panther.

REIGATE: Who?

SON: And your mother wasn't exactly a bluebell, either.

REIGATE: My mother? You've never seen my mother.

SON: Of course I have.

REIGATE: Oh, don't be so simple. That good, honest woman isn't my *real* mother.

SON: (*Puzzled.*) Noah called her 'Mrs Reigate'. I heard him distinctly.

REIGATE: Noah only knows what's good for him to know. That was no more my mother than you are.

SON: Who was she then?

REIGATE: Just the dear, good, old soul who promised to look after me.

SON: When?

REIGATE: When they smuggled me out of Russia, after the revolution. They smuggled me out in a wickerwork trunk. I was ten days and nights on the rack in the carriage of the Siberian Railway. Then we got to Paris…

SON: I thought Siberia…

REIGATE: They tried to shoot us in Paris. Me and my brother. But we got away, across the frozen river.

SON: I understood Siberia was in the other direction.

REIGATE: And escaped to England. This honest chemist and wife took care us. Swear you won't tell anyone?

SON: All right.

REIGATE: By the blood of my father?

SON: If you like. I just heard from my parents, actually. Something pretty sensational.

REIGATE: Oh, yes?

SON: I think they're probably – getting divorced.

REIGATE: (*Interested.*) Honestly?

SON: Honestly.

REIGATE: Why? Are they unfaithful?

SON: Oh, always. And I told you. My mother goes to cocktail parties…

REIGATE: (*Admiringly.*) You'll be having a broken home, then?

SON: (*Casually.*) Oh, yes. I expect I will…

(*The two boys go together.*)

(*Grown up, to the audience.*) But when I got home, nothing had changed. My home remained imperturbably intact. And, in the bracken on the common, Iris had built me a house.

(*The lights come up on another part of the stage where IRIS is kneeling, building a house under the upturned garden table.*)

IRIS: What do you learn at school?

SON: We learn Latin.

IRIS: What else?

SON: Greek.

IRIS: Say, 'Good morning, what a very nice morning,' in Latin.

SON: I don't know how.

IRIS: All right. In Greek…

SON: I can't.

IRIS: Why not?

SON: They're not those sort of languages.

IRIS: What's the point of them then?

SON: They train – the mind…

IRIS: How's your mum and dad?

SON: Quarrelling.

IRIS: I never see them quarrel.

SON: Oh, it's life… They come back from parties, and they quarrel. Don't ask me to explain.

IRIS: I didn't.

SON: Well – don't.

IRIS: I shan't.

SON: It's just possible, they're not my parents. A very honest couple, but not…

IRIS: Of course they're your parents. Don't be ignorant.

SON: I'm not ignorant.

IRIS: What do you know, then?

SON: I know the second person plural future passive of rogo.

IRIS: What is it?

SON: Rogobamini.

IRIS: What's that mean?

SON: It doesn't mean anything. It's just the future passive of rogo – that's all it is…

IRIS: (*After a pause; pointing to the house.*) Why don't we get in now?

SON: (*Shrugs his shoulders.*) What for?

IRIS: To be Mothers and Fathers.

SON: I think I might find that a bit painful, well, what with the situation at home. Anyway, I haven't got time.

IRIS: Haven't you?

SON: Someone's coming over to see me today.

IRIS: Who's that?

SON: His name's Reigate, actually.

IRIS: Don't you want to be Mothers and Fathers… Tell you what. I'll let you see… (*She lifts up her skirt.*)

SON: No, thank you. Reigate's coming to stay...
  (*IRIS goes. REIGATE comes in.*)
REIGATE: You start then.
SON: Bill...
REIGATE: Who is it...
SON: It's me, Bill. It's Harry.
  (*MOTHER enters.*)
REIGATE: Harry!
MOTHER: Where do you want us to sit?
SON: In the stalls.
REIGATE: What comes next?
SON: I can't see you, old fellow.
REIGATE: I can't see you, old fellow. Then what?
SON: You were supposed to learn your lines!
  (*FATHER enters.*)
MOTHER: There now, darling. Did you have a good rest?
FATHER: What's good about a rest. 'My best of rest is
  sleep, and that thou oft provok'st, yet grossly fearest thy
  death which is no more.'
MOTHER: There's going to be a little surprise.
REIGATE: (*To the SON; suspiciously.*) Can't see much sign of
  divorce in this family.
SON: They're putting on a show – for the visitor.
FATHER: (*Pleased.*) Is something happening?
MOTHER: It's the boy talking to Reigate.
FATHER: To whom?
MOTHER: To Reigate – his friend.
FATHER: (*Incredulously.*) The boy has a friend? Welcome,
  Reigate! What's Reigate like, eh? Paint me the picture.
MOTHER: Well, he's quite small, and...
SON: And he's really Russian...
FATHER: (*Impressed.*) Russian, eh? Well, that's something
  of an achievement. (*He pauses.*) When I was at school
  I never minded the lessons. I just resented having to
  work so terribly hard at playing. They don't roast you at
  school nowadays, I suppose? I can't think what I'm
  paying all that money for if they don't roast you from
  time to time...

MOTHER: Do you like school, Reigate?

REIGATE: It's all right. The Headmaster makes us call him Noah.

SON: And his son is Shem.

REIGATE: And we have to call Mr Box and Mr Pearce Ham and Japhet. And we're the animals.

SON: And Mr Bingo Ollard is Mr Bingo Ollard.

FATHER: (*Gloomily.*) Didn't I warn you? Second-rate minds.

REIGATE: Now we're going to do something to keep you from thinking of your great unhappiness.

MOTHER: Our unhappiness...

FATHER: What did he say?

MOTHER: They're going to put on an entertainment.

FATHER: Oh, I like an entertainment. When's it to be?

SON: This afternoon.

MOTHER: Well, you'd better hurry up, because Mr Lean's coming to drive you back to school at six. (*She giggles gently.*) Whatever will they think of...
(*The SON and REIGATE exit.*)

FATHER: What're you laughing at?

MOTHER: At Reigate?

FATHER: Who on earth's Reigate?

MOTHER: I told you, dear. The boy's friend.

FATHER: Is this Reigate, then, something of a wit?
(*The SON and REIGATE enter with a hamper.*)

MOTHER: He does come out with some killing suggestions.

REIGATE: (*Dignified.*) We're going to do a play.

FATHER: What is it? Something out of the *Boys' Own?*

SON: I wrote it.

FATHER: You what?

MOTHER: I'm sure Reigate helped. Didn't you, Reigate?

SON: He didn't help.

MOTHER: What are you supposed to be. Two little clowns?

REIGATE: Actually, we're two subalterns. Killed on the Somme, actually.
(*They take coats, caps and a belt from the hamper and put them on.*)

FATHER: They'll soon be giving us war again. When it comes, avoid the temptation to do anything heroic. What's going on? Make it vivid.

(*The boys exit and return with barbed wire which they set up.*)

MOTHER: They're bringing in some of your barbed wire.

FATHER: My what?

MOTHER: Your barbed wire.

FATHER: Oh, put it back again, won't you. We don't want the cows everywhere.

MOTHER: Reigate's got your greatcoat, and the Boy's wearing your old Sam Browne.

FATHER: How killing!

SON: Lights out! Curtain up!

MOTHER: Well, we can see Reigate's artistic! He's giving a very lively performance.

REIGATE: Actually we're ghosts.

FATHER: Ghosts, eh? What's happening now?

SON: We're meeting after the bombardment.

MOTHER: It's after the bombardment.

FATHER: How very killing!

SON: Bill...

REIGATE: Who is it...?

SON: It's me, Bill. It's Harry.

REIGATE: Harry! I can't see you, old fellow. It's this damn gas, everywhere. Take my hand.

SON: Where are you?

REIGATE: Out here – by the wire. Listen.

SON: What?

REIGATE: They've stopped straffing. I say, if ever we get back to the old country –

SON: What?

REIGATE: – I want you to marry Helen.

SON: You said you'd never let Helen marry a chap who'd funked the top board at Roehampton...

REIGATE: Never mind what I said, Harry. I saw you today on the north redoubt; you were in there, batting for England! You shall have my little sister, boy. My hand on it.

SON: I can't feel your hand, Bill.

REIGATE: I can't see you, Harry.

SON: I'm cold...

REIGATE: I'm afraid we'll never see England again.

SON: What's the matter with us, Bill?

REIGATE: (*Beginning to laugh.*) We're dead, old fellow. Can't you understand? We're both of us – dead!

FATHER: Dead! How killing!

(*The play over the boys bow to the MOTHER and FATHER.*)

MOTHER: That was splendid! Now we must clear away all this barbed wire, but mind your hands.

(*The boys exit with the hamper and costumes, and the barbed wire.*)

FATHER: (*Serious.*) Dead. You know I didn't want to be dead. I never wanted that. When your mother and I got married – at Saffron Walden, they were just about to pack me off to France. Bands. Troopships. Flowers thrown at you...and dead in a fortnight. I didn't want to have anything to do with it. And then, the day before I was due to sail my Old Major drew me aside and said, 'You're just got married, old fellow. No particular sense in being dead!' He'd found me a post in the Inland Waterways! That's my advice to you, if they look like giving us war. Get yourself a job in the Inland Waterways...

(*FATHER exits. REIGATE and the SON enter.*)

REIGATE: Your parents seem to be getting on quite well.

SON: They pretend – for me.

REIGATE: And your mother didn't seem to drink very much either.

SON: Not till the evenings.

REIGATE: You know? I'll tell you something about your father...

SON: What?

REIGATE: He can't see. He's blind, isn't he?

SON: (*Grown up.*) It was a question our family never asked. Naturally I didn't answer it.

(*Dance music starts.*

JAPHET enters with a gramophone on a trolley.)

JAPHET: And – slow, slow, quick, quick, slow – and chassis – chassis! How do you expect to get through life if you can't even do the foxtrot? That's the trouble with education today. It never teaches you anything worth knowing. Do you know, there are boys here who can't even tie their ties, let alone tango... Come on. Sorry you're leaving?

SON: Not altogether...

JAPHET: I'm leaving, too. Perhaps you heard...?

SON: Yes, sir, I know. Lydia left yesterday. We had to make our own beds this morning.

(*The music stops.*)

JAPHET: Yes. Lydia's left. I've resigned. So has the poor old King.

SON: Him as well...?

JAPHET: He broadcast this afternoon. We all heard him on Noah's radiogram. The King has given up everything for love. I told you we had a lot in common. Take my advice. Don't give up everything for love...

SON: No, I won't, sir.

JAPHET: It's just not on – that's all. Just simply not on...

SON: You coming to Noah's talk, sir? It's for all of us leavers.

JAPHET: The one where he tells you the facts of life...?

SON: Yes, sir. I think that's the one.

JAPHET: No. I shall stay away. I've heard quite enough about *them* to be going on with...

(*The HEADMASTER appears, wearing a tweed jacket with leather patches and smoking a pipe. REIGATE comes in and sits on the floor gazing up at him respectfully. JAPHET packs up his gramophone and goes. The SON moves away.*)

HEADMASTER: You are the leavers! In a month or two you will go on to Great Public Schools, away from this cosy little establishment.

(*The SON arrives and stands and knocks.*)

Come in, you're disturbing everybody. Shut the door, boy. Most terrible draught. Ah now, before I forget, Mrs Noah and I will be pleased to see you all to tea on

Sunday. A trifling matter of anchovy paste sandwiches! Do you hear that, eh, Reigate? All boys to come with clean finger-nails, no boy to put butter on his hair.

REIGATE: Please, sir?

HEADMASTER: Yes, Reigate.

REIGATE: Why aren't we to put butter on our hair?

HEADMASTER: Ah! Good question. I'm glad you asked me that! We had that trouble with the native regiments. They used to lick their hair down with butter. It went rancid in the hot weather. Unpleasant odour on parade. There's no law against a drop of water on the comb. Now, what was I going to tell you? Ah! I was warning you about dreams. You'll have them. Oh, certainly you'll have them. And in the morning you may say to yourselves, 'You rotter! To have a dream like that!' Well, you can't help it. That's all. You simply can't help them. Not dreams. Of course, if you're awake you can do something about it. You can change into a pair of shorts and go for a run across country. Or you can get into a bath, and turn on the cold tap. You can always do that. Your housemaster will understand. He'll understand if you should've been up to a French lesson, or Matins or some such thing. Simply say, 'Sir, I had to have a bath', or go for a run, or whatever it is. Just say to Mr Raffles, or Humphrey Stiggler, or Percy Parr, just say, Mr Raffles or Mr Parr, dependant on which school you're at of course, that, sir, is what I felt the need to do. He'll understand perfectly. Now, another thing! When sleeping, always lie on the right side. Not on the face, for obvious reasons. Not on the left side. Stops the heart. Not on the back, brings on dreams. Just the right side – all the time. Now, to the most serious problem you're likely to run up against. Friends. You may find that a boy from another class, or a house even, comes up to you and says, 'Let's be friends', or even offers you a slice of cake. That's a simple one, a perfectly simple one to deal with. You just say very loudly, 'I'm going straight to tell the housemaster'. Straight away. No hesitation about it.

Remember, the only real drawback to our Great Public School system is unsolicited cake – have you got that very clear? Go straight and tell the housemaster.

SON: (*Grown up.*) It wasn't until later that I realized that the Headmaster had been trying to advise us on a subject which my father used to often bring up unexpectedly, in the middle of tea.

FATHER: Sex! It's been greatly overrated by the poets. I never had many mistresses with thighs like white marble.

MOTHER: Would you like your biscuit now, dear?

SON: (*Grown up.*) Now what did he mean? Did he mean that he'd had many mistresses without especially marmoreal thighs – or few mistresses of any sort?

FATHER: 'Change in a trice
The lilies and languors of virtue
For the raptures and roses of vice!'
Where's my bloody biscuit?

MOTHER: I put it in your saucer.

FATHER: 'From their lips have thy lips taken fever?'
'Is the breath of them hot in thy hair...?'

SON: (*Grown up, to the audience.*) What did he know of the sharp uncertainties of love?

FATHER: (*Suddenly laughing.*) 'Is the breath of them hot in thy hair?' How perfectly revolting it sounds! Sex is pretty uphill work, if you want my opinion.

SON: I don't agree.

FATHER: You don't agree?

SON: I don't happen to agree.

FATHER: Who's that?

MOTHER: The Boy!

SON: I don't think sex has been overrated exactly.

FATHER: I'll tell you a story. A lover, a wife and an angry husband...

MOTHER: (*Calmly.*) Not that one, dear. (*To the SON.*) You'll have some tea?

FATHER: Why ever not?

MOTHER: It's not very suitable. (*To the SON; vaguely.*) Do you like sugar? I always forget.

SON: Nothing.

FATHER: The husband returns and discovers all! He summons the lover into the dining-room. The wife waits, trembling, terrified, for the sounds of fighting, the smashing of crockery. Silence. She tiptoes down the stairs. There's the husband and the lover side by side at the dining table, perfectly contented, drinking light ale. Suddenly, she bursts out at both of them – 'You ungrateful brutes!' They both listen as the door slams behind her. Then they open another bottle of light ale. (*Pause. The SON looks down.*)

SON: Did that really happen? I don't believe that ever really happened. We've got some new neighbours.

FATHER: It's the ridiculous inconvenience of sex. That's what they never write about. New neighbours? Perhaps we'd better plant some more poplars.

SON: Miss Baker and Miss Cox.

FATHER: Who?

MOTHER: Two ladies who run the new bookshop. By the station. Apparently he went in to buy a book and they found him sympatico...

FATHER: He hasn't invited them back here, has he? (*The SON does not answer.*) He hasn't encouraged them to 'drop in', for a glass of sherry? (*No answer.*) If he has I shall lie doggo! I shall go to earth in the West Copse, I promise you.

MOTHER: He didn't say he was bringing them here.

FATHER: Well, if he does, I shall disappear without a trace. Doesn't he know we dread visitors? Poor boy! He'll miss the evening foray after earwigs. What exactly did he say?

MOTHER: He didn't say anything.

FATHER: Well, I think I'd better go and cut off dead heads – at the far end of the border. (*FATHER and MOTHER exit.*)

SON: Miss Baker and Miss Cox! One was as soft and feathery as Carol Lombard. In the other I found Joan Crawford's merciless sensuality. They both smelt of

Imperial Leather soap and talked of distant days in
the South of France. I spent afternoons deciding which
I should first seduce.

(*MISS COX and MISS BAKER enter.*)

MISS COX: I could have kissed you when you first came
into our shop.

SON: Could you really?

MISS BAKER: And actually bought a book!

(*The SON wheels on a trolley with drinks and a radio.*)

MISS COX: Most people come in for pamphlets. A
hundred things to do with dried egg – published by the
Ministry of Food. Is your family out?

SON: I'm afraid so. Would you like a drink?

MISS BAKER: Please.

MISS COX: I'd adore a *Pernod*. Bill and I got used to
Pernod in Cassis.

SON: Who's Bill?

MISS BAKER: I'm Bill. She's Daphne. (*She looks out across
the garden.*)

SON: I'm afraid we're out of Pernod!

MISS COX: Sherry would be lovely. Did you say your
family were out?

SON: I'm afraid so. Cocktail parties.

MISS COX: We've never actually met your father.

MISS BAKER: No. We looked over the gate one evening
and shouted. He was busy doing something with a
bucket.

SON: Probably the earwigs.

MISS COX: What?

SON: He drowns earwigs every night. Cheerio! It's quite a
small house really, isn't it? I mean, you know, when you
consider the size of the garden.

(*Pause.*)

Oh!

(*Pause.*

SON switches on the radio. Charles Trenet starts to sing.)

I adore Charles Trenet, don't you?

MISS COX: Bill and I once danced with Charles Trenet. In
Cassis.

RADIO: (*Making a sudden announcement.*) What do I do if I come across German or Italian broadcasts when tuning my wireless? I say to myself: 'Now this blighter wants me to listen to him, so I'm going to turn this blighter off!' (*The SON turns off the radio.*)

MISS BAKER: Bloody war. I've been called up!

MISS COX: Bill's been called up. They're putting her on the land.

MISS BAKER: I'll probably ruin the crops.

MISS COX: It's the war, Bill. We all have to make sacrifices. (*To the SON.*) Bill doesn't care much for this war. We were more keen on the war in Spain.

MISS BAKER: They've got me down for a pig farm, near Godalming.

MISS COX: All our friends were awfully keen on the war in Spain. Stephen Spender and all that jolly lot.

SON: Oh. I love Stephen Spender.

MISS COX: I expect you'll go into the Fire Service.

SON: Why?

MISS COX: All our friends go into the Fire Service.

MISS BAKER: They get a lot of time for writing, waiting about between fires.

(*MOTHER passes through with a bucket of water.*)

MOTHER: We forgot the bucket for the drowning.

FATHER: (*Off.*) Have you abandoned me?

MOTHER: Coming, darling.

(*The MOTHER exits.*)

MISS BAKER: Well, I expect you'd like us to…

SON: Please, my father always says that in time of war one should avoid the temptation to do anything heroic.

MISS COX: One day we'd like to meet him.

FATHER: (*Off.*) Did you manage to get rid of them?

MOTHER: (*Off.*) Ssh!

MISS COX: The Fire Service. That's where you'll end up. It gives everyone far more time to write.

MISS BAKER: Is that what you're going to be then, a writer?

(*MISS COX, MISS BAKER and SON exit.*
FATHER and MOTHER enter.)

MOTHER: Isn't there an easier way of getting rid of earwigs?

FATHER: Sometimes I think women don't understand anything. Easier way!

(*SON enters. MOTHER exits with the trolley and returns.*)

MOTHER: Did you enjoy your visitors, dear?

FATHER: (*After a pause.*) Is that you?

SON: Yes, it's me.

FATHER: What're you doing?

SON: Helping you.

FATHER: Consider the persistence of the earwig. Each afternoon it feasts on our dahlia blooms. Each evening it climbs into our flower-pots to sleep. We empty the flower-pots and drown the earwigs – yet still they come. Nature's remorseless.

SON: I may be a writer...

FATHER: If we did this for one million years all over the world, do you think we would make some small dent in the pattern of evolution? Would we produce an earwig that could swim? (*After a pause.*) You'd be far better off in the law...

SON: I'd like to write...

FATHER: You'll have plenty of spare time! My first five years in chambers, I did nothing but *The Times* crossword puzzle. Besides, if you were only a writer, who would you rub shoulders with? (*With contempt.*) Other writers? You'll be far better off in the law.

SON: I don't know...

FATHER: No brilliance is needed in the law. Nothing but common sense, and relatively clean finger-nails. Another thing, if you were a writer and married, think of your poor unfortunate wife...

SON: What?

FATHER: Well, she'd have you at home all day! In carpet slippers. Drinking tea and stumped for words! You'd be far better off down the tube each morning, and off to the Law Courts. Now, how many have we bagged today?

SON: (*Looking down into the bucket.*) About a hundred.

FATHER: A moderate bag. I'd say. Merely moderate. You know, the law of husband and wife may seem idiotic at first sight. But when you get to know it, it can exercise a vague, medieval charm. Learn a little law, won't you? Just to please me.

(*FATHER exits.*)

SON: It was my father's way to offer the law to me – the great, stone column of authority which has been dragged by an adulterous, careless, negligent and half criminal humanity down the ages – as if it were a small mechanical toy which might occupy half an hour on a rainy afternoon. (*To the audience.*) He never used a white stick – but his clouded malacca was heard daily, tapping the stone corridors of the Law Courts. He had no use for therapy, dogs nor training, nor did he adapt himself to his condition. He simply pretended that nothing had happened.

(*SON goes. MR BOUSTEAD enters, robed, and carrying his wig. The JUDGE enters and sits.*)

BOUSTEAD: Good morning.

MOTHER: Good morning.

FATHER: Who's that?

MOTHER: It's Mr Boustead, dear. He's for the husband.

FATHER: Agin me, Bulstrode. Are you agin me?

BOUSTEAD: Boustead.

FATHER: Excuse me. Boustead, of course. Where are you?

BOUSTEAD: Here, I'm here…

FATHER: I have studied your case pretty closely and I have a suggestion to make which you might find helpful.

BOUSTEAD: Really?

FATHER: What I am suggesting, entirely for your assistance, of course – is that you might like – my dear boy – to throw in your hand. Now, is that a help to you?

BOUSTEAD: Certainly not! I'd say we have some pretty valuable evidence…

(*The lights change.*
In the witness-box appears MR THONG, a private detective of crafty appearance.
BOUSTEAD stands questioning him. The MOTHER leads the FATHER to his seat and sits behind him.)

Now from the vantage point which you have already described, Mr Thong, will you tell my Lord and the Jury exactly what you saw?

(*The FATHER turns and speaks in a loud stage whisper to the MOTHER.*)

FATHER: Throat spray!

(*The MOTHER puts a small throat spray into the FATHER's hand. THONG consults his notebook.*)

BOUSTEAD: Yes, Mr Thong, in your own words.

FATHER: (*In a loud whisper.*) Thank you.

THONG: (*Monotonously, reading his notebook.*) From my point of vantage, I was quite clearly able to see inside the kitchen window...

BOUSTEAD: Yes?

THONG: And...

(*The FATHER opens his mouth and starts, very loudly, to spray his throat.*)

JUDGE: Speak up, Mr Thong, I can't hear.

THONG: My Lord. I was able to distinguish clearly the Respondent.

JUDGE: Yes...

THONG: In the act of – (*His mumble is again drowned by the FATHER's work with the throat spray.*) – with a man distinguishable only by a small moustache... I now recognize him as the co-respondent, Dacres.

BOUSTEAD: In the act of what, Mr Thong?

THONG: In the act of...

(*The FATHER works the throat spray very loudly.*)

BOUSTEAD: If my learned friend would allow us to hear the evidence...

FATHER: (*Puts down the throat spray and whispers deafeningly to BOUSTEAD.*) I'm so sorry. My dear boy, if *this* is the valuable evidence you told me about, I shall be quiet – as the tomb...!

BOUSTEAD: (*Firmly.*) Mr Thong.

FATHER: (*Half rising to address the JUDGE.*) By all means, my Lord. Let us hear this *valuable* evidence.

JUDGE: Very well.

THONG: I distinctly saw them...
(The FATHER drops his malacca cane with a clatter.)
FATHER: Oh, my God. How can I apologize.
JUDGE: Distinctly saw them what?
THONG: Kissing and cuddling, my Lord.
BOUSTEAD: And then...
THONG: The light was extinguished...
BOUSTEAD: Where?
THONG: In the kitchen.
BOUSTEAD: And a further light appeared?
THONG: In the bedroom.
JUDGE: For a moment?
THONG: Merely momentarily, my Lord.
BOUSTEAD: So...
THONG: So the house was shrouded in darkness. And the co-respondent, and this is the point that struck us, had not emerged.
BOUSTEAD: And you kept up observation until...
THONG: Approximately, dawn.
BOUSTEAD: *(Very satisfied, as he sits down.)* Thank you, Mr Thong.
(The FATHER rises, clattering. Folds his hands on his stomach, gazes sightlessly at THONG and then allows a long pause during which THONG stirs uncomfortably. Then he starts quietly, slowly working himself up into a climax.)
FATHER: Mr Thong, what price did you put on this valuable evidence?
THONG: I don't know what you mean...
FATHER: You have been paid, haven't you, to give it?
THONG: I'm a private enquiry agent...
FATHER: A professional witness?
THONG: Charging the usual fee.
FATHER: Thirty pieces of silver?
BOUSTEAD: *(Rising; indignantly.)* My Lord, I object. This is outrageous.
JUDGE: Perhaps that was not entirely relevant.
(BOUSTEAD subsides.)
FATHER: Then let me ask you something which is very relevant. Which goes straight to the secret heart of this

wretched conspiracy. Where was this lady's husband during your observations?

THONG: Captain Waring?

FATHER: Yes. Captain Waring.

THONG: He had accompanied me...

FATHER: Why?

THONG: For the purpose of...

FATHER: For the purpose of what...?

THONG: Identification...

FATHER: And how long did he remain with you?

THONG: As long as observation continued...

FATHER: Till dawn...

THONG: Until approximately five-thirty a.m.

FATHER: And did he not storm the house? Did he not beat upon the door? Did he not seize his wife's paramour by the throat and hurl him into the gutter?

THONG: According to my notebook. No.

FATHER: And according to your notebook, was he enjoying himself?

BOUSTEAD: (*Driven beyond endurance, rising to protest.*) Really...!

FATHER: Please, Mr Bulstrode! I've sat here for three days! Like patience on a monument! Whilst a series of spiteful, mean, petty, trumped-up, sickening and small-minded charges are tediously paraded against the unfortunate woman I represent. And now, when I rise to cross-examine – *I will not be interrupted.*

JUDGE: Gentlemen! Gentlemen, please. (*To the FATHER.*) What was your question?

FATHER: I've forgotten it. My learned friend's interruption has had the effect he no doubt intended and I have forgotten my question!

BOUSTEAD: This is intolerable...

FATHER: Ah. Now I've remembered it again. Did he enjoy the night, Thong, in this field – from which he was magically able to overlook his own kitchen...?

THONG: This plot of waste ground...

FATHER: Up a tree, was he?

THONG: What?

FATHER: Was he perched upon a tree?

THONG: We had stepped up, into the lower branches.

FATHER: Was it the naked eye?

THONG: Pardon?

FATHER: Was he viewing this distressing scene by aid of
the naked eye?

THONG: Captain Waring had brought a pair of field-glasses.

FATHER: His racing glasses?

THONG: I...

JUDGE: Speak up, Mr Thong.

THONG: I imagine he used them for racing, my Lord.

FATHER: You see Captain Waring has already given
evidence in this Court.

BOUSTEAD: (*Ironically.*) On the subject of racing glasses?

FATHER: (*His voice filled with passion.*) No, Mr Bulstrode.
On the subject of love. He has told us that he was
deeply, sincerely in love with his wife.

THONG: I don't know anything about that.

FATHER: Exactly, Mr Thong! You are hardly an expert
witness, are you, on the subject of love? May it please
you, my Lord, Members of the Jury. Love has driven
men and women in the course of history to curious
extremes. It tempted Leander to plunge in and swim the
raging Hellespont. It led Juliet to feign death and
Ophelia to madness. No doubt it complicated the
serenity of the Garden of Eden and we are told started
the Trojan War: but surely there is no more curious
example of the mysterious effects of the passion than the
spectacle of Captain Waring of the Royal Engineers,
roosted in a tree, complacently viewing the seduction of
his beloved through a pair of strong racing binoculars...
(*The SON enters.*)
Is not the whole story, Members of the Jury, an
improbable and impertinent tissue of falsehood...?
(*The SON is lit downstage as in the upstage darkness, the
JUDGE, the FATHER, and the MOTHER go and the courtroom
furniture is moved away.*)

SON: (*To the audience.*) He sent words out into the darkness,
like soldiers sent off to battle, and was never short of

reinforcements. In the Law Courts he gave his public performance. At home he returned to his ritual of the potting shed, the crossword puzzle and, when I was at home, the afternoon walk. The woods were dark and full of flies and we used to pick bracken leaves to swat them, and when I was a child he told me that we carried cutlasses to hack our way through the jungle. I used to shut my eyes at dead rats, or magpies gibbeted on the trees: sights his blindness spared him. He used to walk with his hand on my arm. A small hand, with loose brown skin. From time to time, I had the urge to pull away, to run and hide among the trees...to leave him alone, lost in perpetual darkness. But then his hand would tighten on my sleeve; he was very persistent...
(*The FATHER enters, takes the SON's arm, and they walk round slowly.*
The lights come up.)

FATHER: I've had a good deal of fun – out of the law.

SON: Have you ever been to the South of France?

FATHER: Once or twice. It's all right, except for the dreadful greasy food they can't stop talking about.

SON: Bill and Daphne say the worst of the War is that they can't get to the South of France.

FATHER: Who're they?

SON: The ladies from the bookshop.

FATHER: The ones who downed all our sherry?

SON: That's right.

FATHER: My heart bled for you on that occasion.

SON: Daphne's Miss Cox.

FATHER: And Bill?

SON: Bill's Miss Baker.

FATHER: Damned rum!

SON: They practically lived in Cannes before the War. They met Cocteau...

FATHER: Who?

SON: He smoked opium. Have you ever smoked opium?

FATHER: Certainly not! Gives you constipation. Dreadful binding effect. Ever seen those pictures of the wretched poet Coleridge? Green around the gills. And a stranger to the lavatory. Avoid opium.

SON: They may find me a war job.

MOTHER: Who may?

SON: Miss Baker and Miss Cox.

MOTHER: Why, is old 'Bill' on the General Staff?

SON: They have a friend who makes propaganda films for the government. He needs an assistant.

FATHER: You're thinking of entering the film world?

SON: Just – for the duration.

FATHER: Well! At least there's nothing heroic about it.

SON: No.

FATHER: Rum sort of world, isn't it – the film world?

SON: I expect so.

FATHER: Don't they wear their caps *back to front* in the film world?

SON: You're thinking of the silent days.

FATHER: Am I? I expect I am. Your mother and I went to a silent film once. In Glastonbury.

SON: Did you?

FATHER: Yes. We were staying there in an hotel. Damn dull. Nothing to do in the evenings. So we sallied forth, to see this silent film. The point was, I invariably dressed for dinner, when in Glastonbury. Follow?

SON: I follow.

FATHER: And when we entered this picture palace – in evening dress, the audience burst into spontaneous applause! I believe they took us, for part of the entertainment! Rum kind of world, I must say. Now where are we?

SON: At the bottom of Stonor Hill.

FATHER: Good. I'll rest a moment. Then we'll go up to the top.

(*The SON moves him to the right of the platform and sits him down.*)

SON: Will we?

FATHER: Of course we will! You can see the three counties from the top of Stonor Hill. Don't you want to see three counties…?

SON: All right.

FATHER: See everything. Everything in Nature… That's the instinct of the May Beetle. Twenty-four hours to live, so spend it – looking around.

SON: We've got more time…

FATHER: Don't you believe it! It's short – but enjoyable! You know what?

SON: What?

FATHER: If they ever say to you, 'Your old father, he couldn't have enjoyed life much. Overdrawn at the bank and bad-tempered and people didn't often visit him…' 'Nonsense', you can say. 'He enjoyed every minute of it…'

SON: Do you want to go on now?

FATHER: When you consider the embryo of the liver-fluke, born in sheep's droppings, searching the world for a shell to bore into for the sake of living in a snail until it becomes tadpole-like and leaves its host – only to be swallowed up by a sheep again! When you consider that – complicated persistence, well, of course, I've clung on for sixty-five years. It's the instinct – that's all. The irresistible instinct! All right. We'll go up. Watch carefully and you'll see three counties…

(*The FATHER puts out his hand. The SON pulls him up and they go off.*

The lights change.

MISS BAKER and MISS COX enter, carrying a picnic basket and a bird in a large cage. They settle down to a picnic.)

MISS COX: Our last picnic…

MISS BAKER: Oh, for God's sake, Daphne. I mean they're not sending me to the Western Desert. Now, let's find a bit of shade for Miss Garbo. (*She finds a place for the bird.*)

MISS COX: Did we *have* to bring her?

MISS BAKER: She likes the air here. Up Stonor Hill. Where's the sandwiches? Thanks.

MISS COX: (*Putting out sandwiches sadly.*) I know you will…

MISS BAKER: You know I will what? (*Gives a bit of sandwich to the bird.*) Do you know this bloody bird gets all my butter ration.

MISS COX: Fall for some carrot-haired number – with dung all over her jods.

MISS BAKER: Why should I?

MISS COX: She'll be washing you down in the evenings. In front of the fire.

MISS BAKER: I'm not going down the mines either!

MISS COX: I know. (*Half laughing, half starting to cry.*) It's going to be bloody lonely.

MISS BAKER: Cheer up, old thing. Keep smiling.
(*They lie together, MISS BAKER feeding MISS COX with the remains of her sandwich.*
The FATHER and SON enter.)

FATHER: What can you see?

SON: Three counties...

FATHER: Be my eyes then. Paint me the picture.

SON: (*After a pause.*) I can just see three counties. Stretched out. That's all I can see.

FATHER: A fine prospect?

SON: A fine prospect.

FATHER: We've bagged a good many sights today! What've we seen?

SON: We saw that hare. Oh, and the butterfly.

FATHER: Danaies Chrysippus! The one that flaunts a large type of powder-puff. You described it to me.

SON: Shall we go home now?

FATHER: You painted me the picture. (*After a pause.*) We've seen a lot today. We've seen a good deal of the monstrous persistence of nature...
(*The FATHER and SON move away upstage. MISS BAKER takes her hand off MISS COX's mouth, releasing a cascade of giggles, as – the curtain falls.*)

End of Act One.

ACT TWO

As the curtain rises, there is the noise of carpentry, shouting, singing and cursing. SPARKS is sitting on a chair with his feet on the table. The technicians enter bringing a movie camera on a tripod, a microphone on a pole, a case of make-up and a typewriter. The DIRECTOR is smoking a Wills Whiff. The Unit Manager is carrying a clipboard and is a tough, competent, deep-voiced woman.

DORIS: Move over, Sparks.

SPARKS: (*Singing loudly.*) 'Oh Salome, Salome,
    That's my girl, Salome.
    Standing there with her arse all bare...'

DORIS: (*Yelling.*) Let's have a little quiet, please!

SPARKS: (*Singing quietly.*) 'Every little wrinkle makes the
    boys all stare...'

DORIS: (*In a full-throated roar.*) Great Scott, Sparks!

SPARKS: Sorry, Doris.

DORIS: You the new assistant?

SON: Yes.

DORIS: Know your job, do you?

SON: I'm new to movies.

DORIS: Great Scott! You don't have to know anything
    about movies. You're here to fetch the subsistence...

SON: The what?

DORIS: Tea breaks. Coffee breaks. After lunch special
    breaks and in lieu of breakfast breaks. The Sparks have
    tea and ham and lettuce rolls, known to them as
    Smiggett sandwiches. The Chippies take coffee and cakes
    with coconut icing. The director needs *Horlicks*, liver
    pâté sandwiches and Wills Whiffs. Keep your mouth shut
    except to call in a firm and authoritative tone for 'Quiet'
    when we shoot. Any questions?

SON: Yes.

DORIS: What?

SON: Where do I get liver pâté sandwiches?

DORIS: Use your bloody imagination! That's what you
    came into the film business for...

DIRECTOR: (*Calling her from the camera.*) Doris!

DORIS: Coming, Humphrey. (*To the SON.*) Next tea break in ten minutes. (*She goes to chatter to the DIRECTOR.*)
(*The SON runs downstage. SPARKS shouts after him.*)

SPARKS: Hey! You lost something?

SON: Well, actually I'm…

SPARKS: Don't worry. Maybe you left it in the Officer's Mess. You know we've got two ATS in the next scene, don't you?

SON: No, I didn't.

SPARKS: There's two sorts of ATS let me tell you. Cocked ATS and fell ATS. Had it in last night, did you?
(*Two ATS enter.*)

SON: I beg your pardon?

SPARKS: Seen the King last night?

SON: The King? No. (*Innocently.*) Was he here?

SPARKS: Was he here? That's a good one. Who did you say you was out with?

SON: Actually, no-one.

SPARKS: Didn't spend out on her, I hope? Never spend out till you've had it in. Then you can buy her a packet of small smokes.

DIRECTOR: All right, we'll try a rehearsal.

DORIS: Stand by!

SPARKS: What did you say you was looking for?

SON: A liver pâté sandwich.

SPARKS: Liver pâté! You're a caution! That's what you are.

DORIS: Rehearsal!

SPARKS: Lights, Alf!

DIRECTOR: All right, then. Settle down…and – action.

FIRST ATS: Gerry's being a bit naughty tonight then, Hilda.

SECOND ATS: Yes. (*She offers the other a cup of tea.*) Tea, luv?

FIRST ATS: Ta, luv.

SECOND ATS: Sugars, do you?

FIRST ATS: Ta.

SECOND ATS: One or two sugars?

FIRST ATS: Two sugars, ta. (*After a pause.*) Ta.

SECOND ATS: (*After a pause.*) You know, I've been thinking lately.

FIRST ATS: Have you, Hilda?

SECOND ATS: Oh, yes, Sandra, I've been thinking.

FIRST ATS: What about then, Hilda?

SECOND ATS: You know what I reckon this war's all about?

FIRST ATS: (*After a long pause.*) No.

SECOND ATS: It's just our freedom. To talk to each other.

FIRST ATS: Sugar for you, then, Hilda? You want sugar, luv?

DIRECTOR: Cut! That was marvellous. Tremendously real.

SPARKS: Save the lights, Alf!

(*The lights change.*)

DIRECTOR: My God, you couldn't do that with actors! All right, Doris. I'm going for a take.

DORIS: Assistant! Get a bit of silence, will you?

SON: (*Turning away from the tea tray.*) Sorry, Doris.

DORIS: Yell 'Quiet', for God's sake.

SON: (*Moving to the centre of the stage and clearing his throat nervously.*) Quiet, please!

(*The noise of the unit continues.*)

Can we have a little quiet now, please?

(*From this moment the noise intensifies. The two ATS start to dance together, humming 'The White Cliffs of Dover'.*)

We'd appreciate a bit of quiet now, thank you!

(*Noise.*)

All quiet now! We're going to try a take.

(*Noise.*)

Ladies and gentlemen, will you please give us a little *quiet!*

(*Noise.*)

Quiet now, PLEASE!

(*There is increased noise.*)

(*Becoming hysterical and yelling.*) SHUT UP, YOU BASTARDS!

SPARKS: All out!

(*Total silence.*)

SON: No, please.

(*ELIZABETH enters with a typewriter, sits at the table and starts to type. All except ELIZABETH and the SON exit, with equipment.*)

(*Moving towards ELIZABETH.*) Is this the writer's department?

(*The typing continues.*)

They say I'm not cut out by nature to be an Assistant Director. When I yelled for 'Quiet' all the electricians went on strike.

(*The typing continues.*)

They say with me as an Assistant Director the War'd be over before they finished the movie.

(*She stops typing, looks up at him and smiles for the first time. Encouraged, he goes and looks at what she is typing.*) What's the script?

ELIZABETH: It's something Humphrey wants to do. (*She pulls a face.*) There's a character in it called the 'Common Man'. He keeps on saying, 'Look here, matey, what *is* the World Health Organization?'

SON: Sounds ghastly.

ELIZABETH: (*Smiling.*) Yes, it is rather.

SON: Why on earth do you bother to write it?

ELIZABETH: I suppose – the school fees.

SON: Oh, you're studying something?

ELIZABETH: No, you fool. It's my kids. Peter's only got his captain's pay and I can't...

SON: Peter?

ELIZABETH: My husband.

SON: He's overseas?

ELIZABETH: Uxbridge. In Army education.

SON: My father always says that in time of war one should avoid the temptation to do anything heroic.

ELIZABETH: How odd.

SON: What?

ELIZABETH: Odd thing for him to say.

SON: You know, I think after today I'll abandon the film business and take up the Law. My father's a lawyer.

ELIZABETH: Do you always copy your father?

SON: Good God, no!

ELIZABETH: Really? You look the type to agree with Dad.

SON: (*Looking at her.*) Well, there's one thing he says that I don't agree with at all.

ELIZABETH: What's that?

SON: He says that sex has been greatly overrated. By the poets...

(The SON goes. The DIRECTOR enters as the rest of the film unit clear the film gear from the stage.)

DIRECTOR: Is he going to be any use to you, Elizabeth?

ELIZABETH: Who?

DIRECTOR: Our new writer.

ELIZABETH: Oh, I shouldn't think so. Is he going to stay?

DIRECTOR: *(Reading.)* What?

ELIZABETH: Just passing through. That's the feeling I get about him.

(The DIRECTOR and ELIZABETH go.

The lights change.

The FATHER enters half-dressed, without his coat, waistcoat or tie. He hooks his braces over his shoulders, shouts, moves round the stage, his hands out in front of him, groping for the furniture that is not there.)

FATHER: My tie. Oh, God in heaven, where's my tie? Will no-one bring me a waistcoat even? Can't any of you realize the *loneliness of getting dressed?*

(The SON enters with the coat, waistcoat and tie over his arm, finds the FATHER's wandering hand and puts the tie into it.)

Is that you?

SON: Yes. It's me.

FATHER: I suppose you expect me to talk about it.

SON: I know it came as a bit of a shock to you, when Peter divorced Elizabeth.

FATHER: Must have come as a shock to you, too, didn't it? The fact that she was available for marriage must have somewhat cooled your ardour. I mean you're hardly in a state to get married...

SON: Do you want to stop us?

FATHER: Are you asking me to?

SON: Of course not.

FATHER: How long have you been at the bar, exactly?

SON: Nine months.

FATHER: Nine months! I'd been in practice for ten years before I felt the slightest need to marry your mother.

SON: Perhaps – needs weren't so urgent then.

FATHER: Got any work to do?

SON: A little work.

FATHER: Unsuccessful defence in serious case of non-renewed dog licence. That'll hardly keep you in Vim...

SON: But we don't want to be kept in Vim.

FATHER: But you'll have no alternative – once you're married. Your no-income will be frittered away on Vim, saucepan scourers, Mansion polish, children's vests and such-like luxuries...

SON: I'm quite prepared to take on her children.

FATHER: You sound like a railway train. Short stop to take on children. Waistcoat anywhere about?

SON: Wait.

FATHER: Yes. In the course of her life – she has acquired children. Mixed blessings I should imagine, for both of you.

SON: If you're worried about money...

FATHER: My dear boy. I'm not worried about it. I just think you haven't bargained for the Vim. Now how long are you going to deny me my waistcoat?

SON: Oh, here.

(*The SON holds out the waistcoat, helps the FATHER to struggle into it.*)

I know you think we're insane...

FATHER: (*Buttoning his waistcoat.*) You feel the need to be dissuaded.

SON: Of course not.

FATHER: I can't help you, you know.

SON: We don't want help.

FATHER: From what I hear, the children seem quite lively. As children go.

SON: Coat.

FATHER: Of course it won't be I, who has to keep them in rompers. I wonder, should I have a drop of eau-de-Cologne on the handkerchief? I understand your poor girl's coming to tea. We seem nowadays to be totally surrounded by visitors.

SON: You're not going to be rude to her?

FATHER: No, of course not! Your poor girl and I have got a certain understanding.

SON: For God's sake. Why do you keep calling her my poor girl?

FATHER: That's something – I'll have to explain to her after tea.

(*The FATHER takes the SON's arm. They move off the stage together. ELIZABETH enters. She waits nervously in the garden area: lights a cigarette. The SON enters, goes to her quickly, also nervous.*)

SON: They're just coming... (*He pauses.*) It's going to be all right. (*He pauses.*) You won't mind, whatever he says?

ELIZABETH: Will you?

SON: No. Of course not.

ELIZABETH: *Whatever* he says?

SON: I'm used to it. (*He pauses.*) He doesn't mean half of it.

ELIZABETH: Yes, I know. But it's difficult...

SON: What?

ELIZABETH: Telling which half he means.

(*The FATHER enters in his garden hat, his hand on the MOTHER's arm.*)

FATHER: Rhododendrons out?

MOTHER: Yes, dear.

FATHER: A fine show of rhododendrons. And the little syringa?

MOTHER: Just out.

FATHER: Just out. And smelling sweetly. Azaleas doing well?

MOTHER: Well, we can see they're a little brown, round the edges...

FATHER: Azaleas doing moderately well. Is our visitor here?

MOTHER: Yes, dear. Elizabeth's here.

SON: We're both here.

FATHER: And is your visitor enjoying the garden?

ELIZABETH: Very much. Thank you.

FATHER: Good. And is he treating you well?

ELIZABETH: Quite well. Thank you.

FATHER: I've often wondered about my son. Does he treat girls well...?

SON: Why've you wondered that?

FATHER: Well, I once knew a man named Arthur Pennycuick. Like you in some ways. He didn't treat girls well...

MOTHER: Please, dear – Arthur Pennycuick's not quite suitable.

ELIZABETH: Tell us. What did he do to girls?

FATHER: When I was a young man, I was out with this Pennycuick. And he picked up a girl. In the promenade of the old Alhambra Music-Hall. And just before he went off with her, he took out his cuff-links and handed them to me for safe keeping. In her *presence!* I was so sick and angry, seeing him take out his old gold cuff-links. I never spoke to him again. Disgusting!

ELIZABETH: You think if you sleep with someone – you should trust them with your cuff-links?

FATHER: At least not take them out – *in front of the girl!* Well, we can see a fine show of rhododendrons.

MOTHER: Yes, dear. And I showed you the polyanthus.

FATHER: A reward at last, for a good deal of tedious potting up.

ELIZABETH: Why do you bother?

FATHER: About what?

ELIZABETH: I said why do you bother to do all this gardening? I mean when you can't see it...

(*The SON tries to interrupt her protectively.*)

SON: Elizabeth...

ELIZABETH: Well, he can't, can he? Why do you all walk about – pretending he's not blind?

(*The FATHER moves, his hand out in front of him, towards ELIZABETH. He gets to her: touches her arm, feels down her arm, and puts his in it.*)

FATHER: Is this you?

ELIZABETH: Yes...

FATHER: Would you take me to West Copse? I'd like a report on the magnolia. Would you do that? (*He pauses.*) Be my eyes.

ELIZABETH: Come then...

(*She moves away, with the FATHER on her arm.*)

MOTHER: (*Looking after ELIZABETH.*) She has nice eyes.

SON: Yes.

MOTHER: Not at all the eyes of a divorced person.

SON: (*After a pause.*) Does he want to stop us?

MOTHER: Well, it's not easy for him. He's such a household word in the Probate, Divorce and Admiralty Division.

SON: Is he going on about that?

MOTHER: No, no, not at all.

SON: If he could only see her he'd understand why I want to marry her.

MOTHER: Oh, he understands that. I think his main difficulty is understanding why she wants to marry you...

SON: (*Gives half laugh.*) Nice of him!

MOTHER: Would you like to come and help me cut up the oranges? I do so hate making marmalade.

(*The MOTHER exits.*)

SON: (*Shouts after her.*) For God's sake, why don't you buy it? (*SON exits downstage. FATHER and ELIZABETH enter upstage.*)

FATHER: Come over, did you, in your own small car?

ELIZABETH: You've been trying to put him off.

FATHER: Not at all.

ELIZABETH: I told him. You'd put him off.

FATHER: He came to me for advice.

ELIZABETH: And I suppose you gave it.

FATHER: I never give advice. Bit of an asset, don't you find it, that private transport?

ELIZABETH: We've made up our minds.

FATHER: And I believe your children are quite lively. For children...

ELIZABETH: He gets on marvellously with them...

FATHER: And I believe you have your own bits and pieces of furniture. A bedroom suite they tell me. In a fine state of preservation. You're a catch! If you want my honest opinion.

ELIZABETH: Well, then you ought to be glad for him...

FATHER: For him? Look here. Joking apart. You don't want to marry him, do you? I mean he's got no assets – of any kind. Not even – a kitchen cabinet. And here's another thing about it. He won't like it, you know. If you get the flu...

ELIZABETH: Really...?

FATHER: Most people are sympathetic towards illness. They're kind to people with high temperatures. They even cosset them. But not him! Sneeze once and he'll be off! In the opposite direction!

ELIZABETH: I don't get ill all that much...

FATHER: Well, if you do – he'll run a mile!

ELIZABETH: I thought it was *me* you might disapprove of...

FATHER: Why ever...?

ELIZABETH: Think he's marrying someone unsuitable...

FATHER: You have particularly nice eyes they tell me.

ELIZABETH: Thank you.

FATHER: And your own bits and pieces of furniture...

ELIZABETH: Not much.

FATHER: And as you told me yourself, your own small run-about.

ELIZABETH: Very bashed.

FATHER: All the same. Not many girls with assets of that description. Couldn't you do better, than someone who bolts if you go two ticks above normal?

ELIZABETH: Well, I hadn't thought about it.

FATHER: Oh, do think. Think carefully! There must be bigger fish than *that* in your own particular sea. You are, I mean, something of a catch. You could catch better fish than *that*. I'm prepared to take a bet on it...
(*He shivers slightly.*) It's getting cold.

ELIZABETH: (*Unsmiling.*) I'll take you in.

(*The FATHER gets up and ELIZABETH leads him off the stage. The SON enters, wearing a black coat and striped trousers.*)

SON: (*To the audience.*) In that case his advocacy failed. In time he became reconciled to me as a husband for his daughter-in-law.

(*GEORGE enters. He is on his way home.*)

Any work for me tomorrow in court, George?

GEORGE: Come now, sir. We were in Court last week. We mustn't be greedy.

SON: No. I suppose not. Good night, George. Don't work too hard.

(*GEORGE goes and ELIZABETH enters.*)

(*To the audience.*) My father was right, though. I hadn't bargained for the Vim.

ELIZABETH: Made lots of money this week?

SON: Ten guineas. For a divorce.

ELIZABETH: That's marvellous, darling! I had to get them new vests.

SON: What in the hell do they do with their vests? You know, it's my opinion they eat their vests.

ELIZABETH: And knicker linings. I put them on the account at John Barnes.

SON: The account at John Barnes is assuming the proportions of the national debt.

ELIZABETH: You ought to be rich.

SON: Ought?

ELIZABETH: I am up all night. Typing your divorce petitions. They must be paying you – for all those paragraphs of deep humiliation and distress.

SON: You don't get paid for years. In the Law.

ELIZABETH: Can't you ask for it?

SON: Of course you can't.

ELIZABETH: Why not?

SON: You just can't knock on someone's door and say, 'Can I have ten guineas for the divorce.'

ELIZABETH: I'll go and knock if you like…

SON: Anyway, George collects the fees…

ELIZABETH: Who's George?

SON: Our clerk. It's his department.

ELIZABETH: I thought his name was Henry.

SON: It is but my father calls him George.

ELIZABETH: Whatever for?

SON: Because he once had a clerk called George, who was killed on the Somme. So when Henry took over my father continued to call him George.

ELIZABETH: Well, Henry doesn't much like that, if you ask me.

SON: He doesn't mind.

ELIZABETH: You always think no-one minds – about your father...

SON: Let's go to the pub.

ELIZABETH: What on?

SON: The Family Allowance.

ELIZABETH: All right. Shall we play bar billiards?

SON: Like that night when Peter walked in. Remember?

ELIZABETH: And said, 'This is the end of our marriage. I see you have become entirely trivial.'

SON: Do you miss Peter?

ELIZABETH: No. Do you?

SON: No. (*After a pause.*) Of course not!

ELIZABETH: I'm sorry.

SON: What about?

ELIZABETH: About John Barnes.

SON: That's marriage.

ELIZABETH: What's marriage.

SON: An unexpectedly large expenditure on Vim, children's vests and suchlike luxuries...

(*ELIZABETH smiles knowingly at him.*)

ELIZABETH: And who's that a quotation from?

(*ELIZABETH exits. GEORGE enters, sits silently at the table, and dozes off. The SON crosses to him, leans over, opens his drawer and takes out a cheque.*)

GEORGE: We have been going, sir, to our personal drawer!

SON: But, George, it's a cheque, for me...

GEORGE: We should have given it out to us, sir, in the fullness of time...

SON: Fifteen guineas! Thank God for adultery.

GEORGE: We have never had a gentleman here in chambers, sir, that had to grub for money in our personal top drawer...

SON: But, George, we're desperately short of Vim.

GEORGE: These things take time.

SON: And what's the point of keeping good money shut up with a box of old pen nibs and a Lyons Individual Fruit Pie. I mean, what's it meant to do in there – breed or something? Don't look at me like that, George. If only you could get me some more work.

GEORGE: We can't expect much. We must wait until a few clients learn to like the cut of our jib.

SON: I have a talent for divorcing people.

GEORGE: It's not our work. It's our conversation to solicitors that counts. While we're waiting to come on, at London Sessions.

SON: Conversations?

GEORGE: Do we ask about their tomato plants? Do we remember ourselves to their motor mowers? Do we show a proper concern for their operations and their daughters' figure skating? That's how we rise to heights in the Law.

SON: My father doesn't do that.

GEORGE: Your father's a case apart.

SON: (*Rather proud.*) My father's obnoxious, to solicitors.

GEORGE: (*Suddenly shouts.*) 'The devil damn thee Black, thou cream-faced loon!'

SON: (*Taken aback.*) George!

GEORGE: He said that to Mr Binns, when he'd forgotten to file his affidavit. Yes. Your father is something of an exception.

SON: Yes.

GEORGE: I sometimes wonder. Does he realize I'm one of the many Henrys of the world?

SON: (*Reassuring.*) I'm sure he does, George.

(*GEORGE looks at the SON more sympathetically. There is a pause.*)

GEORGE: Mr Garfield goes down to the Free Legal Centre, Holloway Road. That's where he goes of a Thursday. He picks up the odd guinea or two, on poor persons' cases. And I don't have him in here, sir, ferreting about among my packed meal, sir.

SON: Mr Garfield lives with his mother – he spends nothing at all on Vim!

GEORGE: He takes the view he might rise to fame from the Free Legal Centre. He says a murderer might rush in there off the streets any day of the week...

(*The lights change. The SON moves forward and speaks to the audience.*

GEORGE exits. A table, chair and portrait of George VI is set. MISS FERGUSON, a social worker, with glasses, chain-smoking over a pile of files, enters.)

SON: So I went to the Free Legal Centre and I waited in a small room which smelt of gym shoes and coconut matting and I used to pray that a murderer, still clutching the dripping knife, might burst in from the Holloway Road begging urgently for Legal Aid. Any murderers for me tonight, Miss Ferguson?

MISS FERGUSON: I'm just away to send you in my Mr Morrow. I chose you out for him specially.

SON: Why me?

MISS FERGUSON: He makes Mr Garfield faint. Mr Morrow!

(*MISS FERGUSON exits. MR MORROW enters.*)

MR MORROW: You the lawyer?

SON: Mr Morrow? Is it matrimonial?

MR MORROW: Yes, sir. In a sense...

SON: Now, you were married on...?

MR MORROW: The sixth day of month one. I prefer not to use the heathen notation.

SON: Nineteen-forty?

MR MORROW: Nineteen-forty.

SON: I have to write it down on this form, you see. (*He pauses.*) Now, what is the trouble?

MR MORROW: The corpuscles.

SON: But there's no place on the free legal form for corpuscles.

MR MORROW: Which is, however, the trouble. That's what I want, sir. The legal position... She's on to the red ones now. I could just about stand it when she only took the white. And my child, sir. My Pamela. I have a very particular respect for that child, sir, who is now losing her hearty appetite.

SON: What is your wife doing, exactly?

MR MORROW: She is eating our red corpuscles.

SON: Mr Morrow, if you're not feeling well...

MR MORROW: She drains them from us, by the use of her specs, sir. That is how she drains them out. She focuses her rimless specs upon our bodies and so our bodies bleed.

SON: Mr Morrow...

MR MORROW: I was standing upon my hearth rug, sir, which lies upon my hearth. I looked down and I saw it there. The scarlet flower. There was the stain of blood all over my white fleecy rug, sir.

SON: Have you spoken to your wife about this at all?

MR MORROW: I haven't spoken to her, sir. But she is forgiven. All the same I feel she has let me down. When it was only the white she focused her eyes on, it was more or less immaterial. But now she's after my vital strength.

SON: But you see, legally – there's not a great deal I...

MR MORROW: A man stands entitled to his own blood, sir, surely. It must be so.

SON: I know of no case decided on this particular issue.

MR MORROW: So you're advising me to go to Doncaster?

SON: You might as well.

MR MORROW: It's your considered and expert opinion, her destructive eye won't be on me in Doncaster?

SON: Why not give it a try, anyway?

MR MORROW: Very well, sir, I will. I bow to your honest opinion. I shall discontinue all legal proceedings and proceed at once to Doncaster. Will you require my signature to that effect?

SON: Well, no, I hardly think so.

MR MORROW: That's just as well, as it so happens. I never
   sign – ethical reasons.
   (*MR MORROW exits. MISS FERGUSON enters.*)
MISS FERGUSON: Oh uhhu. Mr Morrow looks well
   contented.
SON: He should. He has absolutely no need of the law.
   (*MISS FERGUSON exits. The FATHER enters.*)
FATHER: 'Let's talk of graves of worms and epitaphs.'
SON: Back in chambers my father, smelling of eau-de-
   Cologne and occasional cigars, sat among his relics, the
   blown duck egg on which a client's will had once been
   written, the caricatures of himself in famous cases. He
   wrote a great textbook on the law of wills, becoming
   expert in the habits of mad old ladies who went fishing
   for gold under their beds and left all their money to
   undesirable causes.
FATHER: 'Let's choose executors and talk of wills.
   And yet not so... For what can we bequeath?
   Save our deposed bodies to the ground.
   Our lands, our lives and all are Bolingbroke's.
   And nothing can we call our own but death
   And that small model of the barren earth...
   Which serves as paste and cover to our bones.'
   You're back from lunch.
SON: Yes.
FATHER: You took a long time.
SON: I went to see a man – who might want to put on my
   play...
FATHER: Possibly you would work harder if you were a
   woman barrister.
SON: Possibly...
FATHER: I've often said to George, 'Why don't we have a
   woman in chambers?' Women work so much harder than
   men. They can be imposed on so much more easily.
   Look how seriously girls' schools take lacrosse! They'd
   treat the law like that. I could get a ridiculous amount of
   work from a woman pupil.
SON: What does George say?

FATHER: He says there's not the toilet facilities. Enjoying the law, are you?

SON: Not all that much.

FATHER: Plays are all very well. Photographs in the paper may be very fine and large. But you need something real! Hold hard on the law.

SON: Are you sure the law's real?

FATHER: What on earth do you mean?

SON: No-one seems to need it – except lawyers...

FATHER: The law's not designed for imbeciles, or for your friends who combine the art of being called Bill with membership of the female sex. It's not exactly tailor-made for the poet Percy Bysshe Shelley. No! The whole point of the Law is – it's designed for the ordinary everyday citizen seated aboard the ordinary, everyday Holborn tramcar.

SON: I don't think they have tramcars in Holborn any more.

FATHER: That's hardly the point.

SON: No tramcars and no ordinary common-sense citizens sitting on them. No. They're all busy thinking about the things that really worry them, like the shapes on the ceilings and the stains on the carpet, and, do you know, they only pretend to be ordinary common-sense citizens when they need lawyers. It's a disguise they put on, like the blue suit and the old Boy Scout button, and the pathetic voices they use when they take the Bible oath. They're fooling us, that's what they're doing. Because they think if they play our game we'll let them off their debts, or we'll order their wives to permit them sexual intercourse, or we'll liberate them from old pointless crimes no-one holds against them anyway. No, honestly, all this legal language we're so proud of, it might just as well be Chinese...

FATHER: (*Conciliatingly.*) Oh, come now, I mean – you can get a lot of innocent fun out of the law. How's your cross?

SON: What?

FATHER: Your cross-examination. In Court – have you the makings of a cross-examiner?

SON: I don't know.

FATHER: Timing is of great importance. In the art of cross-examination.

SON: That's show business.

FATHER: How do you mean?

SON: It's an expression, used by actors.

FATHER: (*Without interest.*) Really? How very uninteresting. Now I always count, in silence of course, up to forty-three before starting a cross-examination.

SON: Whatever for?

FATHER: The witness imagines you're thinking up some utterly devastating question.

SON: Are you?

FATHER: Of course not. I'm just counting. Up to forty-three. But, it unnerves the gentleman in the box. Then, start off with the knock-out! Don't leave it till the end: go in with your guns blazing! Ask him...

SON: What?

FATHER: Is there anything in your conduct, Mr Nokes, of which, looking back on it, you now feel heartily *ashamed?*

SON: Is that a good question?

FATHER: It's an excellent question!

SON: Why exactly?

FATHER: Because if he says 'yes' he's made an admission, and if he says 'no' he's a self-satisfied idiot and he's lost the sympathy of the Court.

SON: Anything else?

FATHER: Suppose you have a letter from him in which he admits something discreditable – like, well having apologized to his wife for instance. Now then, how're you going to put that to him?

SON: Did you, or did you not –

FATHER: Not bad.

SON: – write a letter apologizing to your wife?

FATHER: Well, I suppose you're young.

SON: Isn't that right?

FATHER: Not what I'd call the *art* of cross-examination.

SON: Then how...?

FATHER: You be Nokes.

SON: Right.

FATHER: You behaved disgracefully to your wife, did you not?

SON: No.

FATHER: In fact, so disgracefully that you had to apologize to her.

SON: I don't remember.

FATHER: Will you swear you did not?

SON: What?

FATHER: Will you swear you didn't apologize to her?

SON: All right.

FATHER: Now just turn to the letter on page twenty-three. Just read it out to us, will you?

SON: I see. (*He pauses.*) But what's the point of all this, actually?

FATHER: (*Standing up; very positive.*) The point? My dear boy, the point is to down your opponent. To obliterate whoever's agin you. That's what the point of it is... And, of course, to have a little fun, while you're about it. (*Tapping with his stick, the FATHER feels his way off. The SON moves downstage and speaks to the audience.*)

SON: My father got too old for the train journey to London...

(*A Robing-room Man comes in with a wig and gown, stand-up collar and bands; and stands by the SON. As he speaks the SON unfixes his own collar, hands it to the man and takes the collar which is handed to him and puts it on, ties the bands and is robed in the wig and gown. A JUDGE is sitting in wig and gown. A Lady WITNESS, in a flowered hat and gloves, is waiting be questioned.*)

My father retired on a pension of nothing but credit, optimism and the determination not to think of anything unpleasant. His money had gone on cigars and barrels of oysters and eau-de-Cologne for his handkerchief and always first class on the railway and great, huge Japanese cherry trees which flowered for two weeks a year in a

green-white shower he never saw. He left me all the
subtle pleasures of the law.

JUDGE: (*Loudly to the SON.*) Do you want to cross-examine
this witness?

SON: (*Turns round as if woken from a reverie and enters the
courtroom scene.*) Most certainly, my Lord.

JUDGE: Very well, get on with it.

SON: (*Turning to the witness.*) Now, madam...

WITNESS: Yes.

SON: (*Starting to count under his breath.*) One – two – three –
four – five – six – seven...

JUDGE: Are you intending to ask any questions?

SON: I'm sorry, my Lord?

JUDGE: If you have a question to ask, ask it. We can't all
wait while you stand in silent prayer, you know.

SON: Now, madam. Is there anything in your conduct of
which, looking back on it, you now feel heartily ashamed?

WITNESS: (*After a pause.*) Yes.

SON: Ah. And what are you ashamed of?

WITNESS: Well, I once wrote up for an autograph – with
picture. You know the type of thing. At my age! Well,
I began off, 'Am heartily ashamed to write up but...'

JUDGE: Have you any relevant questions?

SON: Now, madam, would you be so kind as to read this
letter? – which I am about to hand you.

WITNESS: Oh, yes. Thank you.

SON: Will you read it out to us, please, madam.

WITNESS: I can't...

SON: Madam. The Court is waiting...

WITNESS: I really can't.

SON: Is there something in that letter which you would
rather not remember?

WITNESS: No. Not exactly...

SON: (*Very severely.*) Then read it to us, madam!

WITNESS: Then, could I borrow your glasses?

(*All on stage except the SON, laugh.*)

SON: It was years before it got any better.

(*The members of the court exit, removing and replacing the
courtroom furniture.*)

But then quite suddenly all the judges seemed to get younger. I forgot my father's timing, and I began to enjoy a modest success.

(*The SON exits. The FATHER enters, then the MOTHER, the FATHER carries a newspaper.*)

FATHER: Elizabeth?

MOTHER: No.

(*ELIZABETH enters.*)

They're giving him a lot of briefs.

ELIZABETH: Yes.

MOTHER: It's hard to believe. Of course his father would so have enjoyed Clarkson *v.* Clarkson.

ELIZABETH: Oh, yes, I'm sure he would.

MOTHER: It must be keeping you very busy.

ELIZABETH: Me? Why me?

MOTHER: Don't you help him with his cases?

ELIZABETH: Oh, he's got a secretary now. He hardly ever discusses his work: he thinks I take it too seriously.

MOTHER: Of course his father misses going to London. He used to get such a lot of fun, out of the divorce cases.

FATHER: (*Opening his eyes.*) What's that?

MOTHER: I said you missed going to London, dear.

FATHER: It's my son, you know. He's pinched all my work. Are we still waiting?

MOTHER: Yes, dear, we're still waiting. Children all settled?

ELIZABETH: Yes, they're all settled.

MOTHER: And how's our little Jennifer?

ELIZABETH: Your little Jennifer's fine, and the same goes for our little Daniel and Jonathan.

MOTHER: Jenny's so pretty. I'd like to have done a drawing of her. Perhaps a pastel.

ELIZABETH: Well, why don't you?

MOTHER: Oh, I gave up drawing when I got married. You have to, don't you – give up things when you get married...

ELIZABETH: Do you?

MOTHER: Of course now there's no time...

ELIZABETH: (*Looking at the FATHER and whispering.*)
   Doesn't he ever leave you half an hour to yourself?

MOTHER: He doesn't like to be left. I suppose I often
   think. Some day I'll be alone, shan't I. You can't help
   thinking.

ELIZABETH: What'll you do? Travel. Go to France.

MOTHER: Well, I shan't dig the garden for one thing.
   (*The SON enters with a tray of champagne and glasses.*)

SON: (*Pause.*) The traffic was Hell!

ELIZABETH: What happened, darling?

SON: I won – Clarkson *v.* Clarkson, after five days.

FATHER: (*Smacking his lips.*) Five refreshers!

SON: They insisted on fighting every inch of the way.
   Terribly litigious...

FATHER: The sort to breed from – those Clarksons!

SON: I brought champagne...

MOTHER: Oh, how festive.

SON: For a small celebration.

ELIZABETH: (*Muttering.*) Just like a wedding.

SON: What did you say?

ELIZABETH: Nothing.

MOTHER: Isn't it festive, dear?

FATHER: Festive indeed!

MOTHER: He's offering you a glass of champagne.

FATHER: I'm glad you can afford such things, dear boy.
   I suppose you're polite to solicitors?

SON: Occasionally.

FATHER: I could never bring myself... Pity. If I'd gone to
   dinner with solicitors I might've had something to leave
   you – beyond my overdraft. I remember after one case,
   my solicitor said to me, standing on the platform of
   Temple Station, 'Are you going west, old boy, we might
   have dinner together?' 'No', I lied to him, I was so
   anxious to get away, 'I'm going east.' I ended up with a
   sandwich in Bethnal Green. It's been my fault... The
   determination to be alone. You know what'd go very
   nicely with this champagne?

MOTHER: What, dear – a dry biscuit?

FATHER: No.

SON: The crossword.

MOTHER: One across. The N.C.O. sounds agony.

FATHER: The N.C.O. sounds agony. How many letters?

MOTHER: Two words – eight and ten.

FATHER: Corporal punishment.

MOTHER: That's very clever!

FATHER: Oh, I have this crossword fellow at my mercy.
  (*The FATHER and MOTHER exit.*)

ELIZABETH: And you're very clever, too, darling.

SON: Thank you.

ELIZABETH: The only thing is…

SON: What?

ELIZABETH: I thought – I mean in that Clarkson *v.*
  Clarkson – you were for the husband?

SON: Of course I was for the husband.

ELIZABETH: Wasn't he the man who insisted on his wife
  tickling the soles of his feet. For hours at a stretch…

SON: Yes, but it was only while they watched television.

ELIZABETH: With a contraption! A foot tickler…

SON: It was most ingenious actually. The whole thing was
  worked out by a system of weights and pulleys. The
  actual act was performed by an old pipe cleaner.

ELIZABETH: Ought he to have won?

SON: (*Correcting her.*) *I* won.

ELIZABETH: Yes, but ought you…?

SON: The Judge said it was part of the wear and tear of
  married life.

ELIZABETH: Yes, but how did *they* feel about it. I mean,
  I suppose they're still married, aren't they?

SON: They did look a little confused.

ELIZABETH: Perhaps they didn't appreciate the rules of
  the game…

SON: Oh, I enjoyed it…

ELIZABETH: You enjoy playing games, don't you?

SON: Yes, I do.

ELIZABETH: You know what?

SON: What?

ELIZABETH: (*Quite loudly.*) You get more like him. Every day.
(*The FATHER and the MOTHER enter.*)

SON: In his old age, my father's chief sport was starting
arguments!

FATHER: Music! I can't imagine anyone actually *liking*
music. (*He pauses.*) The immortality of the soul! What a
boring concept! I can't think of anything worse than
living for eternity in some great transcendental hotel,
with nothing to do in the evenings – like that place in
Glastonbury. (*He pauses.*) What's the time?

MOTHER: Nearly half past nine.

FATHER: Ah! Time's nipping along nicely. (*He pauses.*)
Nothing narrows the mind so much as foreign travel.
Stay at home. That's the way to see the world.

ELIZABETH: I don't know that that's true.

FATHER: But of course it's true! And I'll tell you
something else, Elizabeth. Just between the two of us.
There's a lot of sorry stuff in D H Lawrence.

ELIZABETH: I don't know about that either.

FATHER: Oh, yes, there is. And a lot of damned dull stuff
in old Proust. (*He pauses.*) Did you hear that, Elizabeth?
Lot of damned dull stuff in old Proust.

ELIZABETH: Yes. I heard.

FATHER: Well, I'll say one thing for you – you're an
improvement on the ones he used to bring home. Girls
that would closet themselves in the bathroom for hours
on end. And nothing to show for it. None of them lasted
long.

ELIZABETH: I wonder why?

FATHER: Yes. I wonder. At least my son's someone to talk
to. Most people get damned dull children.
(*FATHER puts his hand out, feels the SON's hand.*)
Is that you?

SON: Yes. It's me.

FATHER: That play of yours came across quite well they
tell me.

SON: Yes.
(*A pause.*)

MOTHER: Would you like a hot drink?

SON: Nothing, thank you.

(*A pause.*)

FATHER: I see that other fellow's play got very good reviews. You want to watch out he doesn't put your nose out of joint. (*He pauses.*) I haven't been sleeping lately. (*He pauses.*) And when I can't sleep, you know, I sometimes like to make a list of all the things I really hate.

MOTHER: Elizabeth, would you like a hot drink?

ELIZABETH: Is it a long list?

FATHER: No. Not very. Soft eggs. Cold plates. Waiting for things. Parsons.

SON: Parsons?

FATHER: Yes. Parsons. On the wireless. If those fellows bore God as much as they bore me, I'm sorry for Him...

ELIZABETH: My father's a parson.

FATHER: I know. (*He pauses.*) 'Nymph, in thy orisons be all my sins remembered.'

(*There is a pause. He smacks at the air with his hand.*)

Is that a wasp?

MOTHER: Yes. (*She flaps at the wasp.*)

FATHER: What's it doing?

MOTHER: It's going away

FATHER: After you've been troubled by a wasp, don't you love a fly? (*He pauses.*) Don't the evenings seem terribly long now you're married? Aren't you finding it tremendously tedious? What do you do – have the wireless?

ELIZABETH: We don't get bored, exactly.

SON: We can always fight.

FATHER: You know, I was surprised about that play of yours.

SON: Were you?

FATHER: Yes. When you told us the story of that play, I said, 'Ha. Ha. This is a bit thin. This is rather poor fooling.' Didn't I say that?

MOTHER: Yes, dear.

FATHER: 'This is likely to come very tardy off.' But now it appears to have come across quite well. Didn't that surprise you, Elizabeth?

ELIZABETH: Well...

SON: She doesn't like it.

FATHER: What?

SON: Elizabeth doesn't like it very much.

FATHER: (*Interested.*) Really? That's interesting. Now tell
me why...

ELIZABETH: Not serious.

FATHER: You don't think so? You think he's not serious.

ELIZABETH: He plays games and he tells jokes. When the
time comes to say anything serious it's as if...

SON: Oh, for heaven's sake!

FATHER: No. No. Go on.

ELIZABETH: Well, it's as if there was something stopping
him. All the time...

FATHER: Is that so? I wonder why that should be...

ELIZABETH: Well, I should think you'd know.

FATHER: Why?

ELIZABETH: Because you've never really said anything
serious to him, have you? No-one here ever says
anything. They tell stories and they make jokes – and
something's happening.

SON: Elizabeth. It doesn't always have to be said.

ELIZABETH: Sometimes. Sometimes it has to.

FATHER: Very well. What would you like to hear from
me? What words – of wisdom?
(*Silence. They all look at the FATHER. He rises, moves upstage
and sings softly.*)
'She was as bee-eautiful
As a butterfly
And as proud as a queen...'
(*The SON rises and moves down.*
The MOTHER and ELIZABETH exit.)

SON: (*To the audience.*) He had no message. I think he had
no belief. He was the advocate who can take the side that
comes to him first and always find words to anger his
opponent. He was the challenger who flung his glove
down in the darkness and waited for an argument. And
when the children came to see him he told them no
more, and no less, than he'd told me...

(*A young GIRL and two BOYS enter.*)

FATHER: Ha, ha, and who have we here?

GIRL: I'm Daniel...

FATHER: Oh really, and you're...

FIRST BOY: (*Falsetto.*) And I'm Jennifer.

GIRL: I'm Daniel, honestly.

SECOND BOY: She's a liar.

FATHER: Oh, come now. I mean, if she says she's Daniel –
shouldn't we take her word for it?

FIRST BOY: Tell us again...

FATHER: About what?

SECOND BOY: The Macbeths...

GIRL: (*With relish.*) Yes, the Macbeths!

FATHER: Dunsinane! What a dreadful place to stay...for
the week-end. Draughts. No hot water. No wireless, and
the alarm bell going off in the middle of the night when
you least expect it. And finally...the dinner party!

GIRL: Go on! Tell us!

FIRST BOY/SECOND BOY: Tell us...

FIRST BOY: About the dinner party!

FATHER: Oh, a most embarrassing affair. Dinner with the
Macbeths. And everyone's sitting down...quite comfortably.
And his wife says, 'Come and sit down, dear.'

FATHER/CHILDREN: 'The soup's getting cold...'

FATHER: And he turns to his chair and sees – someone –
something horrible! Banquo! (*His voice sinks to a terrifying
whisper.*)

'The time has been

That, when the brains were out the man would die

And there an end, but now they rise again

With twenty mortal murders on their crowns

And push us from our stools...'

SON: I used to scream when he did that to me.

(*The CHILDREN are quiet. The FATHER mouths stories
to them.*)

(*To the audience.*) His mind was full of the books that he'd
read as a boy, lying in the hot fields in his prickly
Norfolk jacket. He told them of foggy afternoons in

Baker Street and sabres at dawn at Spandau Castle, and Umslopagas and Alan Quartermaine and She Who Must Be Obeyed. He spoke to them of the absurdities of his life...

FATHER: My old father was a great one for doing unwelcome acts of kindness! Recall his rash conduct in the affair of my Uncle George's dog...

(*During this story which the CHILDREN know by heart, they prompt him.*)

SECOND BOY: It's the dog...!

FIRST BOY: Go on about the dog.

FATHER: My poor Uncle George fell on evil days – and had to sell his faithful pointer. And my father, thinking Uncle George was heartbroken, went furtively about – to buy the animal back. It was a most...

FATHER/GIRL: Lugubrious hound...

FATHER: With a long powerful rudder! It seldom or never smiled. It was not so much dangerous as...

FIRST BOY: Depressing!

FATHER: Depressing indeed! And when he saw it again my Uncle George took himself off to Uxbridge where he got himself a post with good prospects and diggings at which, unfortunately, animals were not permitted. He shed no tear, to my old father's great surprise, at this second parting from his dumb friend who then took up residence with us. A most...

FATHER/CHILDREN: Unwelcome guest...!

(*ELIZABETH enters with three waterproofs.*)

ELIZABETH: Come on, now. It's time to go home.

GIRL: Oh, no, Mum. It's the one about the dog...

SECOND BOY: Let's finish the dog.

ELIZABETH: Oh, the dog!

FATHER: We offered the dog to anyone who would provide a good home for it. Then we said we'd be content with a thoroughly bad home for the dog. (*He laughs.*) Finally, we had to pay someone a large sum of money to have the animal taken away. But my mother and I used to remember terrible stories – about faithful hounds that were able to find their way home...

FATHER/CHILDREN: *Over immense distances!*

ELIZABETH: Come on now, we must go really.

(*The MOTHER enters carrying a diary and joins the others in waving. The FATHER, ELIZABETH and the CHILDREN exit.*

The MOTHER sits at the table. The SON moves down, facing the audience.

The lights change.)

SON: The enormous garden became dark and overgrown in spreading patches. My father continued, daily, to chronicle its progress in the diary he dictated to my mother.

MOTHER: (*Reading from the diary.*) June twenty-fifth. We put sodium chlorate on the front path. We had raspberry pie from our own raspberries. The dahlias are coming into flower. The jays are eating all the peas...

SON: Willow herb and thistles and bright poppies grew up. The fruit cage collapsed like a shaken temple and wood supported the tumbled netting. The honeysuckle and yew hedges grew high as a jungle, tall and dark and uncontrolled, lit with unexpected flowers...

MOTHER: (*Reading.*) Thomas came and we saw him standing still among the camellias...

SON: A boy was hired to engage the garden in single combat. His name was not Thomas.

MOTHER: (*Reading.*) July fifteenth. We planted a hundred white begonias and staked up the Malva Alcoa. A dragonfly came into the sitting-room. Thomas was paid. Am laid up. The pest officer arrived to eliminate the wasp nests.

(*The SON goes out and returns with the FATHER in a wheelchair. ELIZABETH enters with a book.*)

Unhappily we couldn't watch the destruction...

SON: In the summer, with the garden at its most turbulent, my father became quite suddenly very old and ill...

ELIZABETH: (*Reading.*) 'What are you going to take for breakfast, Mr Phelps?' said Holmes. 'Curried fowl, eggs, or will you help yourself?' 'Thank you, I can eat nothing', said Phelps. 'Oh, come. Try the dish before you.' 'Thank you, I would really rather not.' 'Well, then', said Holmes, with a mischievous twinkle.

'I suppose you have no objections to helping me?' Phelps raised the cover, and as he did so, uttered a scream, and sat there staring with his face as white as

the plate upon which he looked. Across the centre of it was lying a little cylinder of blue-grey paper...'

FATHER: (*Breathing with difficulty; gasping.*) The Naval Treaty!

ELIZABETH: Yes. (*She closes the book.*)

FATHER: I'm afraid – you find that story a great bore.

ELIZABETH: Of course not. It was very exciting.

FATHER: Dear Elizabeth. I'm so relieved to find that you can lie as mercifully as anyone.

(*ELIZABETH goes.*)

(*Suddenly with a great effort he tries to get out of the chair.*) I want a bath! Take me to the bathroom. Cretins!

(*The SON holds him, and pulls him gently back into the wheelchair.*)

SON: Sit down. Don't be angry.

FATHER: I'm always angry – when I'm dying.

(*The FATHER's breathing becomes more irregular, then calms down as he falls asleep.*)

SON: It was a hot endless night, in a small house surrounded by a great garden in which all the plants were on the point of mutiny.

(*There is a long pause. The SON looks down on the FATHER, who is now sleeping.*

The DOCTOR comes in, wearing a dinner-jacket and carrying his bag. He nods to the SON and leans over the FATHER and feels his pulse.)

Dr Ellis...

DOCTOR: We've got a territorial dinner. In High Wycombe...

SON: How is he?

DOCTOR: (*To the FATHER.*) Wake up! Wake up! (*To the SON.*) Don't let him sleep. That's the main thing. Come on, wakey wakey! That's better...

SON: But do you think…

DOCTOR: The only thing to do is to keep his eyes open.
(*He leaves FATHER's hand hanging over the arm of the chair.*)
There's really nothing else. (*He pauses.*) I'll come back in the morning.
(*The DOCTOR goes. The MOTHER follows.*
The SON turns back to the chair, he looks at the FATHER and speaks urgently.)

SON: Wake up! Wake up! Please! Please! Wake up! (*He pulls a chair next to the FATHER and sits by him. He arranges FATHER's hand on his lap, and nods off himself.*)
(*There is a silence. Slowly the light fades over the part of the stage where they are. The SON sits up suddenly, leans over, rises and moves down.*)
I'd been told of all the things you're meant to feel.
Sudden freedom, growing up, the end of dependence, the step into the sunlight when no-one is taller than you and you're in no-one else's shadow. I know what I felt.
Lonely.
(*The SON turns and walks slowly away as – the curtain falls.*)

The End.

COLLABORATORS

Characters

HENRY WINTER

KATHERINE WINTER

SAM BROWN

GRISELDA GRIFFIN

Collaborators was first presented by Michael Codron Ltd., at the Duchess Theatre, London, on 18 April 1973, with the following cast:

HENRY, John Wood

KATHERINE, Glenda Jackson

SAM, Joss Ackland

GRISELDA, Gloria Connell

Director, Eric Thompson

Set Designer, Michael O'Flaherty

The action passes in the Winters' house
in North-West London

Time – the end of the 1950s

ACT ONE

Before and as the curtain rises we hear the sound of a record – a group singing in the manner of the late fifties.

RECORD: 'Sweet, sweet, the memories you gave me.
    They're so sweet, the memories you gave me.
    Take a fresh and tender kiss
    And a stolen night of bliss,
    One girl – one boy,
    Two hearts – much joy.
    Mem – oh – ries are made of this...'
    (*The curtain rises on the living-room of a large Victorian house in North-West London at the end of the fifties. Finger-marked white paint, an electric fire with plastic coal, children's drawings and photographs pinned up. Posters for art exhibitions: 'Matisse at the Tate', 'Sculpture in Battersea Park'. A door leads to the kitchen and a children's playroom. Back stage we can see the front door and stairs up to the bedrooms. A large table, on it a typewriter, paper, legal briefs, a dying pot plant, bills, empty bottles, children's clothes, etc., all in a mess. On the other side of the room a telephone on the floor beside the electric fire with the plastic coal. An old sofa. A radiogram which is playing.*
    HENRY WINTER comes in from the kitchen. He is in his thirties. He is carrying a white, elaborate new table lamp, with a base made from a pile of ceramic lemons, a contrast to the other rather old and battered furniture. He plugs it in. Turns off the other lights making the room look slightly more warm and romantic. He goes to a cupboard, finds one candlestick with a candle in it and puts it on the table. The record is still playing.)

HENRY: (*Calling to someone in the kitchen next door.*) When did we last have a dinner party?

RECORD: 'Add the wedding bells,
    Two hearts – where love dwells,
    Three little kids for the flavour...'

HENRY: (*Stumbling over a small plastic fire-engine on the floor.*) For the last ten years I seem to have lived entirely on nursery tea...

RECORD: 'Stir gently through the days,
See how the flavour stays,
Mem – oh – rees are made of this...'

KATHERINE: (*Calling from the kitchen.*) Have you seen Suzannah's plastic knickers?

RECORD: 'Don't forget a small moonbeam,
Stir lightly with a dream.
One man – one wife,
Two hearts – through life,
Mem – oh – rees are made of this...'

HENRY: (*Calling back.*) No! (*He goes back to the cupboard, finds the other candlestick, broken.*) You know what it's like? Living with children? It's like spending your days in a home for very old, incontinent Irish drunks! It's like life in a colony of hostile meths drinkers! They come swaying up to you with their dribble and their deep hoarse cries and you smile – a smile of propitiation – and then they take a great swipe and smash the other candlestick.

(*HENRY puts the bits of broken candlestick back in the cupboard and goes out to the kitchen.*

KATHERINE comes in. She's the same age as her husband – very attractive although at the moment her head is turbaned in a towel. She wears trousers and smokes a lot. She carries a hairbrush. She stops the record-player and squats by the fire to brush her hair.)

KATHERINE: I told you – I've lost Suzannah's plastic pants.

HENRY: (*Off.*) Thank God!

KATHERINE: Why?

HENRY: I can't stand them, that's why.

(*HENRY enters carrying an old Chianti bottle.*)

KATHERINE: You don't have anything to do with them.

HENRY: I see them in the distance. As they retreat I notice our children's bottoms swathed in pixie hoods. It's like an aerial view of American tourists in the rain. (*He fits another candle into the Chianti bottle and puts it on the table.*) I think that looks pretty distinguished. (*He looks at the bookshelves anxiously.*) The children are getting so tall. (*He takes out a book.*) Someone's started to eat the pornography. (*He puts it on a higher shelf.*) I got a new lamp fixed up. (*He moves the new lamp an inch or two, admires it.*)

KATHERINE: (*Looking at the lamp.*) Bloody Hollywood!

HENRY: What? (*He puts the typewriter on the sideboard and clears the table generally.*)

KATHERINE: Did you tell the bank manager you bought a bloody Hollywood lamp? He rang again today. (*In a Scots accent.*) 'Mr MacFeeling of the Westminster this end. Is your husband at home just now? The tide would appear to be going out on his overdraft.' I'm sick of telling him – you're locked in the downstairs loo. Trembling!

HENRY: Why not tell him we've got to live? (*He goes to a cupboard, gets out paper table napkins and glasses, starts to lay the table.*)

KATHERINE: I did. He said that might not be necessary. Why can't you speak to him? I don't think the Westminster Bank believe I've *got* a husband!

HENRY: We've got great news for MacFeeling. It's going to be all right.

KATHERINE: What?

HENRY: Mr Samuel Brown's going to solve…all our problems. (*He puts table napkins, neatly folded, into glasses. Three places.*)

KATHERINE: It's not tonight?

HENRY: (*Looking at her.*) You know damn well it's tonight. That's why you washed your hair – because someone's coming to dinner.

KATHERINE: I washed my hair because no-one's coming to dinner.

HENRY: (*Admiring the table.*) What do you think it looks like?

KATHERINE: Marvellous. Like New Year's Eve at the Rotary Club. Haven't we got any streamers?

HENRY: We don't need streamers. All we need is for you to be reasonably polite to Mr Brown. (*He lays plates, etc., for three places, then tidies the room generally during the following.*)

KATHERINE: No.

HENRY: What?

KATHERINE: No. I don't think so really. I'd rather live with the overdraft.

HENRY: For God's sake! Why?

KATHERINE: He'll – corrupt you.

HENRY: How on earth is he going to manage that?

KATHERINE: (*Standing and combing her hair, looking at her reflection in the glass.*) If you let that Mr Brown in here, he will undoubtedly corrupt you. He wants to change you. I didn't marry a movie writer.

HENRY: You didn't marry me.

KATHERINE: Oh, really?

HENRY: You married someone inexperienced and painfully thin. Who'd never heard of nappy rash or Volpar Jells or Castle Pudding or Farex or Groats or Acute Menstrual Depression. I was someone else entirely.

KATHERINE: And now you'll be someone ghastly.

HENRY: *Who* do you think?

KATHERINE: Someone who drives a white Jag and cashmere polo necks and an identity bracelet and a house in Weybridge...

HENRY: You think Sam Brown'll do that to me?

KATHERINE: And two bloody Hollywood lamps. With a white leather sofa in between them. Full of Miss Rank-Odeon unzipping her plastic tiger-skin ski-pants. I want no part of it.

HENRY: He's not going to change my life.

KATHERINE: No?

HENRY: He's harmless...

KATHERINE: Really?

HENRY: As a matter of fact he's quite civilized. He's someone who listens to radio plays.

KATHERINE: I don't believe it.

HENRY: Why?

KATHERINE: There isn't anybody who listens to radio plays.

HENRY: That's why he rang up. He said he'd heard my play on his car radio. He was stuck in a traffic jam at Marble Arch...

KATHERINE: (*Incredulously.*) For an hour!

HENRY: That's why he asked me to lunch.

KATHERINE: You're a pushover!

HENRY: At the 'Pastoria', Leicester Square.

KATHERINE: And I bet you said 'yes' after the *hors d'oeuvre*.

HENRY: I told you – he's putting together this little package.

KATHERINE: You'll be in it!

HENRY: What?

KATHERINE: Neatly wrapped in brown paper and tied up with string. Has, he ever actually made a film?

HENRY: I think...just commercials so far.

(*HENRY goes out of the door into the kitchen. She shouts to him there and he shouts back.*)

KATHERINE: Tell him you're a respectable lawyer! You don't want anything to do with his little packages.

HENRY: (*Coming back into the room with a bottle of wine which he opens and then puts down by the electric fire.*) I told you. He wants me to write something. That's all. About marriage. It's a subject he thinks might suit me.

KATHERINE: Why?

HENRY: I'm married, aren't I? For God's sake! Why else am I living in a sea of plastic knickers?

KATHERINE: Is that what you're going to write – a commercial – about our marriage?

HENRY: Sam Brown says the aim is to do something truthful. (*KATHERINE shivers.*) What's the matter?

KATHERINE: I'm afraid.

HENRY: Whatever of?

KATHERINE: We've got too many weapons.

HENRY: You know, I haven't got the slightest idea what you're talking about.

KATHERINE: The children. My mother and your mother. My past and your future – your car and my furniture. They're all like loaded guns we can pick up and use – if ever – if ever things get a little – out of control.

HENRY: If ever?

KATHERINE: The shopping and the overdraft and the John Barnes account, all little hand grenades lying about the place…and you want to import a great thousand ton all purpose hydrogen bomb we can throw at each other the day you're feeling a little bored.

HENRY: (*Lighting the candles.*) Dramatize! Dramatize everything…

KATHERINE: It's like standing on the edge of the sea…

HENRY: Doom! Doom! The Lady Macbeth of Belsize Park!

KATHERINE: On the edge of the sea and you have an irresistible urge to walk in, until the water closes over your head.

HENRY: Ring the alarm bell! Lines of murdered children, stretching as far as the eye can reach… It's nothing but a film producer coming for dinner!

KATHERINE: My Aunt Freda drowned herself, in Prestatyn. The sea was very shallow – she was only a small woman but she had to walk out two miles until she could get her head under. I wonder what she thought about all the time she was walking…

HENRY: (*Going to the radiogram and putting on a record.*) Will you stop *acting!*

KATHERINE: What's your part, darling? Little orphan Annie – eagerly waiting for the rich squire to come in and seduce her? It's all laid on, isn't it? Music and candles – how disgusting!

(*The record starts to play. Elvis is singing.*
HENRY starts to dance a slow 1950s jive. He puts out his hand for KATHERINE to dance with him. She shakes her head.)

KATHERINE: I'm not dancing with you tonight. Anyway, it's not your period.

HENRY: What's my period?

KATHERINE: I'd say late Carmen Miranda…

HENRY: (*Stopping dancing, angry, and moving to the kitchen door.*) Try and not be brutal to Mr Brown.

(*HENRY exits to the kitchen.*

KATHERINE picks up the towel, puts it round her neck like a muffler, and also exits. The record goes on playing.

KATHERINE returns with a large wooden clothes horse hung with nappies which she plumps down in front of the electric fire. The front doorbell rings.)

KATHERINE: Oh, shit!

(*KATHERINE blows out the candles then runs off by the entrance leading to the staircase. She returns with a plastic baby bath full of washing and puts it on the table.*

The doorbell rings again. KATHERINE turns off the record, pushes the baby's potty down stage. The doorbell rings a third time. She goes and opens the front door.

SAM BROWN enters – it is difficult to tell his age – sometimes he seems gay and enthusiastic, at others haggard and middle-aged. He speaks with a variable American accent and is wearing an anonymous Brooks Brothers suit, a black knitted tie which he loosens at moments of stress and a small tartan trilby hat. He looks at the domestic chaos.

KATHERINE follows him into the room. A sound of chopping is heard from the kitchen.)

SAM: Brown. Sam Brown. (*He takes off his hat.*) You must be his wife.

KATHERINE: (*Whispers back.*) *Must* I? That's depressing.

SAM: Is it?

KATHERINE: I always thought I exercised a vague kind of choice. I'm sorry about the muddle – kids. You know how it is.

SAM: (*Whispering.*) No. No.

KATHERINE: (*Whispering.*) What?

SAM: I don't know.

KATHERINE: (*Looking at him.*) You haven't got any?

SAM: No. No. I haven't.

KATHERINE: (*Looking at him as though he were some rare phenomenon.*) How extraordinary!

(*Pause.*)

Why're we whispering?

SAM: Your feller's at work. Isn't that the typewriter?

KATHERINE: No. The chopper.

(*SAM looks at her, surprised.*)

SAM: The chopper?

KATHERINE: He's doing his *Pot au feu.*

SAM: Pardon me?

KATHERINE: It's stew. He cuts recipes out of the *Evening Standard.*

SAM: (*After a pause, looking at her, worried.*) You mean, he cooks?

KATHERINE: Practically the whole time.

SAM: This man writes dramatic material for the radio and also cooks!

KATHERINE: (*Picking up baby clothes.*) And dusts and sprays things with Gleam and arranges furniture and administers aspirin to wilting chrysanths.

SAM: Jeezus!

KATHERINE: He doesn't often change nappies or make beds or put washers on taps. That's my work.

SAM: Kerist...!

KATHERINE: Yes. (*She picks up the potty.*) I was just going to settle the children.

SAM: How many – exactly?

KATHERINE: Does it matter?

SAM: No – but...

KATHERINE: More, probably, than you've ever seen in your life. Many, many more.

SAM: Before you go...can I ask you something quite frankly? As Henry's wife? How's his availability?

KATHERINE: His what?

SAM: His availability. How is it?

KATHERINE: Pretty good first thing in the morning. Not so marvellous last thing at night.

SAM: I mean – is he really going to have time to take on this assignment?

KATHERINE: (*Decidedly.*) No.

SAM: What?

KATHERINE: No. He's certainly not going to have time for that.

(*KATHERINE exits upstairs.*
SAM starts to examine the room curiously, as though it were a strange country.
HENRY enters carrying an empty casserole dish from which he is taking a pair of children's plastic pants.)

HENRY: Look, it's unbelievable! An incredible place to find them. (*He throws the pants down into the plastic bath, bangs the dish down on the table.*) Oh, Mr Brown. You're here early.

SAM: What a lovely home you have here.

HENRY: (*Incredulously.*) What?

SAM: This certainly is a lovely home.

HENRY: You're joking?

SAM: Dickensian!

HENRY: You can say that again.

SAM: How would a person find – a truly Dickensian home such as this?

HENRY: Only by mistake. Have a drink? (*He goes to the bottle of wine by the fire.*)

SAM: Maybe later...

HENRY: (*Pouring himself a glass and holding it up to the light.*) Something shy and anonymous from the off licence.

SAM: Mr Winter. May I call you Humphrey?

HENRY: If you like. My name's Henry actually.

SAM: Henry. I'm Sam. And I have already met your lovely lady.

HENRY: Oh? (*He drinks quickly.*)

SAM: She let me into your front door and was gracious enough to engage me – in conversation.

HENRY: (*Picking up the clothes horse and carrying it out.*) She seems to have turned the place into a kind of steam laundry.

SAM: Henry. Henry. I want you to tell me something.

HENRY: (*Returning.*) What? (*He picks up the plastic tub of washing, puts the saucepan on top of it.*)

SAM: The process of procreation and childbirth – it's not particularly difficult, is it?

HENRY: (*Putting the dish into the plastic tub, and going out with it into the kitchen.*) No.

SAM: It doesn't call for any special skills or aptitude which I may not possess?

HENRY: (*Coming back into the room.*) I don't think so.

SAM: Or demand arduous training or a long period of study?

HENRY: Certainly not. What's troubling you, Mr Brown?

SAM: How come your wife made me feel so suddenly inadequate?

HENRY: Ah, well now...when you get to know her...

SAM: Something of a ball cutter, is she, your good lady?

HENRY: Well now, Mr Brown.

SAM: Sam. I'm Sam, Henry. Is she the sort that enjoys to cut ball occasionally? I feel we should be very frank with each other at the outset of what I hope will be a long and happy relationship.

HENRY: (*Moving away from him.*) I was just – chopping parsley.

SAM: You are wandering from the point. Something here's a little painful for you to contemplate, is that it? Your lady does not feel that we should work together. She thinks that your schedule is such that you may be unavailable?

HENRY: What?

SAM: She thinks you might have too much on your plate already.

HENRY: Too much on my plate? That's ridiculous. Look. Why don't you sit down, or play a record, or – something. (*HENRY moves towards the kitchen door. SAM follows and stands very close to him.*)

SAM: She also suggested you were cooking.

HENRY: Well, that's right. It's a kind of casserole, quite honestly. It won't take me a minute.

SAM: Where I come from only faggots cook.

HENRY: (*Looking at him, not knowing what to say.*) Do they? Where is that exactly? I know. You told me...

SAM: To cook is always thought of as the hallmark of a fag. (*Pause. HENRY can think of nothing to say.*)
What was your wife doing, Henry – laying such emphasis on your cooking abilities? Was she trying to cut your balls off, feller?
(*The telephone rings.*)

HENRY: Excuse me. (*He goes to the telephone.*) Oh, hullo,
Miss Griffin. Of course I don't mind you ringing me at
home... No, I'm not busy, not really...
(*SAM picks a book from the shelf, is surprised.*)
Oh... It's about our murder. Yes. How's it going?
(*SAM looks up from the book, more surprised.*)
To be committed on Thursday? Well, that doesn't give us
much time.
(*SAM puts down the book and moves closer to him.*)
I mean attempted murder's not a thing we can rush into
– that is, if I'm not going to make a complete and utter
fool of myself.
(*SAM has now moved very close to HENRY and is standing
beside him as he talks to the phone.*)
Look shall we talk about it tomorrow...? Four-thirty.
Fine. (*He scribbles a note on the pad by the phone.*) We'll
have tea in the Kardomah. (*He puts down the phone, finds
he is looking into SAM's anxious face.*)

SAM: Murder? Did you say – attempt to murder?

HENRY: My first time, actually...
(*KATHERINE comes down the stairs.*)

KATHERINE: He's a lawyer. Hasn't he told you?

HENRY: A barrister.

SAM: Henry! You have a barristership?

KATHERINE: No-one gets told everything – about my
husband. (*She pours herself a drink.*) Have you told Mr
Duffield you're writing a film about marriage, darling?

SAM: Who's Mr Duffield?

KATHERINE: He sits every night in the condemned cell,
wondering how the show's going.

HENRY: Not the condemned cell. Brixton. The Hospital
Wing. They get television and tranquillizers.

KATHERINE: Just like us.

HENRY: I'm worried about Bernard Duffield, as a matter of
fact. He seems to have a deep desire to be found guilty.

KATHERINE: Then he's certainly picked the right barrister.
(*SAM makes a private cutting gesture with his hand to
HENRY.*)
Care for a drink, Mr Brown?

SAM: Scotch, please. On the rocks. I'm afraid my blood alcohol is sinking a little low.

KATHERINE: (*Pouring him a glass of wine.*) I'm afraid we've got no rocks.

SAM: Murder, uh? That must be interesting. Tell me...

HENRY: 'How do you defend a person you think's really done it?'

SAM: How did you know I'd ask you that?

HENRY: Everyone does. Well, the answer is – I just don't make up my mind.

KATHERINE: He finds that perfectly easy. Not making up his mind comes quite naturally to Henry.

HENRY: It's just a question of suspending belief...

KATHERINE: That was his belief you passed in the hall, it's been hanging up there for years!

SAM: I guess the movie business calls for a little more sincerity.

KATHERINE: Sincerity? We must get some of that in for the next time you call. (*To HENRY.*) Write it on the blackboard, darling. (*To SAM.*) He has a little blackboard in the kitchen. He writes down things he's short of. Garlic, sweet and sour sauce, sincerity...

SAM: (*Very seriously.*) Add one more quality, Katherine.

KATHERINE: What?

SAM: Hard work. It's pretty ruthless. The Show Business.

KATHERINE: You'll find murder gentle by comparison?

SAM: You go to Honolulu at all?

KATHERINE: Not regularly.

SAM: Katherine, let me tell you something. The brain of a dolphin is half as big again as the brain of man!

KATHERINE: No kidding!

SAM: They have this great Dolphinarium in Honolulu. And you should see these fish perform! Better than actors. They solve mathematical problems. They dance the – Da Da Da Da Pom – you know!

KATHERINE: (*Helpful.*) The Skaters' Waltz.

SAM: Yes. Well, in the hotel there the Maître D offered me 'Mai Mai steak'. Very good. Natural, sustaining and delicious food. Until I asked what was 'Mai Mai' exactly. You know what they told me?

KATHERINE: You were eating those unfortunate dolphins that couldn't do Strauss waltzes?

SAM: Right! She's right! Kinda frightening, though, isn't it?

HENRY: (*Refilling SAM's glass.*) Is it?

KATHERINE: Oh, Henry's not frightened. He'll whistle and ring bells and dance the waltz even if there's no water in the tank. I'll get the stew...

(*KATHERINE goes into the kitchen, banging the door after her. SAM is left looking at HENRY. HENRY brings down his own chair and sets it at the table.*)

SAM: Know what I told you, feller? (*He drinks.*) Professionally. A modern marriage. What a great story. (*KATHERINE enters with a casserole and plates, which she puts on the table.*
The three sit to eat, SAM in the middle.
The lights fade, then come up as before. Dinner is over. SAM is explaining to KATHERINE.)
I tell you this group – this group I've done commercials for – they've become so big in footwear they're investing in talent...! They want to make something really interesting. (*He yawns.*)

KATHERINE: About marriage?

SAM: They figure – a subject that concerns everyone...

KATHERINE: Like feet...

SAM: I believe – if we can put a script together that they go for – they'll find us finance, Henry. No question. It will be found eventually...

HENRY: Well, finance would certainly come in useful.

KATHERINE: (*To SAM.*) I thought you wanted *him* to do it.

SAM: What?

KATHERINE: I thought Henry was going to put the script together...

SAM: We'll work together, won't we, feller? Knowing each other as we do – we'll work together as a team. It's a challenge!

HENRY: (*Unenthusiastically.*) Yes. I suppose it is.

SAM: It's not going to be easy. I'm not going to kid you about that. We'll have our bad moments, sure. We'll cry together, but have our laughs also, let's hope. (*He gets up.*) Well, you lovely people. It was a pleasure and a privilege to enter your home. (*He punches HENRY lightly on the shoulder.*) Great stew. You did a great job.

KATHERINE: He'll make a lovely wife. (*She moves away from them, pours herself a glass of wine.*)

SAM: (*Looking after her.*) What a subject! (*He moves with HENRY towards the front door.*) Ring me next week, uh? (*Goes.*)

(*As SAM exits, KATHERINE starts to laugh. HENRY sees her, pushes the front door. It does not shut. HENRY goes towards KATHERINE and puts his arm round her. They both laugh.*)

HENRY: Cry together! Do you think we have to?

KATHERINE: What did he propose to you at lunch, actually? Sounds to me as if he proposed marriage. (*She stops laughing.*) He's ruthless! (*She moves away from him.*)

HENRY: Probably.

KATHERINE: Russian, of course.

HENRY: He's not Russian!

KATHERINE: What is he then?

HENRY: I believe he was born in a small office off Wardour Street.

KATHERINE: With an American accent!

HENRY: They learn that. In the Berlitz School, Tottenham Court Road. Anyway, why should an American accent make him Russian? (*He drains the wine bottle into his glass, drinks.*)

KATHERINE: That's his cunning.

HENRY: Oh, yes?

KATHERINE: You can't believe a word he says.

HENRY: That's true.

KATHERINE: Pretending to be a film producer!

HENRY: People who pretend to be film producers *become* film producers. It's the only way.

KATHERINE: Modern marriage! What a ridiculous idea!

HENRY: Exactly. If people want marriage they can do it quietly amongst themselves. They don't need to go out and watch other people at it.

KATHERINE: Did you tell him that?

HENRY: Of course I did. Didn't you hear me?

KATHERINE: You kissed his arse!

HENRY: (*Sings.*) 'Here we go again
Moaning low again!!'

KATHERINE: 'Yes, Mr Film Producer. No, Mr Film Producer. Three bags full, Mr Film Producer. Mr Film Producer, do tell us about footwear all over again, Mr Film Producer.' Kissing his arse.

HENRY: I suppose you pick up that revolting language from the children.

KATHERINE: I saw the utter contempt – in his cold Slavic eyes. He'll be round for a work session.

HENRY: No. No, he won't.

KATHERINE: Lying all over the furniture in his stockinged feet. Surrounded by little men from Freeman, Hardy and Willis. Talking through the story line. What's your contribution going to be? The semi-colons? Come to think of it Brunowski probably never heard of a semi-colon.

HENRY: He's gone.

KATHERINE: What?

HENRY: And he won't be coming back.

KATHERINE: Or German. Probably a German. They always pretend to come from Austria.

HENRY: He never mentioned Austria.

KATHERINE: That was his cunning! You were so bloody polite. Collaborating with the Germans... That's very typical.

HENRY: I'm not going to!

KATHERINE: You're not going to what?

HENRY: I've decided – I shall ring up and say I'm not interested.

(*KATHERINE looks at him sympathetically.*)

KATHERINE: (*After a pause.*) Poor darling... You have that feeling, don't you?

HENRY: What feeling?

KATHERINE: That he's got away. That you might be missing something – the bus.

HENRY: It's my life! Standing there full of regrets as the bus draws away into the distance. I remember once. I was at a party.

KATHERINE: When?

HENRY: Long ago. Before we met.

KATHERINE: (*Singing quietly as she starts to clear the table.*) 'Long ago and far away
I dreamed a dream one day...'

HENRY: I had an introduction to some people called Bottle. They lived in Enfield. I was told they 'swung'. I was innocent at the time. Of what 'swinging' meant.

KATHERINE: And imagined you'd find the whole family Bottle suspended from the ceiling on trapezes.

HENRY: Anyway, they invited me to this party. I was standing in the loo when I became aware of many of me. All in similar attitudes. The loo chez Bottle was as rich in mirrors as the Palace of Versailles. When in burst Mrs B.

KATHERINE: Beatrice...?

HENRY: Bernice Bottle. Gold lamé trousers, stiletto heels, a stretched jersey top. Her front teeth lightly tinted with carmine lipstick.

KATHERINE: I know. She made a proposition. The most boring thing about marriage is having to share your fantasies.

HENRY: No, it's true! I promise you it's true! 'Well,' I said, 'well, if you really feel like that – urgently.'

KATHERINE: Always modest.

HENRY: 'If you feel like that,' I said, 'let's get the hell out of here and back to my small room in Kilburn High Road.'

KATHERINE: That room! Your imaginary heaven.

HENRY: (*Replacing the dining chair.*) She was horrified, as if I'd committed some ghastly social blunder. 'What?' she said. 'Are you suggesting I leave my guests?' As I went out of the door I had the impression she was naked in the dimmed light of the lounge, handing round twiglets.

Since then I've felt I've missed some vital experience…
It was rather like that when Mr Brown left us.

KATHERINE: Do they really do that in Enfield? (*She picks up SAM's hat.*)

HENRY: I believe most Fridays. Except when they're watching Wimbledon.

KATHERINE: He's left his hat.

HENRY: What?

KATHERINE: (*Looking inside it.*) Prizunic! M'sieur Brown's left his little tartan hat. (*She puts it down.*)

HENRY: Women don't have fantasies…

KATHERINE: Oh, all the time.

HENRY: What's your fantasy?

KATHERINE: You.

(*He looks pleased. He pours them both another drink. They drink. He goes to the radiogram.*)

I was coping with some sort of reality. The war. Paul away fighting for his country in army education. I was queuing up for orange juice and dodging doodle bugs. And then I met you. The fantasy began.

HENRY: New Year's Eve. (*Finding an old record.*) The Cathedral Hotel, Guildford.

KATHERINE: A fantasy meal, in time of shortage.

HENRY: Black Market Communion wine. (*He puts the record on the radiogram.*)

KATHERINE: Gin and altars.

HENRY: Whale steak.

KATHERINE: Moby Dick and chips. (*The record starts to play softly.*)

HENRY: All the men having been called up to study Kafka with your husband…

KATHERINE: Eve Tish and her Squadronettes!
(*They start to dance – a slow foxtrot with lots of Victor Sylvester turns. KATHERINE sings 'Small Hotel'. The front doorbell rings. They don't hear it.*)

HENRY: Who wants people?

KATHERINE: (*Breaking away from him.*) You do! You do, apparently! You want to populate our lives with people!

Why do you *tell* me all the time? That's what I don't
understand… Why *tell* me? (*She turns off the record.*)

HENRY: I haven't told you anything.

KATHERINE: You bring it all back like a little dog –
reverently laying corpses, mauled birds, half a rat, on the
hearth rug. For Mother to see!

HENRY: (*Singing.*) 'Here we slide again
Ready to take that ride again…'

KATHERINE: Notes on cheque-books! Love letters on the
backs of menus! Shirts which you carefully mark with
lipstick before you come home at night. For my benefit!
Why should I care what weird people you fancy. Just
don't bring them all home.
(*The front doorbell rings again. Intent on quarrelling they
do not answer it.*)

HENRY: I don't fancy him.

KATHERINE: What?

HENRY: I don't actually fancy Sam Brown.

KATHERINE: (*Picking up the notepad by the telephone.*)
Griselda. *Who is Griselda Griffin?* Tea four-thirty.

HENRY: Who do you think she is?

KATHERINE: A floosie! A popsie! A little bit of fluff! Tea!
How charming. How utterly delightful. Just when I'm
reading *Noddy in Toyland* to Henrietta with one hand and
prodding groats into Seraphina while she squats on her
potty with the other, you'll be giving it to Miss Griselda
Griffin in some tousled bed-sitting-room in Oakley
Street. And then stagger back for a strong drink and
sympathy after a hard day at work. With your pockets
full of messages for me to read! (*She throws the pad down.*)

HENRY: (*Calmly.*) Miss Griselda Griffin is articled to a
solicitor of the Supreme Court.

KATHERINE: You're lying!

HENRY: We shall be meeting in the Kardomah, Fleet Street.

KATHERINE: Why do you have to lie?

HENRY: Why do you have to pretend?

KATHERINE: Pretend what?

HENRY: That it's disaster. Fire. War. Pestilence. That you're
drowning yourself. That the water is closing over your head.

KATHERINE: Bastard! I am not drowning myself. You're drowning me!

HENRY: How?

KATHERINE: With your lies. Do you think I mind about Gristle? Of course I don't mind about Gristle. It's the lies I mind, that's all. Why can't you tell the truth for once in your life!

HENRY: We've chosen the Kardomah so that we can go through forty-two passionate positions under the pastry trolley...what do you want?

KATHERINE: What do *you* want?

HENRY: Freedom. For five minutes. Not to answer questions.

KATHERINE: (*Shouting.*) Are you? Are you having it off with Gristle? Just say you are. Tell the truth!

HENRY: (*Shouting back.*) All right. Yes. I'm having it off with Gristle.

KATHERINE: I hate you!

HENRY: All right. No! I'm not having it off with Gristle.

KATHERINE: Liar!

HENRY: (*With very carefully assumed, and maddening, patience and calm.*) You could just let me know exactly what it is you want me to say.

KATHERINE: Bloody... Barrister!

(*KATHERINE picks up the lamp. As she rips it out of the wall there is a flash and darkness as the light fuses. There is a crash in the darkness and then KATHERINE cries. KATHERINE and HENRY collapse behind the sofa with the lamp, which breaks. There is a great deal of laughter and giggling which changes to sighs and murmurs.*

The front doorbell rings again and SAM enters, returning to retrieve his hat, and strikes a match.

Somewhere in the gloom SAM sees HENRY and KATHERINE apparently locked in a death struggle on the floor: he blows out the match, darkness.)

You're drowning me!

(*After a moment there is the sound of a Hoover. As the lights come up to daylight, the whine of the Hoover rises to a crescendo, then dies. When we can see her, KATHERINE is alone on the stage, moodily trying to repair the broken Hoover plug with a knife. The front doorbell rings. KATHERINE drops the plug, puts the knife on the table, then opens the door. SAM enters.)*

Oh, it's you.

SAM: Where's the genius?

KATHERINE: If you mean Henry. He's out. *(She starts to roll the cord of the Hoover up.)*

SAM: Oh. Oh, I see. Did he say where...?

KATHERINE: He said – to the Uxbridge Magistrates' Court.

SAM: Oh. So that's where he's gone.

KATHERINE: Not necessarily. Where he goes and where he says he goes only coincide occasionally. *(She pushes the Hoover out into the kitchen as SAM is speaking.)*

SAM: He called me. He left a message on my answering service. About our project, I guess.

KATHERINE: *(Coming back from the kitchen.)* He's not going to do it. *(She picks up a doll from under the table, walks a few paces, then throws it back where it was.)*

SAM: What?

KATHERINE: *(Turning off the electric fire.)* He phoned to tell you. He's not going to do it.

SAM: He's not. Any reason in particular?

KATHERINE: We've got too much on our plates.

SAM: Pardon me?

KATHERINE: Too many – people. We can't take on you as well. Either of us. I'm sorry. Look. What's the time? I've got to collect the kids from nursery and...

SAM: Look. Mrs Winter – Katherine. *(He moves nearer to her.)* Are you scared of me or something?

KATHERINE: Yes.

SAM: What?

KATHERINE: Yes, I'm scared of you, or something.

SAM: It's only a script. It's only a little job of work, God dammit. Aren't you being overly possessive?

KATHERINE: Possessive? Me? Possessive...?

SAM: Are you afraid I'm going to take your husband off you?

KATHERINE: (*Looking round for an escape.*) I've got to get all round John Barnes' Food Department and...

SAM: Look, Katherine, are you being exactly fair to Henry?

KATHERINE: (*Puzzled.*) Fair? I'm married to him, aren't I? What's being fair got to do with it?

SAM: I remember. First thing off... You suggested to me that he was never out of the kitchen... In his apron! Well, our boy seems a fairly normal type of individual...

KATHERINE: Our boy! (*Almost laughing in spite of herself.*) Our sweet little fellow. Look – if I don't get these kids out of the nursery by three they strap them down on to their pots and read them Bible stories...

SAM: Katherine! (*He looks at his watch.*) It's only midday by now.

KATHERINE: (*Desperately, looking hopelessly at the door.*) We're standing still... The day's going on for ever!

SAM: I'd like you to think of me as a human being... Forget the film tycoon and all that crap. Ignore the Head of Wardour Screen Promotions and all that bugaboo. Okay, I'm the guy who's in a position to offer your husband remunerative employment. Just think of me as a human person who accidentally got an insight into your private life.

KATHERINE: Accidentally?

SAM: That night after dinner, as it so happened, I forgot my hat. Well, your door doesn't seem to shut properly...

KATHERINE: We're open to the public.

SAM: No-one answered the bell. I thought I'd retrieve it unobtrusively.

KATHERINE: You were here! When...

SAM: You didn't notice me?

KATHERINE: No – no.

SAM: You were busy, I guess.

KATHERINE: (*Outraged.*) You were spying on us!

SAM: (*Putting a hand on her shoulder.*) Katherine, I am offering you my concern.

KATHERINE: (*Moving away from him; angrily.*) Not today, thank you!

SAM: Not...?

KATHERINE: That's what I have to say to all of you.

SAM: All of us?

KATHERINE: All of you who come here offering me offers. I'm stuck here like an Aunt Sally for offers. Once you get your sharp little feet inside the door. Special suction brushes. Cut-price Brillo Pads! Slightly soiled copies of the *Encyclopaedia Britannica*. Gaily coloured books on the subject of Blood, free from Jehovah's Witnesses – and your Concern! Thank you very much. Not today. No, thank you.

SAM: You're not happy, are you?

KATHERINE: Oh, for God's sake!

SAM: You think you can tell me why?

KATHERINE: Because I can't get anyone to put a new plug on the Hoover. If I got another life it'd be – married to an electrician.

(*The phone rings. KATHERINE picks it up. SAM stands watching her. She is tense, gripping the instrument.*)

No. He's not back yet... The Magistrates' Court. That's what he said... Yes... Yes, I'll tell him.

(*She puts the phone down. SAM looks at her.*)

(*With deep contempt.*) Gristle!

SAM: (*Moving to the door.*) Well. You've got the kids to fetch...

KATHERINE: (*Reluctant now to let him go.*) Not till three. Not for hours, actually...

SAM: I'd better go – and think about another writer...

KATHERINE: Don't go. If you don't have to...

SAM: (*Moving back into the room.*) I thought I wasn't entirely welcome.

KATHERINE: Oh, you're better than the other things.

SAM: Thank you very much! What other things?

KATHERINE: Encyclopaedia men. Jehovah's Witnesses – telephone calls – from Miss Griselda the articled clerk. Why does he have to arrange for her to phone me every hour on the hour? Just in case I might forget her existence...

SAM: Would you like to talk?

KATHERINE: Yes. Yes, I'd like to – I think.

SAM: About Henry?

KATHERINE: About anything. It gets so quiet here during the day. Sometimes – sometimes the only way I can hear a bit of intelligent conversation is by switching on the Archers...

SAM: You know – I'm not really close to Henry. Not intimate. As yet. But from the few times I've met your feller – he struck me – I must say if I'm honest...

KATHERINE: How did he strike you?

SAM: As amiable. Extremely amiable.

KATHERINE: You know how he struck me? Hard. Did I make a joke? (*She shivers.*) How disgusting! It must be infectious. Amiable?

(*KATHERINE hears the front door opening and without looking round, raises her voice a little.*)

Oh, certainly. Until he starts throwing the furniture.

SAM: Is *that* what happened?

KATHERINE: Didn't you notice? When you were spying on us?

(*The hall door opens. HENRY comes into the room. He is wearing a dark suit and carrying a brief-case.*

KATHERINE goes on as if unaware he's arrived.)

Until he rips the lamps from the wall and uses them – as ammunition!

(*HENRY goes to the table and puts his brief-case down on it.*)

HENRY: I hear myself say the most incredible things.

KATHERINE: (*Moving away and standing by the electric fire and the mantelpiece.*) So do I.

HENRY: In court! I open my mouth and for God's sake Marshall-Hall rides again! There was Bernard in the dock...

SAM: Hello, Henry. Who...?

HENRY: Bernard Duffield and I pointed to him – with a finger trembling with emotion...

KATHERINE: Such emotional fingers!

HENRY: 'Give him justice', I heard myself say. 'The justice he has waited and prayed for all these months. But let it

be justice tempered with that mercy which is the
hallmark of the Uxbridge and Hillingdon District
Magistrates' Court...'

(*HENRY laughs. The other two do not.*)

KATHERINE: Was Gristle with you?

HENRY: What? (*He unpacks some briefs, a typescript, pencils
and bills in envelopes, together with children's bricks, from his
case.*)

KATHERINE: Was the learned Miss Articled Solicitor
Griselda in court with you? In your hour of triumph.

HENRY: Well, as a matter of fact... (*He smiles at her.*) Yes.

KATHERINE: Then why does she keep ringing me up – to
find out where you are?

HENRY: Oh – well. She had to rush away actually. To an
indecent assault in Dagenham...

KATHERINE: Tell her to leave me alone, will you?

HENRY: I suppose she was curious about the result.

KATHERINE: However curious she is. Just tell her to lay
off the telephone.

HENRY: (*Remembering with a smile.*) 'Justice – tempered with
that mercy which is the hallmark of the Uxbridge...'

SAM: Pretty good, that. Did they let him off?

HENRY: They sent him for trial – at the Old Bailey.

SAM: You want to be careful, old friend.

HENRY: What?

SAM: Careful they don't send you for trial. Katherine's been
telling me...

HENRY: What...? What's she been telling you?

SAM: Only what I saw – with my own eyes.

KATHERINE: He came back after his little tartan hat. The
day the Hollywood lamp met an untimely death...

HENRY: Oh. Oh, I see.

SAM: And I couldn't help noticing...

HENRY: What?

SAM: It appeared to me, chum. Just from the casual glance
I took. That you were assaulting your lady wife.

HENRY: Really?

SAM: Striking Katherine.

HENRY: Is that the impression you got?

SAM: I have lived a hell of a lot of life, friend. But I can think of no defence to using physical force against a woman.

HENRY: Can't you really?

SAM: None whatsoever.

HENRY: Poor Bernard.

SAM: Who the hell's Bernard?

HENRY: Bernard Duffield. My most important client. Come to think of it, by and large my only client. He set out to murder his wife. A huge and ambitious project. Something calling for the full fire-power of the NATO alliance.

SAM: And you are defending him.

HENRY: Brutal Bernard, the Rickmansworth Ripper!

SAM: Inhuman.

HENRY: He bought a long sharp kitchen knife, Sam – and he stole a heavy iron bar from his place of work, and he provided himself with what he describes as a short strangling cord.

SAM: Jesus.

HENRY: He then went to the *Cricketers* to announce his intentions to at least twenty witnesses, meanwhile absorbing eleven pints of Guinness, nineteen double brandies and twenty-two 'Blue Heavens', which turn out to be a mixture of Babycham, port, rum and blackcurrant juice. With his will strengthened, our Bernard set out to commit the crime of the century.

SAM: (*Hurt.*) Henry, baby – I have been sharing you with this criminal.

HENRY: He climbed up on the roof of the coal bunker and entered the bedroom to deal his wife Maisie instant death…

SAM: You're not suggesting, I hope, that these Duffields are typical of thousands of perfectly normal married couples all over the world.

HENRY: Now Maisie had a lover. A Mr Meatyard, the twenty-stone manager of Tescos. Huge and indestructible as herself. And when this vast pair started up in bed Bernard, terrified, fell seventeen feet.

KATHERINE: Poor little fellow.

HENRY: And so was arrested on his hands and knees, crawling across the allotments with a terrible hangover and two broken ankles. And his victim without a scratch! There is no justice!

KATHERINE: Justice? Is that what you care about?

HENRY: But we have a defence. A cast-iron defence. They've got the wrong man.

KATHERINE: I know what you're going to say. His wife did it.

HENRY: Of course. Bernard's innocent! Can't you see? She planned it all.

KATHERINE: Our poor boy. Married to the Boston Strangler!

HENRY: Mrs Duffield carefully, ruthlessly engineered Bernard's appearance on the roof of the coal bunker, stuffed to the gills with murder weapons and port and Guinness and Babycham and she well knew in her wicked scheming mind that he'd fall and break his fragile little neck.

(*Pause. SAM looks at HENRY, sadly again.*)

SAM: Henry – I guess you know I'm feeling sore – sore at you, Henry. Was it a nice way to behave?

HENRY: To Katherine? We're not going all through that again.

SAM: To me! I've been waiting – for a telephone call. Three whole days I waited – for a call. Day and night I waited, feller.

KATHERINE: He's what you might call casual – in human relationships.

SAM: And now after keeping me dangling. Katherine says you're about to give me a no-no...

HENRY: Did *she* say that? *She* said it?

SAM: What does that mean exactly?

KATHERINE: It probably means he'll do it. It's when he says 'yes' you know nothing's going to happen. He said 'yes' to putting a new plug on the Hoover.

HENRY: I didn't say 'yes'. I said, 'Get a man in.'

KATHERINE: (*Looking at SAM, speaking in a wildly upper class accent.*) 'Get a man in' – what a perfectly splendid idea! It solves all the problems of married life, doesn't it – getting a man in. Are you going to get a man in to write Sam's script?

HENRY: No. No, of course not. (*To SAM.*) I've been thinking about it. I have really. It's a good idea...

SAM: Does that mean you'll do it?

KATHERINE: What do you think? Of course it does. Once he'd met you he couldn't bear to let you go.

SAM: Well. It was certainly a great evening the three of us had together.

KATHERINE: (*Singing to herself.*) 'Some enchanted evening You will see a stranger...'

SAM: There was a sort of empathy, I guess. Among the three of us.

KATHERINE: I knew Henry'd cling on to you. For dear life.

SAM: I'd be around, Henry. For whenever you'd need me.

KATHERINE: You're something he can't bear to miss. He doesn't want to see you vanish into his fantasies, stark naked and carrying twiglets.

SAM: Pardon me. Katherine, I don't know what you're suggesting. But I'm simply interested in your husband as a writer. (*To HENRY.*) What do you say, old friend? Are we going to work together?

HENRY: I don't know exactly. (*To KATHERINE.*) Do you want me to?

KATHERINE: (*With sudden outrage.*) *Don't ask my permission!* (*She is trembling and SAM moves towards her, speaks comfortingly.*)

SAM: I want you to feel yourself – included – Katherine.

KATHERINE: In what?

SAM: I'm deeply concerned. You shouldn't feel left out. Am I right? Your husband's work causes you loneliness.

KATHERINE: He causes me loneliness. Not his work.

SAM: I am concerned about that. I'd like you to know that, Katherine. Deeply concerned... I am here. Whenever either of you need me. (*To HENRY.*) Will you do it? (*HENRY looks up at KATHERINE. She looks back at him.*)

KATHERINE: You say, darling. Your need's greater than mine.

HENRY: All right. We'll start tomorrow.

(*The lights fade.*

SAM exits, taking his hat.

HENRY brings the typewriter from the sideboard to the table, removes his jacket, and sits. KATHERINE sits near the fire. The lights come up to evening, artificial light. HENRY starts to build a tower with the children's bricks. KATHERINE is tense, starts to speak a number of times, stops herself, then finally speaks.)

KATHERINE: Why can't we talk?

HENRY: I'm thinking...

KATHERINE: What about?

HENRY: The work. The work in progress. (*He puts another brick on to the tower.*)

KATHERINE: Why can't we ever say anything to each other?

(*Pause.*)

Have a conversation...

(*Pause. HENRY puts on another brick.*)

You don't ever talk, you tell jokes. When do we ever talk – about our lives?

HENRY: For a living.

KATHERINE: What?

HENRY: I talk...for a living.

KATHERINE: (*Stands up, walks about, bored.*) Oh, that's your cases. And you tell jokes. When do we ever talk – about our lives?

HENRY: When I tell jokes.

(*The tower falls over, he looks at it ruefully.*)

All right then. (*He gets up, goes to the sofa, lies down on it.*)

KATHERINE: What?

HENRY: All right. Let's talk.

(*Pause. Neither of them says anything.*)

Who's going to begin? (*He pulls an imaginary coin out of his pocket.*) Toss for service. (*He spins the coin, looks at it.*) Toss for service. (*He spins the coin, looks at it.*) Heads. You talk first. Toss me a subject.

(*Silence.*)

You're very quiet.

KATHERINE: Yes.

HENRY: (*Pretending to protest.*) Why can't we ever have a conversation...

KATHERINE: Because you don't ever *mean* anything.

HENRY: I've got to *mean* what I say? Talking's not enough but I've got to mean it. Now that's a simply impossible demand...

KATHERINE: For you.

HENRY: Forget me.

KATHERINE: Yes.

HENRY: Just forget me for a moment all together. You say something. With meaning. I'll listen.

KATHERINE: Sam Brown talks. When Mr Brown comes here I hear his voice rising and falling. He seems to be talking to you with some sort of passion.

HENRY: What am I doing? When Mr Brown's carrying on?

KATHERINE: Agreeing with him!

HENRY: That's right. In the faint hope he'll shut up. One word of argument and he's good for another three hours.
(*Pause.*)

KATHERINE: He's rather attractive.

HENRY: I thought we were supposed to say what we meant.

KATHERINE: I did.

HENRY: Oh, yes...

KATHERINE: I just mean I find Mr Brown rather attractive.

HENRY: Lovely! If you've got a thing about little tartan hats.

KATHERINE: He's solid. There's something particularly solid about him...

HENRY: Totally solid, I agree. Underneath the hat.

KATHERINE: Don't be so bloody patronizing!

HENRY: (*Frowning.*) It's a little bit...late. (*He closes his eyes.*)

KATHERINE: I want to talk.

HENRY: All right. Prise my eyelids open with matchsticks. Swing the desk light in my direction... (*With a German accent.*) 'Mr Winter we have ways and ways of making you keep up a conversation...'

KATHERINE: Tell me. (*She sits on the sofa, leaning over HENRY.*)

HENRY: What?

KATHERINE: What you feel. What you actually *feel*.
(*His eyes are closed. He does not answer. Silence.*)
Nothing...
(*She moves away from him and sits below the fire. Pause.*)

HENRY: (*Very quietly.*) What exactly was the matter with your Aunt Freda?
(*KATHERINE becomes tense, does not answer.*)
What did she want to do it for? I've often wondered.
I mean, ladies don't just walk into the sea – for no reason at all... What was up with her exactly?

KATHERINE: What do you think?

HENRY: Perhaps she needed a man.

KATHERINE: (*Deliberately.*) You are disgusting.

HENRY: (*Sleepily.*) Am I?

KATHERINE: That's all any woman ever needs, isn't it?
Their oats. Their greens. Nookey. Hearthrug pudding.

HENRY: Is that what you want? I'm a bit sleepy actually.

KATHERINE: She was an old lady. She pressed flowers and she painted in water colours. She lived with two cats in a small cottage near Prestatyn and what upset her was the war. She was frightened of the Germans! She thought they had her on a black list because she was too old for a brothel and too weak for a labour camp and after the invasion she thought they'd take her into Cardiff and put her down! Because she was useless. She would have found absolutely no consolation in hearth-rug pudding...

HENRY: If you could wait till the morning. I don't know what it is. I feel distinctly more sprightly in the morning.

KATHERINE: With Henrietta coming into our bed at six o'clock, you're quite safe feeling sprightly in the morning.

HENRY: (*Almost asleep.*) Tomorrow – I'll do some work for Sam.

KATHERINE: I never bargained to be married to a writer.

HENRY: What did you think you'd married?

KATHERINE: As a matter of fact – a gardener.

(*The lights fade to a spot on KATHERINE.*
As KATHERINE speaks, HENRY takes his jacket and exits
up the stairs.)

You remember – that extraordinary little house. A square
house in a field near Guilford. Paul rented it – for what
was it during the war? Something? Nothing... And –
well, we'd only met once before at that dance. New Year's
Eve. In the Cathedral Hotel. And, quite unexpectedly
I looked out of the window. It was late afternoon. In
winter. Quite misty. And I saw him walking up the
garden in gumboots.

(*In the darkness SAM enters and sits on the sofa, a small*
screwdriver in his hand, putting a new plug on the Hoover.
The lights fade up to bright afternoon.)

SAM: Saw who?

KATHERINE: Henry. Henry, of course.

SAM: In what? And he was wearing – what?

KATHERINE: Rubber boots. And an old tweed jacket. With
leather patches on the elbows. That's when I decided to
marry him.

SAM: Rubber boots! That's a great image. Go on...

KATHERINE: I thought. We'd live in the country. With oil
lamps! The children'd all be sitting round, doing their
homework. And I'd hear the soft, slow sound of his
gumboots on the gravel. I thought! He'd be standing at
the back door – with his hands full of vegetables...! You
know what? He never wore those clothes again.

SAM: Not the rubbers?

KATHERINE: Or the coat with leather patches. It's my
belief he'd hired them. From Moss Bros. Just to come
walking up our front garden. How was I to know he'd turn
into a man who cooked – and threw lamps at people?

SAM: It strikes me, quite honestly...you've been misled...

KATHERINE: Misled? Totally.

SAM: You know, that's a worthwhile theme. For the movie.
The woman who was deceived – as to the true identity of
her husband.

KATHERINE: By a pair of gumboots!

SAM: They're a great image – those rubbers. They've sparked off ideas in me.

KATHERINE: They sparked off ideas in me, too. More's the pity.

SAM: How wrong can you be – on the subject of a person! You know how I had you cast the first day I stepped in here...

KATHERINE: Cast?

SAM: As the heavy. The early Bette Davis part. The woman who makes men feel either fags or impotent. Preferably impotent fags. It was Henry's fault.

KATHERINE: That's what – he led you to believe?

SAM: Does she cut ball? – if you will pardon my French. That's what I said to your husband.

KATHERINE: He agreed, of course.

SAM: I mean. He didn't bother to argue.

KATHERINE: How very amiable!

SAM: He didn't argue.

KATHERINE: If only he would! That's all I want. If only he'd decide something for himself. Of course – he has to think of me like that.

SAM: You mean – if he gave you the Debbie Reynolds part he'd have to take a few decisions? (*He finishes the Hoover plug.*)

KATHERINE: Debbie Reynolds! I'm not her, am I?

SAM: Of course not! You're unique. Very unique. (*He gets up, moves close to her.*) Look. Katherine. I'd like to talk to you about this – married couple. It's something I feel we ought to get into. In some kind of depth.

KATHERINE: (*Looking at him gratefully.*) You want to talk?

SAM: The way I see it this isn't going to be just another movie. Any movie. It's something I feel deeply about. Like my own flesh and blood. You know how I see it?

KATHERINE: Tell me.

SAM: As two people who got each other wrong, from the beginning.

KATHERINE: Yes!

SAM: I feel we should have some further talks. Maybe just the two of us.

KATHERINE: You want – conversation?

SAM: Could we maybe – go to dinner?

KATHERINE: (*Doubtful.*) Dinner?

SAM: Just the two of us one night...

KATHERINE: (*Nervously.*) Not dinner. I don't think so...
(*Looking at the Hoover.*) You've done it?
(*KATHERINE takes the plug as if it were something very precious, and plugs it in. The Hoover lights up and roars. She looks at him with deep gratitude, then unplugs it. They are looking at each other all the time. The telephone rings, breaking into the moment. She answers it.*)
Excuse me? The Westminster... Oh, Mr MacFeeling... No. It's all right... Yes. You can speak to my husband.
(*She suddenly hands the phone to SAM, who takes it, surprised. KATHERINE quickly pushes the Hoover out of the room to left of the stairs.*)

SAM: (*Into the phone, helplessly.*) Hullo?... No. I'm sorry. No – I'm just someone who happened – to be here.
(*SAM replaces the receiver and exits through the front door, looking upstairs as he goes.*
The lights fade.
HENRY enters and sits at the table, picks up a script and starts to read it. SAM enters with a similar script, reading. The lights come up to evening, with artificial lighting on. HENRY gets up nervously, and looks over his shoulder anxiously to see SAM's reaction. There is none. SAM puts the pages carefully on the table.)
You want to talk a little?

HENRY: Not really.

SAM: I mean, audiences today weren't born yesterday, old chum. They're going to be two jumps ahead.

HENRY: What of?

SAM: Of you! 'This is another one', they will say, 'about two people who are married.' It'll empty the Odeon, Leicester Square quicker than 'God Save The Queen'.

HENRY: But they are.

SAM: What?

HENRY: Married.

SAM: Look, this is just spit balling – just off the top of the milk. Suppose they're *not* married. Suppose they're shacked up. Interesting? More of today?

HENRY: I thought we wanted to investigate what keeps a marriage going.

SAM: All right. You tell me. What does?

HENRY: (*After a pause.*) Fear.

SAM: Fear? Fear of what exactly?

HENRY: If they knew that...

SAM: Well?

HENRY: They'd probably leave each other. Are you drinking today?

SAM: Just coffee. Let's just think about the big box-office grossers. Can't we work a brutal car chase in here somewhere?

HENRY: (*Looking round the room.*) I should think so. We've had almost everything else. I'll make you some coffee.
(*HENRY exits to the kitchen.*
There is a pause, then SAM jumps up excitedly and goes to shout to HENRY through the kitchen door.)

SAM: What about this, Henry? I think I'm on to something! Oh, Christ! I am *very* excited. It's a funny bugger, isn't it?

HENRY: (*Off.*) What?

SAM: Inspiration! Suppose they're... Listen to this carefully, baby. Suppose *our* baby are – our married people. We make them – a couple of fellers!
(*HENRY comes back from the kitchen.*)

HENRY: I'm afraid coffee's out of the question.

SAM: What?

HENRY: Another part of the house has given up the struggle.

SAM: Forget it. My idea! What's your reaction?

HENRY: A couple of fellers? That's exactly what they are.

SAM: (*Looking at him with sad disapproval.*) Henry. I think I know you well enough now to say this. Do you treat marriage with sufficient respect?
(*KATHERINE comes down the stairs into the room. She has changed, looking very smart, carrying a handbag, ready to go*

*out. She pauses a moment to look at her face in the mirror
over the fireplace.)*
I'm not asking you for gimmicks, Henry. Okay, forget
two queens shacked up which could be interesting.
Forget the action sequences. Forget the box-office even.
Try and imagine two people mistaken about each other
from the start.
*(KATHERINE goes and finds a new packet of cigarettes
hidden away among the books.)*
Does that thought surprise you?

HENRY: *(Looking at KATHERINE.)* My couple – understand
each other only too well.

SAM: Henry – I can tell by these thirty pages. You need
help with this one. Two heads is what you need, Henry.
My friend, I think you'll like what I'm going to suggest.

HENRY: What're you going to suggest?
*(KATHERINE goes and sits in a central position – takes a
case out of her handbag and carefully fills it with the cigarettes.
The two men are on each side of her, looking at her as they
discuss her.)*

SAM: A collaboration? With your wife?

HENRY: *(After a pause; looking at SAM, amazed.)* You want
Katherine? To write your movie?

SAM: To help you. I figure it's a pretty good team.

HENRY: Have you asked her – by any chance?

SAM: Not yet. Do you think I'll get a 'No. No'?

HENRY: Samuel. If you were shooting a TV Commercial...

SAM: I have done so. The greatest...

HENRY: And if you approached the Vatican and asked the
Pope to raise his arms over Saint Peter's Square at Easter
and give a short plug for fully fashioned Gossamer
Durex... Do you think you'd get a 'No. No'?

SAM: You mean the actual Pope? Live?

HENRY: You want my wife live, don't you? Dead or alive?

SAM: Do you have anything – against this project, Katherine?

HENRY: *(Coming in before KATHERINE can answer.)* It's not
a project to her. It's the beginning of the end. It's the
Black Death. The dry rot in the basement. The start of

group sex in the children's playroom and Mescalin in the Ostermilk. She fears it. She detests it. It makes her blood run cold...

KATHERINE: So why do you do it?

HENRY: You really want to know?

SAM: Your motivation, old chum.

HENRY: Money. (*He goes over to the table, tosses up a pile of bills like autumn leaves.*)
Rates. Light! Gas! This small corner of Belsize Park is about to opt out of the Industrial Revolution.

KATHERINE: There's always enough – for a bloody Hollywood table lamp.

HENRY: (*To SAM.*) You've heard of places where old people go to die? This is where they go to be born. All those millions of spermatozoa – which usually float off into innocent waste – say, 'Look, this is seventy-nine Alexandra Drive. Cling on, darling. They buy bikky pegs here by the shipload'. This isn't a home, Sam. It's a reservoir for an expanding population. (*He goes to the table, picks up the script, looks at it sadly.*) Is there a bit of it you like?

SAM: You want me to be brutally frank?

HENRY: I'd rather have a little dishonest praise.

SAM: (*Putting a hand on HENRY's shoulder.*) Why don't we wait, until I get Katherine's reaction?
(*KATHERINE stands up. They both look at her, expectant.*)

KATHERINE: I think it's disgusting!

HENRY: You haven't read it...

KATHERINE: This is Sam's project. It's like his child. He's nursed it. Cared about it. Deeply. And you stand there and tell him your only interest in his story of married life is paying the gas bill. It's sordid! That's what you are – mercenary!

HENRY: (*Outraged.*) *Me?* And who's always on – day in, day out about MacFeeling at the Westminster?

KATHERINE: Mr MacFeeling's been spoken to – which is more than you'd ever do. (*She moves to the front door.*) Shall we go now, Sam?
(*SAM moves with her.*)

HENRY: What's happening?

KATHERINE: Sam's taking me to dinner.

HENRY: We'll have to get a baby sitter.

KATHERINE: We've got one.

HENRY: Who?

KATHERINE: You. There's nothing much except
Seraphina's ten o'clock feed.

HENRY: Well, about that. It might be difficult...

KATHERINE: Why not ask Gristle to help? Or don't
articled ladies qualify in changing nappies? (*Almost
hopeful.*) Don't you want me to go – are you going to
argue?

HENRY: No. Of course you can go. I'll be all right.
(*KATHERINE and SAM move towards the door.*)
Where are you going, actually?

KATHERINE: Trattoria Alfresco. The one you thought
looked nice. By the tube station.

HENRY: Enjoy yourselves.
(*SAM and KATHERINE exit.*)
(*As the front door shuts on them.*) Good-bye. Feller.
(*They have gone. He rushes to the telephone, dials a number,
speaks in an absurd Army officer's voice.*)
Hullo. North Thames Gas Board, Emergency Service?...
This is an emergency. My name's Winter. Henry Winter.
Seventy-nine, Alexandra Drive, and I've been overseas.
Central Africa, actually. Government service. I returned
to find my gas cut off... Well, I never got my gas bill.
How would I get a gas bill in Central Africa? There's an
almighty cheque – in the post. Tomorrow morning you'll
be astonished and delighted and be able to open a new
gas works, most probably... Look, I've got starving
children here. I'm desperate... Well, yes. I suppose so.
Yes. A person can still be desperate, even if he's got an
electric kettle.
(*He puts down the phone. It rings.*)
(*Answering it.*) Oh, it's you. It's you. Miss Griffin,
darling... Bernard? Bernard Duffield... Yes... Yes, of
course we need the doctor... To say that Bernard was

incapable of forming the intention of blowing his nose. That he had no idea of right and wrong. That he couldn't tell the difference between a kiss on the mouth and a bash over the head with an iron bar. Just like the rest of us. Yes, I am a bit peculiar tonight. My wife's gone off. With a fat, old film producer from Yeovil. Well, not all that fat actually, or old... See you? Of course I want to see you... At the Kardomah... We've got a date, haven't we? Miss Griffin... Where have you gone, Miss Griffin? (*He listens to the cut-off phone.*) Vanished. (*He puts down the phone. Then, bored, dials a longer, country number.*) Hullo... Hullo, Mum... Well, I've been busy. Rather busy... No, I haven't been irritating Katherine... Yes. I have been treating her well. I'm writing a film... A film... Well, a film *is* photographs, Mother... Yes. But you have to write words for the people to say... Yes... Yes, it is rather killing, actually. No, Mother, it is not an opera singer... Yes, I know you saw Grace Moore in *Love Me Tonight*... No, I don't suppose it will be as good as that. This one is about *us*. Me and Katherine... Why are you laughing, Mother? You think that's a funny idea? I hope it turns out funny. Well, not as funny as that. Look, what I was ringing you up about. You can't think of any sort of simple dinner you can cook in an electric kettle... Please... Please stop *laughing,* Mother!

(*He puts down the telephone. Bored, he goes to the waste-paper basket, takes out the wine bottle, puts it to his eye and gets the last drop in it, drops it back into the waste-paper basket. He goes out into the kitchen and returns immediately with the plastic bath which now contains a baby's bottle, nappies, an alarm clock, an electric kettle, a tin of Ostermilk, measuring jug and ladle. He winds up the clock and puts it on the mantelpiece. Looks up at the book shelves and thinks of something. Climbs on a chair, finds an old black address book carefully concealed behind the books on the top shelf and dials a number with excitement.*)

(*On the phone.*) Stella, Stella, that's exactly what I like... Well, is it seven years, is it, really? Well, a few children.

Well, about twenty... No, what I like is, what I really appreciate, Stella, is that you're *there!* When I ring. Waiting! No nonsense about it. Well now, Stella. What are you doing?... Cooking a chicken. It's nearly cooked. Well, why don't you wrap it all up in that silver paper stuff and bring it round... Yes. I'm alone. To all intents and purposes, totally alone. In the world... Oh, you're cooking it for Brownjohn. Oh, *Brownjohn*. Who's he?... You married him. Not the man who used to leap out and hit the car with an umbrella every night when we turned into your road?... Am I desperate? Of course I'm not desperate. As a matter of fact, it's pretty eventful – life in Belsize Park.

(*The alarm clock goes off.*)

I have to rush now. People coming. Ring me again some time.

(*He puts down the phone and hurries to turn off the clock. Then he plugs in the electric kettle. He has the address book in his mouth as he starts to make up the food. He sits at the table with the chart beside him and ladles out about eight measures, getting it all over his trousers and the table. He puts back one scoopful, puts the lid on the tin, brushes the powder off his trousers, then brushes it from the table on to his trousers again. He gives up in despair, takes the book out of his mouth, glances in it, gives a little whistle of surprise and, on an impulse, dials a number.*)

Is Mr Bottle there, please?... Oh... Edwin Bottle that end? This is Henry... Don't you remember? Henry Winter... Yes... Yes, indeed. Very long time no see. Look, what I wanted to ask you was – you're not having a party tonight by any chance?... Oh well, I just thought you might... How's Bernice?... (*Incredulously.*) She's *what?* (*Hushed and solemn.*) I'm sorry... No, I hadn't heard. I'm really sorry. (*He puts down the phone.*) Bernice. Dead...

(*The kettle starts to give a low whistle. He is about to pick it up when the doorbell rings. He switches off the kettle and goes to answer the door.*

GRISELDA GRIFFIN enters, carrying a brown paper carrier bag and a briefcase. She is young, enthusiastic, a solicitor's articled clerk, pretty, with a rather breathless, upper-class accent.)

GRISELDA: You're really alone?

HENRY: Alone. Yes. Totally. Of course. (*He quickly switches off the main lights and turns on the electric fire, producing a romantic glow.*) Are you going to stay a little while?

GRISELDA: I can't believe it. (*She puts the paper bag on the table, looking round.*)

HENRY: No, I can't, either.

GRISELDA: (*Afraid.*) She really isn't here.

HENRY: As you see.

GRISELDA: I'm afraid of your wife.

HENRY: I know you are. (*He takes her brief-case and puts it down by the sofa, then helps her off with her coat and puts it over the back of the chair.*) We all are. I'm afraid of my wife. Come to think of it, my wife's scared to death of my wife. Why don't you sit down?

GRISELDA: No reason. (*She sits suddenly on the sofa in front of the electric fire, warms her hands, shivering.*) I rang the doctor for Bernard.

HENRY: For Bernard? Well, we've got to look after Bernard, haven't we? I worry about him naturally, most of the time. (*He sits beside her on the sofa then slides, romantically, down on to the floor.*)

GRISELDA: Why? He's not your only case, is he?

HENRY: (*On the defensive.*) My only case? Of course not. I've got others... I've got cases – some other cases...
(*There is the sound of a door banging upstairs and a number of children shouting.*)

GRISELDA: (*Frightened.*) What was that?

HENRY: Mice.

GRISELDA: I wouldn't've come. If you hadn't said you were alone.

HENRY: No. No, of course not... (*He takes her hand.*) Well now, about Bernard.

GRISELDA: Mr Fidella thinks he ought to plead guilty.

HENRY: Nonsense. We've got a defence. No men's rea...

GRISELDA: What?

HENRY: His mind – was on something else at the time.

GRISELDA: On what?

HENRY: Who knows?

GRISELDA: Mr Fidella said that Bernard Duffield must be taken to have intended the natural and probable consequences of his act.

HENRY: Oh, yes?

GRISELDA: The natural and probable consequences. That's what he says.

HENRY: (*Gently stroking GRISELDA as he talks.*) So when Bernard courted Maisie, when he placed a hand on those huge knickers in the quiet back row of the Essoldo, he no doubt intended it should all end up in a short strangling cord and him with a pair of broken ankles crawling across the allotments... I mean any fool could see that coming a mile off. Is that what Mr Fidella says?

GRISELDA: Well...

HENRY: Come to think of it it's something I've never done.

GRISELDA: What?

HENRY: Intended the natural and probable consequences of my acts.

GRISELDA: You never told her, did you?

HENRY: What?

GRISELDA: You never told your wife. Not about me.

HENRY: Of course not.

GRISELDA: What would've happened. If you had?

HENRY: (*Casually.*) Oh, I suppose... Bloodshed.

GRISELDA: What?

HENRY: Armageddon! An explosion which would have rocked the very foundations of Belsize Park. The casualties would have been enormous.

GRISELDA: (*Looks at him.*) Are you lying? I think you tell her everything. Bring everything home to Mum. (*She gets up and looks in the mirror.*)

HENRY: You are all alike! It's extraordinary. Wherever one looks there is another one of you standing there. (*He rises and looks at her thoughtfully.*)

GRISELDA: I couldn't have put up with it, if you'd told her. Of course, I wouldn't mind now.

HENRY: Now?

GRISELDA: Now she's gone.

HENRY: Gone?

GRISELDA: Hasn't she? With a film producer?

HENRY: Yes. Yes, of course. Sit down. Don't look so gloomy, Miss Griffin. From now on life's going to be simple. Calm – simple. We shall sit in the Kardomah and not care who knows it... (*He puts his hand on her shoulders.*)

GRISELDA: And go out in the evenings?
(*They sit on the sofa.*)

HENRY: And go out in the evenings, most probably... And there will be no feelings of impending disaster. Why is it that I seem to have filled all the women I've met with feelings of impending doom? I'm cheerful, basically. Naturally cheerful. Oh, yes, and we'll get Bernard off. The future, Miss Griffin, is incredibly bright. (*He starts to stroke her gently.*)

GRISELDA: (*Looking up at him admiringly.*) Tell me...

HENRY: Yes, Miss Griffin.

GRISELDA: How are we going to get Bernard off?

HENRY: He was filled to the eyes with 'Blue Heavens' for a start.

GRISELDA: 'A man cannot wilfully deprive himself of an intention...' R. *v.* Snoddin.

HENRY: Try not to get to know any law, Miss Griffin. You'll find it a great disadvantage in the legal profession.

GRISELDA: 'If he does so he must be presumed to have that intention which he would have had had he not been incapable of such intention.'

HENRY: Let's not get too subtle, Miss Griffin. A criminal act requires a criminal intention. (*He strokes her on the thigh.*)

GRISELDA: But not an intention to do the precise act charged. For example. If I climb down a chimney with the intention of raping the cook...

HENRY: What things you get up to – at Law Society evening classes!

GRISELDA: And it happens to be the cook's night off. (*Triumphantly.*) I have still entered – with felonous intent... 'Although the actus be frustrated.'

HENRY: You little devil! Who said that?

GRISELDA: Lord Bogden of Midhurst. R. *v.* Blenkinhall.

HENRY: Fuck Lord Bogden of Midhurst.

(*He is about to kiss her – she breaks away, goes to her carrier bag.*)

GRISELDA: I brought this... (*She takes a short orange nylon baby doll nightdress out of the carrier bag and holds it up in front of her.*)

HENRY: Why?

GRISELDA: You've never seen it before. When you said you were all alone – I thought. Now I can at least wear a nightie.

(*GRISELDA turns and, carrying the nightie, goes quickly upstairs.*)

HENRY: No... No, please... (*He goes quickly to the telephone, dials three figures.*) Enquiries? I want an alarm call, please. Would you wake me up – (*He looks at his watch.*) – in thirty seconds time... Just a cat nap actually.

(*GRISELDA is back, in panic, carrying her nightdress.*)

GRISELDA: There's a child, standing on the stairs. (*She stuffs the nightdress back into the bag.*)

HENRY: Look. Miss Griffin...

GRISELDA: Looking at me with accusing eyes. Is it one of yours?

HENRY: Do you want me to check?

(*The telephone rings.*)

(*Answering it.*) My alarm what?... (*He remembers, and speaks as if to KATHERINE.*) Oh, hullo, darling... Tonight? No – well, yes, darling... Yes, I suppose so... No... The children... Yes – yes, of course I understand... All right. (*He replaces the receiver and looks sadly at GRISELDA.*) She's coming back!

GRISELDA: When?

HENRY: Now.

GRISELDA: (*Replacing the nightdress in her case.*) But her film producer.

HENRY: Apparently – let her down...

GRISELDA: (*Picking up her bag.*) Oh, God, will it tell her?
(*HENRY tries to get her into her coat, but keeps missing the armhole. Finally he puts the coat under one of her arms and the bag under another and pushes her up to the door, all during the following speeches.*)

HENRY: What?

GRISELDA: That child! That child'll tell her I was here, and there'll be – what did you say? Total war?

HENRY: Don't worry, Miss Griffin. The children are completely uninterested in our activities. All the same – you'd better go.
(*GRISELDA goes.*
HENRY gets the bottle and Ostermilk tin out of the plastic bath and goes on with his preparations.
The front door opens. GRISELDA is back. She grabs her paper bag.)

GRISELDA: I left this. (*She looks at him.*) You didn't want her to find it, did you?

HENRY: No. No, of course not. But if she did – and if war broke out – would I intend the natural and probable consequences of my acts? Can you tell me that, Miss Griffin – from a legal point of view?

GRISELDA: I'm frightened.

HENRY: I'm – I'm sorry.
(*A taxi is heard stopping in the street outside.*)
Go on – run for safety, Miss Griffin. Out through the garden. They're coming over now. Things are hotting up. Take cover.
(*HENRY grabs GRISELDA and pushes her through the kitchen door, hearing the taxi door slam as he returns.*
HENRY rushes to the main lights and switches them on, then picks up the kettle.
KATHERINE and SAM enter through the front door.)
Did you have a good time?
(*KATHERINE takes the kettle.*)

KATHERINE: I'll do Seraphina's food. (*She pours water into the bottle.*)

(*There is an awkward pause.*)

SAM: How are you, feller...?

HENRY: Quite well, thank you. (*He goes to the radiogram, looks among the records for something to play.*) Nice dinner, Katherine?

KATHERINE: I didn't notice.

HENRY: Well, Did you get a 'no-no'?

SAM: Katherine has agreed – to come into the project. She has a whole lot to offer – in the way of perception and genuine understanding.

HENRY: Corruption!

SAM: What?

HENRY: Didn't she tell you, she'd get corrupted?

KATHERINE: I might get rescued.

(*HENRY looks at her, says nothing.*)

SAM: Of course we'll be glad to have your help, Henry. On a purely working basis. Katherine agrees. You still have something to offer.

HENRY: Big of her.

SAM: I told her... You might find it too painful.

HENRY: What?

SAM: Working along with Katherine and me. Might be just too painful for you. Under the circumstances. It's sure going to be a tough one for you, feller.

HENRY: It's only a film, isn't it? I mean. (*Looking at records.*) For God's sake. It's only a story.

KATHERINE: Not exactly. (*She puts the teat on the bottle and shakes it.*)

HENRY: What do you mean?

KATHERINE: Oh, it's not just tonight. You know it's been going on ever since we met.

HENRY: Going on? What's been going on exactly?

KATHERINE: Battles... Lies... Plotting and scheming! I'm tired. I'm tired out. I want peace, that's all. I want to wake up in the morning and know it's not going to be a war...

HENRY: Why don't you say it?

KATHERINE: All right. I'm going to marry Sam.

125

SAM: Naturally, old friend, we wanted you to be the first to know.

(*HENRY puts on the record. Buddy Holly starts to sing.*)

RECORD: 'Do you remember, baby

Last September, baby

How you held me tight –

(*HENRY sits on the sofa.*)

– Each and every night?

Well – WOOPS A DAISY

How you drove me crazy

But I guess it doesn't matter any more.'

HENRY: (*Quietly.*) Be my guest.

(*The song continues, as the curtain slowly falls.*)

End of Act One.

ACT TWO

The same.

Before and as the curtain rises, the record is playing. KATHERINE, SAM and HENRY are in exactly the same position as at the close of Act One.

RECORD: 'You go your way and I'll go mi-i-ine
   Now and for ever till the end of time.
   Golly gee! What have you done to me?
   But I guess it doesn't matter any more.
   There's no use in me a cry-y-y-ing
   I've done everything 'n now I'm sick of trying.
   I've lost all my nights
   'N wasted all my days
   Over YOU-OU-OU...'
   (*KATHERINE goes to the radiogram and switches it off.*)
KATHERINE: Don't you think we ought to talk?
HENRY: Thrash it around a bit? I expect you'd enjoy that.
KATHERINE: Just for once in your life – couldn't we have a serious discussion?
HENRY: Oh. Is *that* why you're doing it?
KATHERINE: What?
HENRY: So we can have a serious topic for discussion. I mean, isn't that going rather far? Couldn't we just think up a few good debating subjects?
KATHERINE: (*To SAM.*) It's hopeless. He'll never talk.
HENRY: Talk? Of course I'll talk. I'll talk for hours. It's my one talent. 'This House Believes that Sex Without Marriage is like an Egg Without Salt.' I will now call upon Mr Samuel Brown of Keble College to propose the motion.
KATHERINE: (*To SAM.*) He won't say anything...
HENRY: What is there to say? I suppose you've given this matter some thought?
SAM: Thought? It's more of a gut reaction. Where I come from people are accustomed to think with their guts.

127

HENRY: How peculiar. I suppose they digest in their skulls and their mouths, as you would so elegantly say, are full of shit.

KATHERINE: That wasn't funny. That was disgusting and not very funny.

HENRY: Where was it then? This land of gastronomic cerebration?

SAM: Poland.

KATHERINE: Sam grew up in New York. The West Side...

HENRY: Universal man?

SAM: All right, Hank. Where were you raised?

HENRY: The rough end of Godalming. Want to make something of it?

KATHERINE: (*Sighing.*) Very funny.

HENRY: I don't see why there's anything necessarily funny about Godalming.

KATHERINE: For six long years I've been looking for a man without a sense of humour.

HENRY: Well, you've certainly found one.

KATHERINE: He means what he says. It isn't a joke, thank God.

HENRY: Oh, he means it. That doesn't mean it isn't a joke.

KATHERINE: Jokes! I hate jokes. I've been drowning in jokes, sinking in them. Smothered by them! When our children fall over they don't cry, they make jokes which is what he taught them.

HENRY: (*To SAM.*) She'd rather they cried.

KATHERINE: Oh, yes. Yes, much rather. You don't know how I look round this family and long for tears. Tears would be like rain in a desert of puns.

HENRY: You and old Sam Brown have learnt to cry together?

KATHERINE: I honestly think he's serious.

HENRY: (*Rising.*) Are you, Sam? Are you serious? (*He inspects SAM closely.*) Yes. He's serious. (*To KATHERINE.*) Do you fancy him, quite honestly?

KATHERINE: I feel – seriously involved.

HENRY: (*Sitting again.*) Oh, really, and when did you get hooked? Has old Sam been dropping in then, most afternoons when I'm down in the Temple? Has he helped

you pick up the kids from playgroup in the back of the
old Apha? How did you do your courting? Across a
crowded bathroom, launching plastic ducks and
towelling down my daughters in front of the electric
fire? 'Don't interrupt, Henrietta – Mummy's getting a
proposal of marriage.' You make my blood cold.

KATHERINE: Doesn't it remind you of something?

HENRY: What?

KATHERINE: You used to come round in the afternoons –
when I was married to Paul. You used to sit on the edge
of the bath, but you made jokes...

HENRY: I'm sorry. I should have made sounds of serious
concern.

SAM: I am seriously concerned – about your wife, Hal.

HENRY: Concerned! And I suppose your concern's better
than my concern. Yours is real genuine, loving Hi Fi,
Three D, fully stereo, gorgeous Panavision concern and
mine's only small time mini concern from Godalming.
Why should we have finer feelings – just because he
never makes a joke?

KATHERINE: Sam was concerned by that appalling
incident.

HENRY: What incident?

SAM: That was a pretty lethal lamp you threw at her, feller.

HENRY: (*Incredulously.*) I threw? I? (*To KATHERINE.*) You
believe that, don't you...?

SAM: You could have done Kate a permanent injury.

KATHERINE: He's proud of that. 'Put poppies round that
crack in the plaster', he said, 'and blow the last post there
on Armistice Day.'

HENRY: Did I? Did I say that...?

KATHERINE: He loves to get sentimental about our old
battles.

SAM: Look, Henry. We've talked about this, Kate and I. Over
and over. And we can't see any other way out.

HENRY: It's bigger than both of you.

KATHERINE: Shut up!

SAM: It's a pretty sizeable thing. Yes. Of course, you'll fight
like hell to keep her. I respect that.

HENRY: Do you?

SAM: Sure. Been a fighter all my life. A Polack kid – raised in a country where every man and boy was competing for his territory...

(*HENRY begins to hum Western film music – the tune from 'The Big Country'.*)

We *had* to fight.

HENRY: From Wyoming to Montana. From Devil's Gulch to the Old Red River –

KATHERINE: Shut up!

HENRY: – I look around and I'm mighty proud to tell you, boy, it's Sam Brown's country!

KATHERINE: Stop it...

SAM: You'll fight me over this, naturally.

KATHERINE: Are you sure he will? (*She turns her back on them and the audience.*)

HENRY: Or is it hopeless? Am I a loser, eh, Sam? Samuel. May I call you Mr Brown? What're you offering my wife? Concern? Deep – deep emotions – like money?

SAM: I certainly hope to bring Katherine happiness.

HENRY: Happiness? Dear Mr Brown. That's your first boob, if I may say so. Bring my wife happiness and she won't even bother to unwrap the parcel. She doesn't want happiness. She wants tragedy. She wants war! Every morning when she gets up she goes over the top, with incredible courage and her teeth gritted to breakfast. She doesn't want perfume. She wants the smell of gunpowder. Death and destruction. With explosive electric light fittings flying through the air. She won't walk beside you down an English lane, old chum...but all the long way into the sea at Prestatyn. Leave your clothes here, brother. With a little note for your relatives.

(*KATHERINE runs into the kitchen and bangs the door. SAM goes quickly into the kitchen after her.*)

SAM: (*Calling from the kitchen.*) Look out! She's turning on the gas taps... She's got the oven open. She's turning on the gas.

HENRY: Let her.

(*There is the sound of a struggle from the kitchen.*)

SAM: (*Off.*) Kate! Come away from them! Now leave it, honey. Life's good, darling. Life's going to be very good to us from now on. Sam's got you now. Sam's going to take good care of you... *Leave those gas taps alone!*

HENRY: Let her turn them on...

(*SAM appears at the kitchen door.*)

SAM: Did you say, 'Let her turn them on'?

HENRY: Why not? They've cut off the gas.

SAM: You *bastard!*

(*KATHERINE comes out of the kitchen, walks past SAM.*)

KATHERINE: I went to make coffee, that's all.

SAM: Is that right?

HENRY: She went to make some coffee, that's all.

SAM: In the oven? Do you make coffee in the oven?

KATHERINE: I was looking for the gas.

HENRY: They've removed it. You see, I haven't paid the bill.

KATHERINE: (*To SAM.*) You grabbed hold of me. I don't know why you grabbed hold of me. I just thought it was time...we all had some coffee.

SAM: You haven't paid the bill...

HENRY: It's been waiting here. For you.

SAM: What?

HENRY: I understand you are about to take over this leaking enterprise? (*To SAM.*) It's all yours. They're upstairs. Waiting for you. All those hungry little mouths. So you want an inventory? Three bright red cast-iron saucepans her mother gave us, a broken iron and an early English washing machine. (*He picks up bills and starts to stuff them into SAM's pockets.*) Here...! Here...! The horrible results of unforeseen quarter days. Look – brown envelopes – fresh and untouched. You can read them together – in the long winter evenings by the dying plastic coal of her ex-husband's electric fire. Samuel Brown. This is My Life! Take it.

(*SAM looks at KATHERINE. She is looking back at him, smiling.*)

Go on. I meant it. Be my guest.

(*SAM stands looking from one to the other, hesitating.*)

SAM: Well now. Wait a minute.

HENRY: What's the matter, Boy? Feeling nervous? Stand straight now. You'll make a wonderful target for table lamps. I wish I could stay here all night. To listen to you two saying meaningful things to each other. But I must go now. There are people waiting for me. I know you'll both be very, very happy. (*He does not move.*)

SAM: (*Looking from one to the other, confused, uncertain.*) I – I – I – I can't do it to you, Henry.

(*SAM turns quickly and exits. The front door slams after him. HENRY and KATHERINE are left alone. A child calls from upstairs.*

KATHERINE exits upstairs to answer the child.

HENRY, all alone, switches on the radio. It is playing the 'Appassionata' sonata of Beethoven. He lets it play, then goes and sits on the sofa. He is smiling as the lights fade to black-out.

When the lights come up again as before, HENRY has gone, the music has stopped, and KATHERINE is sitting crouched in front of the electric fire. She is shivering slightly.

HENRY comes in from the stairs with a tray of children's supper.)

HENRY: Seraphina's settled. I've settled Seraphina. (*He goes into the kitchen, speaking off.*) Seraphina's settled. She actually used her pot. I promised her a bit of chocolate. As a reward. Probably have the most disastrous effect on her future life. At dinner-parties. (*He comes back into the room.*) I mean, every time anyone offers her an 'After Eight' she'll dash off to the loo.

KATHERINE: (*After a pause, seeming a long way off, in a trance.*) What did you say…?

HENRY: Every time anyone offers her an 'After Eight'… Don't bother. (*He goes to the table, finds a brief tied in pink tape.*) Court tomorrow. (*He moves to a chair, sits, pulls the tape off the brief and starts to read it.*) What're you going to do tomorrow?

(*Pause; KATHERINE does not answer.*)

You going to do something nice tomorrow?

KATHERINE: (*After a long pause.*) Approach death. By inches.
(*Pause.*)

HENRY: (*Who has not listened.*) That'll be nice…

KATHERINE: (*Suddenly sinking her face in her hands.*) Oh
my God!

HENRY: (*Not looking up.*) What did you say?

KATHERINE: (*Lifting her desperate face.*) Nothing.
Absolutely nothing.

HENRY: (*Not looking at her.*) Sorry, I thought you said
something. (*He takes out a pencil, starts to mark the brief.*)
It makes a change, doesn't it? I'm in court making
money. Well – somehow we must make money. Now
Sam's left us – and his profitable assignment. I was
relying on Sam for the new kitchen lino.

KATHERINE: (*Looking at him in amazed desperation.*) It's
incredible!

HENRY: (*Not looking at her, reading his brief.*) Italian
ceramic tile lino. Make the bathroom look like the
baths of Caracala.

KATHERINE: You are incredible!

HENRY: (*Working.*) With the original Ancient Roman Ascot
heater. We might have had central heating. Without Sam,
I suppose – we've got to soldier on with the old Ascot…

KATHERINE: (*Getting up and starting to walk about
nervously.*) Talk about something else…

HENRY: What?

KATHERINE: Will you please talk about something else?

HENRY: (*After a pause.*) All right, what?
(*Pause.*)
What would you like me to talk about?
(*Pause.*)
The weather? The kids? Myself? My case? (*He puts down
the brief, looks at KATHERINE.*) I'll tell you about my
case. Would that pass the time? I mean we can't go to
bed yet, can we? It'd be ridiculous – to settle down for
the night before Daniel – shall I tell you?

KATHERINE: If you like.

HENRY: It's an attempted murder.

KATHERINE: (*Positively, agreeing.*) Yes!

HENRY: A husband who tried to murder his wife. I'm defending him.

KATHERINE: Of course!

HENRY: Why?

KATHERINE: It's bloody appropriate!

HENRY: His name is Bernard Duffield.

KATHERINE: His name is *you!*

HENRY: (*Looking at her, surprised.*) What?

KATHERINE: (*Almost shouting.*) *Be my guest!* (*She sits as before.*)

HENRY: Oh, come on...

KATHERINE: You don't want me, do you? You don't want me in the least. Why am I walking slowly? I should run – I should run into the water. Shall I give you that? Shall I? Freedom. Freedom for little nights in Enfield and little afternoons with Gristle and have her round here after you've put Serena on her pot and told Daniel about your heroic feats in the Hendon Magistrates' Court. You wanted to get rid of me!

HENRY: You really minded!

KATHERINE: What?

HENRY: You minded when I said that. 'Be my guest.'

KATHERINE: Minded! (*She sits in the chair.*) Of course I minded.

HENRY: So you ran into the kitchen.

KATHERINE: To make coffee!

HENRY: In the oven?

KATHERINE: I went to make the coffee.

HENRY: And Sam Brown became very embarrassed and bolted. In disarray. I do miss his whiskey – I'm sorry. (*Rising.*) If I said the wrong thing...

KATHERINE: (*Outraged.*) *If!*

HENRY: (*Soothing.*) But it worked! It made Mr Brown run a mile. It was...remarkably successful?

KATHERINE: You're not saying that's why you did it?

HENRY: Of course. I was fighting for you. (*He squats on the floor beside her.*)

KATHERINE: Fighting? You were lying down.

HENRY: That's how the Indians fought the British Raj. That's how Gandhi fought. He lay down in his little loin cloth and the brutal Ghurkas were too ashamed to march over him and break his glasses.

KATHERINE: Oh, I'm sorry. I didn't recognize you. (*She gets up, disgusted.*) Anyone less than Gandhi...

HENRY: The Mahatma was a very sexy person. When young. I am a bit like him. Yes. You see it worked!

KATHERINE: I don't believe you! You're lying again. Always lying. (*She sits by the table.*)

HENRY: People like Sam are very suggestible.

KATHERINE: You're not going to pretend that you were pretending?

HENRY: (*Rising, pleased with his ingenuity.*) You know old Sam. He can't read a book unless it's *Book of the Month*. He can't go to the movies unless there are queues around the block and it's impossible to get in. He won't even have a disease unless it's been sanctified by an article in the *Reader's Digest*. I saw at once. The only way to get rid of him was to pretend you were not exactly the hot little property he'd bargained for. He was expecting to pay the earth for you. He just couldn't put up with the discovery that you were being given away like a Green Shield Stamp.

KATHERINE: You are disgusting!

HENRY: What did you expect me to do? Challenge him to a duel?

KATHERINE: Yes. Yes, I'd've liked that...

HENRY: (*Kneeling beside her suddenly, his arm round her.*) Don't be ridiculous! I had to use some sort of guile. Well, all I'm pointing out to you, darling, is – it worked. It worked superlatively!
(*She smiles faintly.*)
You may laugh – but there's something to be said for a good basic training before the Hendon magistrates...

KATHERINE: (*Almost laughing.*) He did look tremendously confused.

HENRY: I thought so.

KATHERINE: He left quickly.

HENRY: That's the one disadvantage of a nice fixed universe like Sam's. It's tremendously easy to turn upside down.

KATHERINE: (*Looking at him, uncertainly.*) You wanted to get rid of him?

HENRY: Of course.

KATHERINE: Really? Really and truly?

HENRY: Really and truly.

KATHERINE: Very, very clever...

HENRY: (*Satisfied, moving away from her.*) I thought so. (*He looks at his brief again.*) Now – if I could think of something equally good for Bernard... (*He sits to work on his brief.*)

KATHERINE: (*Rising, outraged.*) Aren't you ashamed?

HENRY: (*Working.*) What?

KATHERINE: Ashamed!

HENRY: What of?

KATHERINE: Of what you've done to Sam.

HENRY: What've I done to Sam?

KATHERINE: Corrupted him.

(*Astonished, he puts down his brief and looks at her.*)

HENRY: (*After a pause.*) I thought he was supposed to do that to me.

KATHERINE: He didn't have a chance, did he? He's too simple... Too full of faith!

HENRY: Faith? Who are you talking about, exactly?

KATHERINE: You know... (*She sits on the sofa.*)

HENRY: Not the Sacred Saint Samuel and All Angels? The Blessed Martyr Brown of the Bronx? I'm sorry, I didn't recognize him for a moment.

KATHERINE: You wouldn't understand. He believed, in everything.

HENRY: And when did he convert you? All those little lunches, I suppose at the Trattoria in Belsize Park?

KATHERINE: We never went out to lunch. He used to bring things here. From the delicatessen. Wonderful things! Russian salad and pastrami on rye and strawberry cheesecake and coffee in little plastic cups with lids on them to keep it warm. He used to bring it in a carrier bag. Why don't you ever do that?

HENRY: I'm sorry.

KATHERINE: And we'd sit here. Over there. Where you're sitting.

(*HENRY gets up and moves.*)

And he'd be caring so hard his forehead would be damp, gleaming with sweat and he'd have to undo his tie as if he were being strangled...

HENRY: Was he caring about anything in particular?

KATHERINE: Of course he was! About the Bomb and Suez and the Generation Gap and how he never communicated with his Father and the End of the World...

HENRY: The End of the World has always seemed the least of our worries.

KATHERINE: And about me! That's not one of your worries, either?

HENRY: I wish I'd known...

KATHERINE: You carefully avoided finding out.

HENRY: I could've given him something constructive to worry about. Like the rates...

(*Pause. He goes back to work.*)

There's one thing...

KATHERINE: What?

HENRY: About Sam...

KATHERINE: Let's stop talking about him, shall we?

HENRY: All right. (*He is bored with his brief and goes to the radiogram.*) Do you want some music?

KATHERINE: No.

HENRY: We will now stand in silent prayer to mark the passing of Mr Samuel Brown...

(*Pause. KATHERINE does not answer.*)

He hasn't rung up?

KATHERINE: No.

HENRY: Or written to you at all?

KATHERINE: No. Of course not.

HENRY: I must say I think's that a bloody cheek.

KATHERINE: Do you?

HENRY: I certainly do. All that caring and sweating and loosening his collar at you over the pastrami sandwiches and one little setback and he's off like a bloody butterfly. He's probably up the street – caring about the physiotherapist next door.

(*Pause. She does not react.*)

Do you miss him?

(*There is the sound of a very small child calling from upstairs.*)

KATHERINE: Not particularly. (*She looks at him.*) Do you? It seems you didn't settle her at all!

(*KATHERINE goes up the stairs.*

There is a ring at the front door. HENRY answers it and lets in a reluctant and shamefaced SAM, who is carrying a potted plant.)

SAM: You're going to let me in?

HENRY: We were just wondering where you'd got to.

SAM: You were? Both of you?

HENRY: Of course.

SAM: I brought this...

HENRY: Katherine'll like that. She's just up with the children...

SAM: For you, Henry. I know you like the home to look nice. Well, I couldn't think of a present...

(*HENRY takes the plant.*)

You're not offended?

HENRY: Not at all. It was very – thoughtful. (*He puts it on the mantelpiece.*)

SAM: I had to come round. I had to apologize – heartfelt... I expect you can guess. I've gone in for a bit of self examination. Painful – painful process.

HENRY: I don't know. I've always found it a lot better than examining other people.

SAM: I said to myself, 'Sam Brown,' I said, 'I hope you're proud of what you've done. Oh boy, I surely hope you're proud.'

HENRY: Well, you certainly got further than anyone else I've ever known on a pastrami sandwich.

SAM: (*Pained.*) Henry. Please...

HENRY: I'm sorry.

SAM: This hasn't been easy for me. I'd like you to respect that.

HENRY: I'm very sorry.

SAM: A friend! An actual friend. That's what makes it – so hard to forgive myself. You know, Hank, I've lived around, naturally. I got laid in many quarters of the globe...

HENRY: You're referring to your sexual experiences, naturally – and not the circumstances of your birth?

SAM: Henry!

HENRY: It always sounds so like being hatched out. I really am sorry. What do you want me to say? Congratulations.

SAM: (*Patiently.*) I would like you, Henry, just to try and understand...

HENRY: I will try. I promise...

SAM: I have had broads – from the age of ten on. Well, a man loses count after a while.

HENRY: I wish I could.

SAM: What?

HENRY: Lose count. If only they could merge into one anonymous broad. It's the bloody individuality...

SAM: But this is what I thought. No-one is worth trading for a friend. We had found friendship, Henry. Working together, fighting, making it up, getting to know all each other's little faults and weaknesses... Of course, it hasn't been long.

HENRY: Really? It felt as though it was just coming up to our golden wedding...

SAM: That's right, man! That is absolutely correct. Surpasses the love of woman. (*He puts an arm round him.*)

HENRY: (*Moving away.*) Excuse me...

SAM: Like the Bible says, old chum. It surpasses the love of woman. Don't be English – man.

HENRY: What?

SAM: Don't be bloody English. We are just a little bit more open about this where I come from. A little less

139

easily shocked? A little more psychoanalytically oriented maybe...

HENRY: I'd love to know what you're talking about.

SAM: With us it may be a little more common. You know what is in constant use with us? Packaged foods. All sort of packaged and frozen chicken con carne and suchlike. Well, boy – have these chickens been jammed packed full of hormones! Male and female, both – just packed in at random.

HENRY: Sam...

SAM: Henry...?

HENRY: I'm really quite pleased to see you and thank you for the flowers – but can you tell me what any of this has to do with the hormones in chickens.

SAM: Well...some of our guys are getting a little less like guys than they used to be. I could see that our friendship meant a good deal to you. Katherine has no right to come between us. A woman's love is not so pure. It hasn't got the strength – and the generosity. What did the old Arab do?

HENRY: I don't know, Sam. Is it going to be a joke?

SAM: His friend admired his wife – so he offered the wife to the friend, Henry Winter. You made me ashamed. In a friendship like ours. Women just don't enter into it.

HENRY: Don't they? I suppose they don't.

SAM: They just don't enter in. Friends... That's what counts. (*He holds out his hands.*) And the project!

HENRY: And the project. (*He shakes SAM's hand.*)

SAM: The project still means a lot to me. You don't mind my coming round here again? For work sessions... Well, it's better than an office.

HENRY: Be my guest – I'm sorry.

SAM: Henry. I have another small favour to ask you. If you want to kick me out after I've said this – well, I guess I had it coming.

HENRY: This isn't...something to do with the old Arab?

SAM: Not at all! The fact is – I'm kinda between apartments at the moment. I had this wonderful place in Soho

Square all set up and then this schmuck got married and
– of course I could go to a hotel...

HENRY: (*Smiling, welcoming.*) I wouldn't dream of it.

SAM: I have acquaintances, of course, but not real friends
like you and Katherine...

HENRY: Be my... I'm sorry. Of course. You can sleep on
the sofa.

(*KATHERINE comes in from upstairs. She sees SAM.*)

KATHERINE: Well.

SAM: (*Awkward and guilty.*) Hullo, there! Long time no see.

KATHERINE: You did leave rather suddenly.

SAM: Katherine...

KATHERINE: Of course, my husband has a remarkable
talent for seeing people off the premises. He usually
manages to get us left entirely alone.

(*She moves towards the exotic potted plant she has noticed.*)

SAM: I'm sorry. I called round to say I was sorry. To make
– some sort of amends, I guess...

KATHERINE: Well, Sam. That's very nice of you. It's
beautiful.

HENRY: (*Firmly.*) It's mine. (*He moves in front of the plant.*)

KATHERINE: What?

HENRY: Sam brought that floral tribute, as a personal
present for me. Katherine – I think you'd better find
some blankets.

KATHERINE: Have you gone mad?

HENRY: I have invited Sam to be – to stay with us for a
little while. It seems he's had a little bad luck. He's fallen
between flats.

KATHERINE: (*Looking at them both with amused amazement.*)
Good God! When's the wedding...?

SAM: What?

KATHERINE: (*To HENRY.*) When's the happy day? I mean,
first he brings you flowers – then you tell me he's moving
in.

HENRY: What's the matter? Jealous?

KATHERINE: You're taking him over!

HENRY: Sam and I just happen to have something rather
fine going for us. Surpassing the love of women...

KATHERINE: (*To SAM.*) You're not going to let him do it?

SAM: Do what?

KATHERINE: Have you to live in. As a mother's help!

SAM: (*With dignity.*) I really don't know what you're suggesting, Katherine. I thought I'd move in here so I could get down to work with Henry.

HENRY: If you've got any strong objection...

KATHERINE: Don't let me come between you.

HENRY: Sam just thought it'd be convenient.

KATHERINE: Convenient. For you. I suppose so.

HENRY: For the work, naturally. (*He moves to SAM and gives him a brisk slap on the back.*) Well, old chum. Feel like a work session, do you?

SAM: Ready when you are, feller.

KATHERINE: (*Raising her eyes to heaven.*) Oh, my God!

HENRY: What're you going to do, Katherine?

KATHERINE: What do you suggest? Do you two boys want to be left alone together?

SAM: No. No, of course not...

HENRY: Not necessarily.

KATHERINE: Well, then. I'll just hang around doing something feminine. (*She looks around the room for something to do.*) I'll water the plant...
(*KATHERINE goes into the kitchen.*)

SAM: (*Lying back on the sofa and kicking off his shoes.*) I have been thinking about the project. Pretty hard in the last few days. I feel – our married couple need something.

HENRY: No doubt about it.

SAM: Maybe – an extra problem.
(*KATHERINE enters with a milk bottle containing green washing-up liquid shaken up in it.*)

KATHERINE: An extra problem! That's it. For the couple who have everything. (*She waters the plant, drowning it.*)

HENRY: That shouldn't be too hard. What sort of problem would you suggest?

SAM: A modern problem... Something to give this story a rather contemporary look.
(*Pause.*)
Oh, my God – inspiration!

KATHERINE: It's struck again? (*She sits.*)

SAM: (*To HENRY.*) Look! I wouldn't want to force anything on you, kid, and it's your story, anyway, but suppose – I mean, just suppose we kick this one around a little – I can speak freely in front of you, Katherine?

KATHERINE: I thought you already had.

SAM: Thanks. Well, just suppose this man – this husband in our story – had to face with a great deal of courage. And good taste, of course. The human problem of sexual inversion.

KATHERINE: (*Singing.*) 'Here I go again
I hear the trumpets blow again...'

SAM: Of course, it would have to be tastefully done.

KATHERINE: You mean he's a faggot, Samuel?

SAM: Doesn't that have a certain truthfulness?

KATHERINE: I should say so.

SAM: And her problem is – she feels it her duty to live with a man who is otherwise orientated sexwise, quite frankly.

KATHERINE: Why does she feel it her duty?

SAM: Well, why don't we say... Got it! For the sake of the kids!

KATHERINE: Brilliant!

SAM: Now we are cooking. Doesn't that give her a real dilemma? And warmth. You know what this wife needs?

KATHERINE: What does she need?

SAM: A friend! A sympathetic friend... Say a guy – who knows her really well. I mean, he's really got the hots for her but she's married to a man he greatly respects...and well. He keeps his distance...

KATHERINE: I'll get you some blankets. (*She moves to go out of the room.*) Sounds very moving.

SAM: Doesn't it. I'm glad you think so, Katherine. (*He gets up and starts to follow her.*) We've got something going for us now. A purity – a kind of nobility, even! Want some help?

(*KATHERINE exits upstairs.*)

You know – with a warm dilemma like that we might even get a 'yes' from Deborah Kerr.

(*SAM goes out after KATHERINE.*
The phone rings. HENRY picks it up.)

HENRY: Miss Griffin? Well... Hullo, Miss Griffin darling... (*He looks round the room.*) It's not all that easy actually... Visitors? Yes... Tomorrow. I'll be there at nine... For a nice chat in the cells... No... No, I'm sorry. Of course I can't get out tonight. Well... It's impossible. Not for a long time, I'm afraid. You see. It's happened. Total war! Yes. Daniel told her. (*He whispers.*) The gas oven!

(*KATHERINE comes back with an armful of blankets. SAM follows with pillows.*)

(*Beginning to talk quickly.*) If we could get Bernard's prints on the gas oven we could prove he wasn't at the scene of the crime at all. He was at home with his mother – heating up the steak and mushroom pie. Look into it, will you? (*He puts down the phone.*)

SAM: Has he got an alibi?

HENRY: Always. (*He gets up and moves to the table.*) It's always possible, given a little ingenuity, to prove that you were in two places at any given moment.

(*KATHERINE starts to make up a bed on the sofa.*)

I'm hungry.

KATHERINE: Then why don't you cook us a cosy little snack before we tuck Sam up for the night?

(*HENRY goes into the kitchen.*)

(*Sitting on the pouffe.*) I'm sorry. He's treating you very badly.

SAM: He's being great. It's great of him to have me here. (*He continues with the bed-making.*) Say what you like about Henry. He behaved like a gentleman.

KATHERINE: That's right. Badly.

SAM: What did you mean by that – 'mother's help'?

KATHERINE: He's got you, hasn't he, exactly where he wants you?

SAM: Where's that?

KATHERINE: Here. Doing the tough work. That's what he's always recommended – as a solution for every problem. 'Get a man in.'

SAM: I behaved badly. I blame myself – very much.

KATHERINE: 'Get a man in.' To mend the Hoover and put washers on taps and provide his wife with a bit of an alternative to *Listen with Mother*...

SAM: And when I came back not a word of blame. Not a word!

KATHERINE: Or even to do the real dirty jobs – like saving my life.

SAM: Like what?

KATHERINE: Not a great life saver, our Henry. Shall I tell you a scene? You might be able to use it.

SAM: Go on. Shoot. We're really creative tonight, aren't we?

KATHERINE: I was thinking – of a scene with the children. Perhaps – somewhere on holiday.

SAM: Kids! That's good.

KATHERINE: (*Ignoring him.*) On some huge white beach. In England. With the children swimming. Teeth chattering. Gooseflesh. Swimming, determined.

SAM: And what's he doing?

KATHERINE: What's he always doing? Cooking!

SAM: Making a fire of driftwood on the sand. Frying sausages. The way the kids like it.

KATHERINE: He's got a cook's hat on, maybe – and a striped apron.

SAM: Don't be ridiculous!

KATHERINE: And one of the children...

SAM: One of his?

KATHERINE: One of theirs. Is shouting. Calling from the water. There's a tide on that beach, you see. It pulls you out however hard you swim against it. He never asked about it, he never discovered. He was busy cooking. Anyway, this child is screaming, being carried away. Drowning...

SAM: I like it.

KATHERINE: Extraordinarily quickly.

SAM: I can see it. In visual terms. We shoot down – and this kid's face is actually under the water. We shoot through water. I can see it all!

KATHERINE: So could he! He saw a man – far out to sea. In the direction this child was floating. 'Let him save her', he said. 'He's much nearer to her than I am.' Get a man in.

SAM: Katherine, you make me ashamed.

KATHERINE: You?

SAM: I ran out on you. That night…

KATHERINE: He made you.

SAM: It's just that I couldn't do it. To a sensitive guy like Henry.

KATHERINE: Sensitive? He's about as sensitive as a ten-ton truck. Bashing on his way – regardless.

SAM: (*Moving nearer to her.*) Katherine. Sweet Katherine…

KATHERINE: Yes?

SAM: I want to fuck you.

(*As SAM is speaking HENRY comes in from the kitchen.*)

HENRY: Anyone want a cheese on toast?

KATHERINE: Sam just said, 'I want to fuck you'.

SAM: It's a great line. Don't you think so? For the script I mean.

HENRY: Oh, for the script. Brilliant. And so original.

SAM: Why not be original? Why not say 'fuck'?

HENRY: I've been saying that as long as I can remember.

SAM: But not on the movies, Hank. Don't you see the distinction?

KATHERINE: Do we have to?

SAM: What?

KATHERINE: Do we actually *have* to say it?

SAM: (*Thinking it over.*) Well, you don't *have* to. But it'd be kind of nice if you did.

KATHERINE: Can't we use that word for it they used to use in the Golden Oldies of Movieland?

SAM: What word is that, Katherine?

KATHERINE: 'Dance.'

SAM: Sorry. I'm not with you…

HENRY: Dance. Samuel, where were you brought up, exactly? (*He sings suddenly.*)
'I'm dancing with tears in my eyes
Because the girl in my arms isn't you.'

KATHERINE: 'Say that I will always dance
The anniversary dance with you...'
HENRY: 'They're dancing overhead
Up above my lonely bed.'
(*HENRY starts a tap dance, and as she sings KATHERINE joins in till they are doing, for SAM's benefit, their long-practised version of Fred Astaire and Ginger Rogers.*)
KATHERINE: 'I love my ceiling more
Since it is a dancing floor...'
HENRY: 'I won't dance
How could I?
I won't dance, why should I?
I won't dance, Madame, with you.
My heart won't let my feet do what they want to...'
KATHERINE: 'When you dance you're sweet and you are
gent...le
Especially when you do the CON... TIN... ENT... AL.'
HENRY: 'It's heaven sent...le
And sentiment...le
Heaven...
I'm in heaven...

I won't dance
How could I?
I won't dance. Why should I?
I won't dance, Madame, with you...'
(*They finish the dance in a fine pirouette and, holding hands, bow to SAM who starts, reluctantly, to clap. He goes on clapping. KATHERINE and HENRY exit upstairs.*
SAM takes off his shoes, trousers and jacket and gets into bed on the sofa. He is instantly asleep. The lights fade to a black-out.
When the lights come up again it is daylight. SAM is lying in a heap of blankets. The sound is heard of the children who have visited him earlier. The doorbell rings. SAM rises and staggers out to the kitchen. The doorbell rings again. There is the sound of a tap running, then SAM returns and goes towards the front door. The bell rings again as he reaches it and opens it.
GRISELDA enters.
SAM gets quickly behind the open door.)

GRISELDA: Have I come to the right house?

SAM: The right house for what?

GRISELDA: (*Coming into the room.*) I wanted to see Mrs Winter. It's rather urgent.

SAM: Katherine…?

(*KATHERINE enters downstairs.*)

KATHERINE: Sam. You look terrible. What time did the children get at you?

SAM: Around four, I guess. Look, there's someone…

GRISELDA: Mrs Winter. I had to come and talk to you. Urgently.

SAM: (*Picking up his clothes.*) I'll go. I was just fixing myself a glass of kiddies' orange drink.

(*SAM exits to the kitchen.*)

KATHERINE: (*Calling after him.*) There's some Delrosa rose hip syrup if you like it better. (*To GRISELDA.*) I'm sorry. Our lodger seems to have overslept.

GRISELDA: (*Who has been looking at her.*) You look different.

KATHERINE: Different from what?

GRISELDA: Different from what I expected. You didn't mind my coming?

KATHERINE: No. Should I? (*She gathers the sheets and blankets together and puts them on the back of the sofa.*)

GRISELDA: Henry told me a bit last night. And then this morning. We were having coffee – down at the Old Bailey.

KATHERINE: Henry?

GRISELDA: Your husband, Henry.

KATHERINE: Oh, *that* Henry…

GRISELDA: He told me it all. I just got up and left. Mr Fidella'll have to look after the case – I couldn't stay. I had to set your mind at rest, you see – I had to tell you it's all over. Finished. Completely. With me and Henry. (*Pause.*)

You'll never do that again, Mrs Winter, will you…?

KATHERINE: Excuse me – this may sound awfully rude but – who are you, exactly?

GRISELDA: I'm Griselda – Griselda Griffin. I used to go out with Henry.

KATHERINE: Gristle! My husband actually took you out?

GRISELDA: Well, not *very* much.

KATHERINE: Four-thirty. The Kardomah, Fleet Street. Did he stand you tea? I mean, let's face it, my husband can be bloody mean.

GRISELDA: (*With a faint smile.*) I managed to winkle a cake out of him occasionally.

KATHERINE: The bastard! Didn't he ever buy you dinner?

GRISELDA: Well – once.

KATHERINE: The menu at the Carvery? All you can get on your plate for twelve-and-six?

GRISELDA: You'd taken the children to stay with his mother in the country. You weren't due back till ten. We had to leave before the sweet trolley…

KATHERINE: I can only apologize for my husband. He's got the most despicable manners.

GRISELDA: Oh, it's not your fault. Nothing's your fault, Mrs Winter.

KATHERINE: Please. Katherine.

GRISELDA: All right then. Katherine. I'm so ashamed. About that night.

KATHERINE: What night, exactly?

GRISELDA: The night I came round with my nightie in a bag.
(*Pause.*)

KATHERINE: You came round with *what?*

GRISELDA: In a paper bag. He'd never seen me in any night wear.

KATHERINE: Of course! That night.

GRISELDA: (*After a pause.*) What really is unforgivable is – involving the children! Of course that little child told you. He had every right to tell you. He was protecting himself, that's all. I was a challenge. I realize that. To the whole family stability.
(*Pause.*)
Wasn't I?

KATHERINE: (*Reassuringly.*) Of course you were, dear! A tremendous challenge.

GRISELDA: If – if my child told me he saw a strange woman coming up the stairs with a ridiculous orange nylon slumber wear – which she'd brought in a carrier bag – I'd do it, too.

KATHERINE: Do what, too?

GRISELDA: Put my head in the gas oven.

KATHERINE: Is that what I did?

(*GRISELDA nods miserably. Pause. KATHERINE looks at her.*)

Are you sure that's what I did?

GRISELDA: Sure.

KATHERINE: So let's get this perfectly straight, Griselda. You came round – with your things in a carrier bag.

GRISELDA: Only because you'd left home. He told me that…

KATHERINE: Oh, I see. I'd left home.

GRISELDA: With a film producer.

KATHERINE: And Daniel saw you. Why did you leave?

GRISELDA: Because you were coming back. You'd decided to give your marriage another chance. And I've ruined it all! Ruined! I was there, you see – going upstairs. That's the point.

KATHERINE: And Daniel passed on – all that information?

GRISELDA: Didn't he?

(*Pause.*)

KATHERINE: No.

GRISELDA: But you knew about it?

KATHERINE: Yes.

GRISELDA: Then who told you?

KATHERINE: You.

GRISELDA: What?

KATHERINE: You did. You just have.

GRISELDA: Oh, Mrs Winter! Where've I got myself?

KATHERINE: I have absolutely no idea. I must say it's fascinating.

GRISELDA: What must you think of me?

KATHERINE: Another of my husband's works of fiction.

GRISELDA: Then what was he talking about?

KATHERINE: Who can ever tell?

GRISELDA: He told me – war had broken out. He seemed so, terribly concerned!

KATHERINE: Then he was lying. He's never concerned about the truth.

GRISELDA: Are you going to tell him – I came round?

KATHERINE: I don't think so. He'd be so flattered.

GRISELDA: Flattered?

KATHERINE: Two women. Saying terrible things about him. I don't think he deserves that pleasure, do you?

GRISELDA: I don't – really understand…

KATHERINE: Be grateful. You'll never have to. I wish I'd known, dear. What you were going through. I'd have been round to beg your forgiveness.

GRISELDA: To forgive *you*…?

KATHERINE: For Henry. He shouldn't be let out alone.

GRISELDA: You've been so lovely. I never expected – you'd be so gentle.

(*KATHERINE smiles at her, steps forward, and kisses her.*)

KATHERINE: I hope we can be friends, at least.

GRISELDA: So do I. (*She starts to go.*)

KATHERINE: What about tea, sometime, in the Kardomah?

GRISELDA: You're joking!

KATHERINE: No, Griselda, dear, I never joke.

(*GRISELDA goes.*

KATHERINE stands a moment looking after her. Then she folds the blankets and puts them at the end of the sofa.

SAM comes out of the kitchen, a tumbler of some pink drink in his hand.)

I'm glad you like the Rose Hip.

SAM: It's incredible!

KATHERINE: The children like it.

SAM: What that girl said. What *about* that?

KATHERINE: You heard it?

SAM: The door was open and…

KATHERINE: That's the worst of this house. It's like living on a stage.

SAM: Incredible!

KATHERINE: No, it's not. Once you get to know Henry…

SAM: You think he actually told her…all that?

KATHERINE: Once you get to know my husband you'll believe anything.

SAM: He told her all that…nonsense, about *you*.

KATHERINE: He has to make me responsible, you see. For everything.

(*KATHERINE goes upstairs with the blankets.*

SAM stands for a moment, the glass in his hand, then picks up his shoes.

HENRY enters through the front door with his brief-case.)

HENRY: Isn't it a bit early? To start on the wine?

SAM: It's rose hip syrup.

HENRY: How revolting!

SAM: (*Putting down the glass.*) You're back early. (*He sits to put on his shoes.*)

HENRY: The case finished – rather unexpectedly. Tell me – you haven't seen someone – from my solicitor's office? (*KATHERINE comes down the stairs.*)

SAM: Yes, she was here.

HENRY: Oh.

KATHERINE: Gristle was here. Fascinating! (*Coming into the room.*) You're back early.

HENRY: Yes.

KATHERINE: Did you lose the case?

HENRY: No. No, not really. It was rather funny, as a matter of fact.

KATHERINE: Just for once – couldn't you do something that's not funny?

HENRY: We happened to have hit, Bernard and I, on the opening day of the Old Bailey – one of those quaint ceremonies which make law so lovable and lend such a touch of gaiety to a ten-year stretch. Bernard came up from the cells, blinking like a mole, to be greeted by the sight of a scarlet-ermine-trimmed judge, sniffing his nosegay, being bowed into place by lots of gentlemen in lace ruffles and swords. Apparently he mistook number one court for heaven and shouted 'Hallelujah. I have passed over. The Day of Judgement is at hand.' They made a hospital order. (*He laughs.*)

KATHERINE: I don't think that's funny.

HENRY: (*Dead-pan.*) No. It's not funny, really – quite a reasonable hospital order.

SAM: The Day of Judgement! I should think it is. As far as you're concerned.

HENRY: He'll probably be out for Christmas.

SAM: Your Day of Judgement. I should imagine it's just about due. What did you tell that Miss Griffin?

KATHERINE: (*To SAM.*) You don't understand Henry.

SAM: I certainly don't.

KATHERINE: He just isn't capable of a plain straightforward brush off. I mean, he couldn't even bring himself to say, 'Miss Griffin, darling, you bore me', or 'Don't ring me, I'll ring you', or 'I've met something strange and new from the typing pool and I'll be having tea in Joe Lyons in future'. He wants everyone to go on loving him.

SAM: So?

KATHERINE: So he puts on his best tragic expression and says, 'Don't ring me, darling, because whenever you do...my wife prepares for immolation!'

SAM: You bastard! What've you given that girl? What sort of a hell of a load of responsibility?

HENRY: Responsibility? What for?

SAM: Tragedy. Could've been...

HENRY: Could've been? Could've been farce.

SAM: What the hell did you let her believe...?

HENRY: Anyway. Something interesting.

SAM: What?

HENRY: Not dull. At least it wasn't dull. What we told her.

KATHERINE: 'We?' Don't drag me into it. He has to bring everything home. Didn't I tell you?

HENRY: What did you bring home?

KATHERINE: What?

HENRY: Him!

SAM: Me?

HENRY: Not good enough for you, was it? Not a secret little romance among the paper cups and pastrami sandwiches. You had to make a great announcement! A great scene. You had to drag me into it.

SAM: Is that right, Katherine?

(*Pause. KATHERINE does not answer.*)

(*To HENRY.*) I guess she wanted to try me out – she wanted to watch my reactions.

HENRY: No. She wanted to watch mine.

SAM: Katherine!

(*Pause. Again she does not answer.*)

I was another one, uh? Someone to provide a little dramatic material for both of you! I suppose you think you've given me something which isn't exactly dull. You know what you gave me? Something so damn complicated I couldn't understand a word of it! (*To KATHERINE.*) I wanted to make a grab for you. A plain simple grab to which any man's entitled. And before I knew it you'd got me all confused with lies and stories and 'I don't want her, you have her', and 'No, I didn't mean that really...' And now I see what it was all for. A present for me. Gift wrapped. Uh? Something for me to remember in the long years ahead when we carve our Sunday roast and cook apple pie and pay our mortgages. The glorious, fascinating days when we tangled with the Winters. Dicing with death. Jam packed with thrills and spills. Is that what we're supposed to remember? You know what I think you are? A couple of monsters. (*He sits.*)

HENRY: Not monsters. Just married.

KATHERINE: It makes it difficult, for anyone who comes near us.

HENRY: It makes it much more difficult for us.

SAM: (*Looking at them.*) Well – well – well! Oh, God, I'm sorry for you! I'm sorry you spend so much on wine and little bottles of herbs and casserole dishes and you can't afford the gas. I'm sorry you've got about nineteen kids upstairs who're just about too grown up to join in your games any more. And that includes the baby! I'm sorry you find each other so unsatisfactory that you have to grab people in off the sidewalk for laughs or kicks or whatever the hell it is. I'm sorry for you both. I'm sorry...

HENRY: Very good speech, Sam. (*To KATHERINE.*) Wouldn't you say so? Eloquent.

SAM: What do I have – did you say Mr laugh-a-minute Henry Winter? 'Three D emotions?' 'Feelings in gorgeous technicolor?' Want to swap? Or are you happy with no feelings at all? Feelings you took out and looked at and made jokes about so often that they've sort of faded out and died, haven't they, old chum?

HENRY: Where did you say you came from?

SAM: What the hell does it matter where I came from?

KATHERINE: You came out of nowhere. We didn't ask you. You came here to take us over.

SAM: Big chance! Like a small bicycle repair shop making a bid for General Motors.

KATHERINE: You hear what he called us? He called us General Motors!

HENRY: Eloquent! Sam Brown has become eloquent.
(*Pause.*)
There's something in what he says.

KATHERINE: I told you. If you let him in here he'd corrupt us...

HENRY: The children are much older than we are. I see in their eyes, as I settle them down for the night, looks of remote disapproval.

KATHERINE: (*To SAM.*) You should have left us alone.

SAM: I only wanted you to work. That's all I had, a job of work for you.

KATHERINE: Is *that* why you came?

SAM: You agreed to do it! You took on this assignment. You have a certain responsibility. To the project.

HENRY: The show must go on?

KATHERINE: Why?

SAM: How much work have you done lately? How many pages?

HENRY: I've been busy. Rather – occupied.

SAM: Amusing yourself with attempted murder! You have neglected my story.

KATHERINE: He's right, you know. After all, you took Sam on...

HENRY: *I* took him on...?

SAM: A person can't rely on you, Henry.

KATHERINE: I agree.

HENRY: What?

KATHERINE: I agree – he's not to be relied on. (*To SAM.*) You put out a hand for him – and he's not there. It's like a sudden gap in the staircase and under it – a great, great fall – black nothing...

HENRY: (*To KATHERINE.*) And *you're* so dependable, of course!

KATHERINE: More dependable.

HENRY: Like when I was here alone. All alone – looking after the kids and you came back and announced your forthcoming marriage – to this – this visitor!

KATHERINE: All alone! Only with about ten girls running around with half Neatawear in paper bags.

HENRY: You didn't know that! You absolutely weren't to know.

(*Pause.*)

I couldn't depend on you.

KATHERINE: You're pathetic! If you want to depend on me you'd find me much more dependable.

HENRY: If I didn't want to depend on you I wouldn't care if you were dependable or not.

SAM: (*Shouting at both of them.*) Oh, for God's sake! We've got to find a resolution.

(*Pause.*)

HENRY: What?

KATHERINE: Would you like to suggest one?

SAM: What we really require here – is something upbeat! I mean it's got to be hopeful.

KATHERINE: Are you actually proposing, Sam, a happy ending...?

SAM: A happy ending. With a twist, if possible. Now what would that *be* exactly?

KATHERINE: Divorce.

SAM: Oh, come on, Katherine.

KATHERINE: A happy ending – for them both.

HENRY: And apparently for everyone else around.

KATHERINE: That's it! For everyone, unfortunately around.

SAM: Oh, come on! You're kidding! Divorce? Divorce has got to be sad. Divorce is failure, isn't it? I mean it's by its nature – gloomy.

KATHERINE: Gloomier than marriage?

SAM: Hey, kids. What're you trying to tell me? You're trying to tell me there's a twist – are you? Wait a minute. I'm starting to get it... A loving divorce! A really meaningful divorce. With love. Do you suppose an audience might identify? Look. These two love each other. Let's say. They're crazy for each other. But they can't stop knocking the hell out of each other. So they end up having a loving divorce. Out of compassion. Done with taste. Have I got it?

KATHERINE: I don't know.

(*The lights fade to a black-out. KATHERINE exits to the kitchen; HENRY through the arch; SAM sits below the fire and takes out a buff-coloured script.*

As the lights come up again, to evening, KATHERINE enters from the kitchen with an armful of HENRY's shirts, packaged fresh from the laundry, and HENRY comes in with a suitcase. They meet in the middle of the room and HENRY drops the case, open on the floor. KATHERINE drops the shirts into the case.)

HENRY: How many?

KATHERINE: Twelve! A man with twelve shirts and no moral principles.

HENRY: (*Crouching by the case, arranging the shirts.*) Fifteen.

KATHERINE: What?

HENRY: I own fifteen.

KATHERINE: Three are in the wash.

HENRY: Then I can't go.

KATHERINE: I'll bring them round on Saturday.

HENRY: No! You won't bring them round. I'm not seeing you again, Katherine. Not ever.

KATHERINE: (*With a shrug.*) Just as you like.

HENRY: (*Shutting the case and standing up.*) I want to find myself.

SAM: (*Nodding approvingly.*) That's good!

KATHERINE: (*Looking at him, astonished.*) You like that?

SAM: 'Find myself.' That's very good.

KATHERINE: I think it's ludicrous! As though he'd left himself in a taxi and was just popping round to the Lost Property Office. (*She goes to the table, picks up a typescript and looks through it.*) What comes next? (*She finds her place in the script.*) 'When you're gone I'll have that crack in the plaster mended.' (*She looks at HENRY, puzzled.*)

HENRY: (*Pointing to a chipped and damaged corner of the wall.*) The plaster.

KATHERINE: When you're gone I'll have that crack in the plaster mended.

HENRY: Why don't you keep it as it is? As a memento of the great attack! Put poppies round it and observe two minutes' bloody silence...

KATHERINE: What attack?

HENRY: Your attack!

KATHERINE: *Mine?*

HENRY: (*Moving to the wall.*) This is where an Italian lamp, constructed from a pile of ceramic lemons, and bought with the proceeds from my first play for steam radio to add a new element of Theatrical High Camp to our lives, was flung at my head. And it's no credit to your marksmanship that my brains weren't spattered all over the John Barnes haircord.

KATHERINE: (*Putting down the typescript and starting to laugh.*) Miss Griffin!

HENRY: 'John Barnes haircord.' What an impossible line!

KATHERINE: (*Laughing.*) Miss Griselda Griffin!

SAM: (*Puzzled.*) Is that in the script?

KATHERINE: No! Gristle never made the script. She was more of a noise off, actually.

HENRY: Look. Shall we get on with it?

SAM: (*Quietly, patiently.*) We're here to work, Katherine.

KATHERINE: Yes, of course, Sam. Of course that's why we're here. (*She looks through the script again, speaks to HENRY.*) Do you have to go?

HENRY: (*Moving to the door with the case.*) You know I have to.

KATHERINE: Why? (*She moves to him.*)

HENRY: I suppose – we care too much...

KATHERINE: I know.

HENRY: We're stifling each other, choking each other to death. We have to move away so we can breathe.

SAM: That's great!

KATHERINE: Our divorce will be an occasion for mutual concern.

HENRY: And tenderness.

(*SAM, watching, covers his eyes.*)

KATHERINE: And respect...

HENRY: A lifelong and loving separation.

KATHERINE: We can be ourselves...

HENRY: And not each other.

(*They are close together, reading the script.*)

KATHERINE: Can we – do you think we can make it?

HENRY: We can try. All I can say is... (*Also making a heroic effort to say it seriously.*) Good luck, Katherine! (*He moves tragically to the door, starting to shake with laughter.*)

KATHERINE: Go now, darling. Go quickly. (*She manages to say this, then throws the script down on the table.*) It's ridiculous!

HENRY: (*Moving back towards her.*) Absurd.

KATHERINE: It'll never do. It'll never – never do. (*She looks at SAM who is still sitting with his hand over his face.*) What's happened to Sam?

(*They both move on either side of SAM, looking at him. He does not uncover his face.*)

HENRY: Sam. What's the matter?

KATHERINE: (*Kneeling beside him, concerned.*) Samuel. Samovitch.

HENRY: (*Also kneeling.*) Courage, M'sieur Brun.

KATHERINE: Sam Brown. What's oop?

HENRY: Brown, Braun, Brunovitch.

KATHERINE: Oh, my God! I believe he's deeply moved. (*She moves SAM's head, looks at his face, incredulous.*) Tears! Real, actual, genuine tears.

HENRY: (*Amazed.*) Brunowski's weeping!

(*SAM dries his eyes, blows his nose and embraces them both.*)

SAM: I love you. I love you both.

KATHERINE: He's crying – and he loves us.

SAM: I knew you could do it. I knew you kids could do it. The first time I walked in that door!

(*SAM rises, takes the script and walks towards the front door. KATHERINE and HENRY rise with him. HENRY opens the front door.*)

I'm going to see – if there's anything I can do with this. Don't ring me.

HENRY: Do you think, you might be able to find us, a little finance?

SAM: You two seem to think about nothing but finance! Think about art for a change.

(*SAM goes.*

HENRY shuts the front door and walks back into the room.)

HENRY: 'If there's anything he can do with it.'

(*KATHERINE gathers up the pillows from the sofa.*)

Our lives! Do you think he'll do anything with it?

KATHERINE: I don't know. He seems determined… (*She starts to go up the stairs.*)

HENRY: You mean he cares?

KATHERINE: (*Disappearing upstairs.*) Well. At least we can get this room tidied up.

(*KATHERINE goes.*

HENRY moves quickly to the telephone and dials.)

Miss Griffin?… It was a good result, wasn't it? A pretty good result… Look, I don't know what Katherine told you, but –

(*KATHERINE comes downstairs.*)

– she says some improbable things, you know. Some quite unreliable things. For her own – purposes. (*He puts down the phone slowly.*)

(*KATHERINE watches him.*)

KATHERINE: What did she do? Ring off? Before you could say good-bye? (*She ruffles the cushions on the sofa and sits.*) Well, that's Gristle gone.

HENRY: And Mr Brown?

KATHERINE: Yes. He's gone.

HENRY: Do you miss him? And Bernice. I didn't tell you.

KATHERINE: What?

HENRY: Bernice is dead. I never told you. (*He sits beside her on the sofa.*) Bernice! Of all people..

KATHERINE: We look like being all on our own.

HENRY: Yes. It seems rather quiet. Without old Samuel. And without Bernard.

KATHERINE: Who?

HENRY: Bernard Duffield.

KATHERINE: Oh, yes. The Day of Judgement...

HENRY: It never comes, actually, does it?

KATHERINE: It's come.

HENRY: What?

KATHERINE: Now and for ever. We'll go on paying for it.

HENRY: Paying for what exactly?

KATHERINE: The day you walked up the garden path. In those bloody deceptive gum boots.

HENRY: You're wrong, you know. I wasn't even wearing gum boots.

KATHERINE: Am I – am I really mistaken?

(*The children are heard calling.*)

CHILDREN: (*Off.*) Mummy...! Daddy...!

HENRY: (*Shouting up at the ceiling.*) Leave us alone! We're not doing anything wrong! (*To KATHERINE.*) So – puritanical – those children! They were perfectly ordinary, crêpe-soled, suede-topped, elastic-sided hush puppies!

KATHERINE: (*Looking at him, bleakly.*) One day, just for a change – why don't you try telling me the truth? (*They are looking at each other, as the curtain falls.*)

The End.

THE DOCK BRIEF

Characters

MORGENHALL
an unsuccessful barrister

FOWLE
an unsuccessful criminal

The Dock Brief was first produced by the BBC Third Programme on 12 May 1957, with the following cast:

MORGENHALL,   Michael Hordern

FOWLE,   David Kossoff

Producer,   Nesta Pain

The play was later subsequently produced on BBC television with the same cast and producer.

Michael Codron with David Hall (for Talbot Productions Ltd.) presented the plays in a double bill (with *What Shall We Tell Caroline?*) at the Lyric Opera House, Hammersmith, on 9 April, 1958, and on 20 May, 1958 at the Garrick Theatre. The cast was as follows:

MORGENHALL,   Michael Hordern

FOWLE,   Maurice Denham

Director,   Stuart Burge

Designer,   Disley Jones

The action of the play is in two scenes
and passes in a prison cell

Time – the present

Scene 1

Scene: a prison cell.

The walls are grey and fade upwards into the shadows, so that the ceiling is not seen, and it might even be possible to escape upwards. The door, up one step, is left of the back wall, and there is a small barred window high up in the wall right, through which the sky looks very blue. There is a bed, with a pillow and two dark blankets, against the wall left. A small table stands right of the door, with a Bible on it, and an enamel bucket under it. Right of the window is a towel-rail with a towel. Under the window there is a chair with a stool on top of it.

When the curtain rises, FOWLE, a small, fat man, is standing on the stool on tip-toe, his hands in his pockets. He is peering out of the window at the sky. The bolts of the door shoot back and the door opens. MORGENHALL strides in. He is an aged barrister with appearance of a dusty vulture, dressed in a black gown and bands. He carries a brief-case and his legal wig. He stands by the door and speaks to an unseen warder off.

MORGENHALL: Is this where – you keep Mr Fowle? Good, excellent. (*He turns to the table, puts down his brief-case and wig, moves centre and looks towards the door.*) Then leave us alone like a good fellow. Would you mind closing the door? These old places are so draughty. (*The door closes. The bolts shoot back.*)
(*He looks around.*) Mr Fowle – where are you, Mr Fowle? Not escaped, I pray. (*He looks around and sees FOWLE.*) Good Heavens, man, come down. Come down, Mr Fowle. (*MORGENHALL darts at FOWLE and there is a struggle. He pulls the bewildered FOWLE down.*)
I haven't hurt you? (*He takes the stool from the chair and sets it on the floor left centre.*)
(*FOWLE makes a negative-sounding noise.*)
I was suddenly anxious. A man in your unfortunate position. Desperate measures. And I couldn't bear to lose you. No, don't stand up. It's difficult for you without braces, or a belt, I can see. And no tie, no shoelaces. I'm so glad they're looking after you. You must forgive me if

I frightened you just a little, Mr Fowle. It was when I saw you up by that window…

FOWLE: (*In a hoarse and sad voice.*) Epping Forest.

MORGENHALL: (*Turning to him.*) What did you say?

FOWLE: I think you can see Epping Forest.

MORGENHALL: No doubt you can. But why, my dear chap, why should you want to?

FOWLE: It's the home stretch.

MORGENHALL: Very well.

FOWLE: I thought I could get a glimpse of the green. Between the chimneys and that shed… (*He climbs on to the chair.*)

(*MORGENHALL crosses to FOWLE and there is a brief renewed struggle.*)

MORGENHALL: No, get down. It's not wise to be up there, forever trying to look out. There's a draughty, sneeping wind. Treacherous. (*He draws FOWLE centre.*)

FOWLE: Treacherous?

MORGENHALL: I'm afraid so. You never know what a mean, sneeping wind can do. Catch you by the throat, start a sneeze, then a dry tickle on the chest, I don't want anything to catch you like that before…

FOWLE: Before what?

MORGENHALL: You're much better sitting quietly down here in the warm.

(*FOWLE crosses and sits on the bed.*)

Just sit quietly and I'll introduce myself. (*He takes off his gown and puts it on the upstage end of the bed.*)

FOWLE: I am tired.

MORGENHALL: I'm Morgenhall. (*He sits on the stool.*)

FOWLE: Morgenhall?

MORGENHALL: Morgenhall. The barrister.

FOWLE: The barrister?

MORGENHALL: Perfectly so.

FOWLE: I'm sorry.

MORGENHALL: Why?

FOWLE: A barrister. That's very bad.

MORGENHALL: I don't know. Why's it so bad?

FOWLE: When a gentleman of your stamp goes wrong. A long fall.

MORGENHALL: What can you mean?

FOWLE: Different for an individual like me. I only kept a small seed shop.

MORGENHALL: Seed shop? My poor fellow. We mustn't let this unfortunate little case confuse us. We're going to come to important decisions. Now, do me a favour, Mr Fowle, no more seed shops.

FOWLE: Bird-seed, of course. Individuals down our way kept birds mostly. Canaries and budgies. The budgies talked. Lot of lonely people down our way. They kept them for the talk.

MORGENHALL: Mr Fowle. I'm a barrister.

FOWLE: Tragic.

MORGENHALL: I know the law.

FOWLE: It's trapped you.

MORGENHALL: I'm here to help you.

FOWLE: We'll help each other.

(*There is a pause then MORGENHALL laughs uncontrollably.*)

MORGENHALL: I see. Mr Fowle, I see where you've been bewildered. You think I'm in trouble as well. Then I've got good news for you at last. I'm free. Oh, yes, I can leave here when I like.

FOWLE: Can you?

MORGENHALL: The police are my friends.

FOWLE: They are?

MORGENHALL: And I've never felt better in my life. There now. That's relieved you, hasn't it? I'm not in any trouble. (*He takes his spectacle case from his pocket and puts on his spectacles.*)

FOWLE: Family all well?

MORGENHALL: I never married.

FOWLE: Rent paid up?

MORGENHALL: A week or two owing, perhaps. Temporary lull in business. This case will end all that.

FOWLE: Which case?

MORGENHALL: Your case.

FOWLE: My...

MORGENHALL: Case.

FOWLE: Oh, that – it's not important.

MORGENHALL: Not?

FOWLE: (*Rising.*) I don't care about it to any large extent. Not as at present advised.

MORGENHALL: Mr Fowle. How could you say that?

FOWLE: The flavour's gone out of it.

MORGENHALL: But we're only at the beginning.

FOWLE: (*Crossing to centre.*) I can't believe it's me concerned.

MORGENHALL: But it is you, Mr Fowle. You mustn't let yourself forget that. You see, that's why you're here.

FOWLE: I can't seem to bother with it. (*He moves up centre.*)

MORGENHALL: Can you be so busy?

FOWLE: Slopping in, slopping out. (*He moves down right centre.*) Peering at the old forest. It fills in the day.

MORGENHALL: You seem, if I may say so – (*He rises.*) to have adopted an unpleasantly selfish attitude.

FOWLE: Selfish?

MORGENHALL: Dog in a manger. (*He moves centre.*)

FOWLE: In the...?

MORGENHALL: Unenthusiastic.

FOWLE: You're speaking quite frankly, I well appreciate...

MORGENHALL: I'm sorry, Fowle. You made me say it. There's so much of this about, nowadays. There's so much ready-made entertainment. Free billiards, National Health, Television. There's not the spirit abroad there used to be.

FOWLE: You feel that?

MORGENHALL: Whatever I've done, I've always been mustard keen on my work. I've never lost the vision, Fowle. In all my disappointments I've never lost the love of the job.

FOWLE: The position in life you've obtained to.

MORGENHALL: Years of study I had to put in. It didn't just drop in my lap.

FOWLE: I've never studied. (*He sits on the chair right.*)

MORGENHALL: Year after year, Fowle, my window at college was alight until two a.m. There I sat among my books. I fed mainly on herrings...

FOWLE: Lean years?

MORGENHALL: And black tea. No subsidized biscuits, then, Fowle, no County Council tobacco, just work.

FOWLE: Bookwork, almost entirely? I'm only assuming that, of course.

MORGENHALL: Want to hear some Latin?

FOWLE: Only if you have time.

MORGENHALL: *Actus non sit reus mens sit rea. Filius. Nullius In flagrante delicto.* Understand it? (*He removes his spectacles.*)

FOWLE: I'm no scholar.

MORGENHALL: You most certainly are not. But I had to be, we all had to be in my day. Then we'd sit for the examinations; mods, smalls, greats, tripos, little goes – rowing men fainting, Indian students vomiting with fear, and no creeping out for a peep at the book under the pretext of a pump ship or getting a glance at the other fellow's celluloid cuff.

FOWLE: That would be very unheard of?

MORGENHALL: Then weeks, months of waiting. (*He crosses to left.*) Nerve racking. Go up to the Lake District. Pace the mountains, play draughts – (*He crosses to centre.*) forget to huff. (*He moves up right centre.*) Then comes the fatal postcard.

FOWLE: What's it say?

MORGENHALL: Satisfied the examiners.

FOWLE: Well done!

MORGENHALL: Don't rejoice so soon. True enough, I felt I'd turned a corner, got a fur hood, bumped on the head with a Bible. Told the only lady in my life that in five years' time, perhaps…

FOWLE: You'd arrived.

MORGENHALL: That's what I thought when they painted my name up on my London chambers. I sat down to fill in the time until they sent my first brief in a real case. I sat down to do the crossword puzzle while I waited. Five years later, Fowle, what was I doing?

FOWLE: A little charge of High Treason?

MORGENHALL: I was still doing the crossword puzzle.

FOWLE: But better at it?

MORGENHALL: Not much. Not very much. As the years
pass there come to be clues you no longer understand.

FOWLE: So all that training?

MORGENHALL: Wasted. The talents rust.

FOWLE: And the lady?

MORGENHALL: Drove an ambulance, in the nineteen-
fourteen. A stray piece of shrapnel took her. (*He picks up
his brief-case.*) I don't care to talk of it.

FOWLE: Tragic.

MORGENHALL: It was.

FOWLE: Tragic my wife was never called up.

MORGENHALL: (*Moving down centre.*) You mustn't talk
like that, Fowle, your poor wife.

FOWLE: Don't let's carry on about me.

MORGENHALL: But we must carry on about you. That's
what I'm here for.

FOWLE: You're here to…

MORGENHALL: To defend you. (*He crosses to left centre and
puts the brief-case on the stool.*)

FOWLE: Can't be done.

MORGENHALL: Why ever not?

FOWLE: I know who killed her.

MORGENHALL: Who?

FOWLE: Me.

(*There is a pause. MORGENHALL swings round up left,
and after considerable thought, giggles.*)

MORGENHALL: Really, Mr Fowle, I have all the respect
in the world for your opinions, but we must face this.
You're a man of very little education.

FOWLE: That's true.

MORGENHALL: One has only to glance at you to see that
you're a person of very limited intelligence. (*He crosses to
FOWLE.*)

FOWLE: Agreed, quite frankly.

MORGENHALL: You think you killed your wife.

FOWLE: Seems so to me.

MORGENHALL: Mr Fowle. Look at yourself objectively.
On questions of bird-seed I have no doubt you may be

infallible – but on a vital point like this might you not be mistaken? Don't answer...

FOWLE: Why not, sir?

MORGENHALL: Before you drop the bomb of a reply, consider who will be wounded. Are the innocent to suffer?

FOWLE: I only want to be honest.

MORGENHALL: But you're a criminal, Mr Fowle. You've broken through the narrow fabric of honesty. You are free to be kind, human, to do good.

FOWLE: But what I did to her...

MORGENHALL: She's passed, you know, out of your life. You've set up new relationships. You've picked out me.

FOWLE: Picked out?

MORGENHALL: Selected.

FOWLE: But I didn't know... (*He rises.*)

MORGENHALL: No, Mr Fowle. That's the whole beauty of it. You didn't know me. You came to me under a system of chance, invented, like the football pools, to even out the harsh inequality of a world where you have to deserve success. You, Mr Fowle, are my first Dock Brief.

FOWLE: Your Dock...

MORGENHALL: Brief.

FOWLE: You couldn't explain?

MORGENHALL: Yes, yes, of course.

(*They both cross to left centre.*)

Criminals with no money and no friends exist. Luckily, you re one of them. They're entitled to choose any barrister sitting in court to defend them. The barrister, however old, gets a brief – (*He moves up centre.*) and is remunerated on a modest scale. Busy lawyers, wealthy lawyers, men with other interests, creep out of court bent double when the Dock Brief is chosen. (*He moves down centre.*) We regulars who are not busy sit on. I've been a regular for years. It's not etiquette, you see, even if you want the work, to wave at the prisoner, or whistle, or try to catch his eye by hoisting any sort of little flag.

FOWLE: Didn't know.

MORGENHALL: But you *can* choose the most advantageous seat. The seat any criminal would naturally point at. It's the seat under the window, and for ten years my old friend Tuppy Morgan, bagged it each day at ten. He sat there, reading *Horace*, and writing to his innumerable aunts, and almost once a year, a criminal pointed him out. Oh, Mr Fowle, Tuppy was a limpet on that seat. But this morning, something, possibly a cold, perhaps death, kept him indoors. So I had his place. And you spotted me, no doubt.

FOWLE: Spotted you?

MORGENHALL: My glasses polished. My profile drawn and learned in front of the great window.

FOWLE: I never noticed.

MORGENHALL: But when they asked you to choose a lawyer!

FOWLE: I shut my eyes and pointed – I've picked horses that way, and football teams. Never did me any good, though, by any stretch of the imagination.

MORGENHALL: So even you, Mr Fowle, didn't choose me?

FOWLE: Not altogether.

MORGENHALL: The law's a haphazard business.

FOWLE: It does seem chancy.

MORGENHALL: Years of training, and then to be picked out like a football pool.

FOWLE: Don't take it badly, sir.

MORGENHALL: Of course, you've been fortunate.

FOWLE: So unusual. (*He crosses to the bed.*) I was never one to draw the free bird at Christmas, or guess the weight of the cake. Now, I'm sorry I told you.

MORGENHALL: Never mind. You hurt me, temporarily, Mr Fowle, I must confess.

(*FOWLE sits on the bed, leans back and puts his feet up.*)

(*He moves the stool to centre.*) It might have been kinder to have kept me in ignorance. (*He moves to the table, picks it up and sets it between the stool and the bed.*) But now it's done. Let's get down to business. And, Fowle –

FOWLE: Yes, sir?

MORGENHALL: – remember you're dealing with a fellow man. A man no longer young. Remember the hopes I've pinned on you and try –

FOWLE: Try…

MORGENHALL: – try to spare me more pain.

FOWLE: I will, sir. Of course I will.

MORGENHALL: (*Picking up his brief-case.*) Now. (*He sits on the stool.*) Let's get our minds in order. (*He takes some newspapers, a bottle of medicine, a paper-backed book and an old envelope from his brief-case, puts them on the table, then takes a pencil stub from his pocket, puts the brief-case on the floor and puts on his spectacles.*)

FOWLE: Sort things out.

MORGENHALL: Exactly. Now, this wife of yours.

FOWLE: Doris?

MORGENHALL: Doris. (*He makes notes on the envelope.*) A bitter, unsympathetic woman?

FOWLE: She was always cheerful. She loved jokes.

MORGENHALL: Oh, Fowle. Do be very careful.

FOWLE: I will, sir. But if you'd known Doris… She laughed all day and all night. 'Thank God', she'd say, 'for my old English sense of fun.'

MORGENHALL: What sort of jokes, Fowle, did this Doris appreciate?

FOWLE: All sorts.

(*MORGENHALL writes.*)

Pictures in the paper. Jokes on the wireless set. Laughs out of crackers, she'd keep them from Christmas to Christmas and trot them out in August.

(*MORGENHALL stops writing and looks up.*)

MORGENHALL: You couldn't share it?

FOWLE: Not to that extent. I often missed the funny point.

MORGENHALL: Then you'd quarrel?

FOWLE: 'Don't look so miserable, it may never happen.' She said that every night when I came home. 'Where'd you get that miserable expression from?'

MORGENHALL: I can see it now. There is a kind of Sunday evening appearance to you.

FOWLE: I was quite happy. But it was always, 'Cat got your tongue?' 'Where's the funeral?' 'Play us a tune on that old fiddle face of yours.' Then we had to have our tea with the wireless on, so that she'd pick up the phrases.

MORGENHALL: You're not a wireless lover?

FOWLE: I couldn't always laugh. And she'd be doubled up across the table, gasping as if her lungs were full of water. 'Laugh,' she'd call. 'Laugh, damn you. What've you got to be so miserable about?' Then she'd go under, bubbling like a drowning woman.

MORGENHALL: (*Taking off his spectacles.*) Made meals difficult?

FOWLE: Indigestible. I would have laughed, but the jokes never tickled me.

MORGENHALL: They tickled her?

FOWLE: Anything did.

(*MORGENHALL puts on his spectacles and resumes writing.*)

Anything a little comic. Our names were misfortunate.

MORGENHALL: Your names?

FOWLE: Fowle. Going down the aisle she said: 'Now we're cock and hen, aren't we, old bird?' She laughed so hard we couldn't get her straightened up for the photograph.

MORGENHALL: Fond of puns, I gather you're trying to say.

FOWLE: Of any sort of joke. I had a little aviary at the bottom of my garden. As she got funnier so I spent more time with my birds. Budgerigars are small parrots. Circles round their eyes give them a sad, tired look.

MORGENHALL: (*Looking up.*) You found them sympathetic?

FOWLE: Restful.

(*MORGENHALL writes.*)

Until one of them spoke out at me.

MORGENHALL: Spoke – what words?

FOWLE: 'Don't look so miserable, it may never happen.'

MORGENHALL: The bird said that?

FOWLE: She taught it during the day when I was out at work. It didn't mean to irritate.

MORGENHALL: It was wrong of her, of course. To lead on your bird like that.

FOWLE: (*Rising and crossing to right.*) But it wasn't him that brought me to it. It was Bateson, the lodger.

MORGENHALL: (*Turning in his stool to face FOWLE.*) Another man?

FOWLE: At long last.

MORGENHALL: I can see it now. A crime of passion. An unfaithful wife. *In flagrante...* Of course, you don't know what that means. We'll reduce it to manslaughter right away. A wronged husband and there's never a dry eye in the jury-box. You came in and caught them.

FOWLE: Always laughing together.

MORGENHALL: Maddening.

FOWLE: He knew more jokes than she did.

MORGENHALL: Stealing her before your eyes?

FOWLE: That's what I thought. He was a big man. Ex-police. Said he'd been the scream of the station. I picked him for her specially. In the chitty I put in the local sweetshop. I wrote: 'Humorous type of lodger wanted.'

MORGENHALL: But wasn't that a risk?

FOWLE: Slight, perhaps. But it went all right. Two days after he came he poised a bag of flour to fall on her in the kitchen. Then she sewed up the legs of his pyjamas. They had to hold on to each other so as not to fall over laughing. 'Look at old misery standing there,' she said, 'he can never see anything subtle.'

MORGENHALL: Galling for you. Terribly galling.

FOWLE: I thought all was well. (*He moves centre.*) I spent more time with the birds. I'd come home late and always be careful to scrunch the gravel at the front door. I went to bed early and left them with the Light Programme. On Sunday mornings I fed the budgies and suggested he took her tea in bed. 'Laughter,' she read out from her horoscope, 'leads to love, even for those born under the sign of the virgin.'

MORGENHALL: You trusted them. They deceived you.

FOWLE: They deceived me all right. (*He moves to the chair right and sits.*) And I trusted them to do the right thing. Especially after I'd seen her on his knee and them both looking at the cartoons from one wrapping of chips.

MORGENHALL: Mr Fowle. I'm not quite getting the drift of your evidence. My hope is – your thought may not prove a shade too involved for our literal-minded judge. (*He takes off his spectacles and puts them in the case.*) Old Tommy Banter was a rugger blue in ninety-eight. He never rose to chess and his draughts had a brutal unintelligent quality.

FOWLE: When he'd first put his knee under her I thought he'd do the decent thing. I thought I'd have peace in my little house at last. The wireless set dead silent. The end of all that happy laughter. No sound but the twitter from the end of the garden and the squeak of my own foot on the linoleum.

MORGENHALL: (*Pointing at FOWLE with his spectacle case.*) You wanted...

FOWLE: I heard them whispering together and my hopes raised high. Then I came back and he was gone.

MORGENHALL: She'd...

FOWLE: Turned him out. Because he was getting over familiar. 'I couldn't have that,' she said. 'I may like my laugh, but, thank God, I'm still respectable. No, thank you, there's safety in marriage.' She'd sent him away, my last hope.

MORGENHALL: So you... ? (*He looks at FOWLE and makes a gesture with his spectacle case.*)

FOWLE: (*Nodding.*) I realize I did wrong.

MORGENHALL: You could have left.

FOWLE: Who'd have fed the birds? That thought was uppermost.

MORGENHALL: So it's not a crime of passion?

FOWLE: Not if you put it like that.

MORGENHALL: (*Putting his spectacle case in his pocket.*) Mr Fowle. (*He rises.*) I've worked and waited for you. (*He moves up centre.*) Now, you're the only case I've got, *and* the most difficult.

FOWLE: I'm sorry.

MORGENHALL: (*Moving down right centre.*) A man could crack his head against a case like you and still be far from a solution. Can't you see how twelve honest hearts

will snap like steel when they learn you ended up your
wife because she *wouldn't* leave you?

FOWLE: If she had left, there wouldn't have been the need.

MORGENHALL: There's no doubt about it. As I look at
you, now, I see you're an unsympathetic figure.

FOWLE: There it is.

MORGENHALL: It'll need a brilliant stroke to save you.
(*He moves up left.*) An unexpected move – something
pulled out of a hat. (*He turns and thumps the table.*) I've
got it. Something really exciting. The surprise witness.

FOWLE: Witness?

MORGENHALL: Picture the scene, Mr Fowle. The courtroom silent. The jury about to sink you. The prosecution
flushed with victory. And then I rise, my voice a hoarse
whisper, exhausted by that long trial. (*He picks up his wig
and puts it on.*) 'My Lord. If your Lordship pleases.'

FOWLE: (*Rising and moving centre.*) What are you saying?

MORGENHALL: Good Heavens, man, you don't expect
me do this off the cuff, without any sort of rehearsal?

FOWLE: No...

MORGENHALL: (*Leading FOWLE to the table.*) Well, come
along, man, sit down.
(*FOWLE sits on the table, with his feet on the stool.*)
(*He takes the towel from the rail.*) Now, this towel over
your head, please, to simulate the dirty grey wig. (*He
drapes the towel over FOWLE's head.*) Already you appear
anonymous and vaguely alarming. Now, Fowle, forget
your personality. You're Sir Tommy Banter, living with a
widowed sister in a draughty great morgue on
Wimbledon Common. Digestion, bad. Politics, an
independent moral Conservative. Diversions, snooker in
the basement of the morgue, peeping at the lovers on the
Common and money being given away on the television.
In love with capital punishment, corporal punishment,
and a younger brother who is accomplished at
embroidery. A small, alarmed man. Served with
distinction in the Great War at sentencing soldiers to
long terms of imprisonment. (*He crosses right and stands*

behind the chair.) A man without friends, unexpectedly adored by a great-niece, three years old.

FOWLE: I am?

MORGENHALL: Him.

FOWLE: It feels strange.

MORGENHALL: Now, my Lord. I ask your Lordship's leave to call the surprise witness.

FOWLE: Certainly?

MORGENHALL: What?

FOWLE: Certainly.

MORGENHALL: (*Crossing to left centre.*) For Heaven's sake, Fowle, this is like practising bullfights with a kitten. Here's an irregular application by the defence, something that might twist the trial in the prisoner's favour and prevent you catching the connection at Charing Cross. Your breakfast's like a lead weight on your stomach. The dog bit your ankle on the way downstairs. No, blind yourself with rage and terrible justice. (*He crosses to right and stands behind the chair.*)

FOWLE: No. You can't call the surprise witness.

MORGENHALL: That's better. Oh, my Lord. (*He raises his left arm, facing left.*) If your Lordship would listen to me.

FOWLE: Certainly not. You've had your chance. Let's get on with it.

MORGENHALL: My Lord. Justice must not only be done, but must clearly be seen to be done. (*He lowers his arm and faces front.*) No-one knows, as yet, what my surprise witness will say. (*He faces left.*) Perhaps he'll say the prisoner is guilty in his black heart as your Lordship thinks. (*He faces front.*) But perhaps, gentlemen of the jury, we have trapped an innocent. If so, shall we deny him the one door through which he might walk to freedom? The public outcry would never die down.

FOWLE: (*Snatching off the towel and rising angrily to his feet.*) Hear, hear!

MORGENHALL: What's that?

FOWLE: The public outcry.

MORGENHALL: Excellent. Now, towel back on.
(*FOWLE resumes his seat and puts the towel on his head.*) You're the judge.

FOWLE: (*As the judge.*) Silence! I'll have all those noisy people put out. Very well. Call the witness. But keep it short.

MORGENHALL: Deathly silence as the witness walks through the breathless crowds. Let's see the surprise witness.

(*MORGENHALL slowly looks from left to right. FOWLE follows the look. MORGENHALL looks at the door. FOWLE does the same.*)

(*He crosses to FOWLE.*) Take the towel off.

(*FOWLE rises, moves up centre, stands on the step and takes off the towel. MORGENHALL moves behind the chair.*)

FOWLE: (*Standing very straight.*) I swear to tell the truth…

MORGENHALL: You've got a real feeling for the Law. A pity you came to it so late in life.

FOWLE: The whole truth…

MORGENHALL: Now, what's your name?

FOWLE: (*Absent-mindedly.*) Herbert Fowle.

MORGENHALL: (*Facing left and clapping his hands in annoyance.*) The witness.

FOWLE: Martin Jones.

MORGENHALL: Good, good, yes, very good. (*He faces front.*) Now, you knew Herbert Fowle?

FOWLE: All my life.

MORGENHALL: Always found him respectable?

FOWLE: Very quiet-spoken man, and clean living.

MORGENHALL: Where was he when this crime took place?

FOWLE: He was…

MORGENHALL: (*Turning to FOWLE.*) Just a moment. (*He faces left.*) My Lord, will you sharpen a pencil and note this down.

FOWLE: (*Moving right centre.*) You dare to say that? To him?

MORGENHALL: Fearlessness, Mr Fowle. The first essential in an advocate.

(*FOWLE moves to the table, sits and puts on the towel.*)

Is your Lordship's pencil poised?

FOWLE: (*As the judge.*) Yes, yes. Get on with it.

MORGENHALL: Where was he?

(*FOWLE rises, goes to the step and takes off the towel.*)

FOWLE: (*As the witness.*) In my house.

MORGENHALL: All the evening?

FOWLE: Playing whist. I went to collect him and we left Mrs Fowle well and happy. I returned with him and she'd been removed to the Country and General.

MORGENHALL: (*Crossing to FOWLE.*) Panic stirs the prosecution benches. The prosecutor tries a few fumbling questions. But you stand your ground, don't you?

FOWLE: Certainly.

MORGENHALL: (*Moving behind the chair.*) My Lord. I demand the prisoner be released.

(*FOWLE goes to the table, sits and puts on the towel.*)

FOWLE: (*As the judge.*) Certainly. Can't think what all this fuss has been about. Release the prisoner and reduce all police officers in court to the rank of P.C. (*He takes off the towel, rises, goes to the foot of the bed and sits.*)

(*There is a pause. MORGENHALL takes off his wig and crosses to the table.*)

MORGENHALL: Fowle.

FOWLE: Yes, sir?

MORGENHALL: Aren't you going to thank me?

FOWLE: I don't know what I can say.

MORGENHALL: Words don't come easily to you, do they?

FOWLE: Very hard.

MORGENHALL: You could just stand and stammer in a touching way, and offer me that old gold watch of your father's.

FOWLE: (*Rising.*) But...

MORGENHALL: Well, I think we've pulled your chestnut out of the fire. We'll just have to make sure of this fellow Jones.

FOWLE: (*Moving left centre.*) But...

MORGENHALL: Fowle, you're a good chap, but don't interrupt my thinking.

FOWLE: I was only reminding you...

MORGENHALL: Well, what?

FOWLE: We have no Jones.

MORGENHALL: Carried off in a cold spell? Then we can get his statement in under the Evidence Act.

FOWLE: He never lived. We made him up.

MORGENHALL: (*After a pause.*) Fowle. (*He moves right centre.*)

FOWLE: Yes, sir?

MORGENHALL: It's a remarkable thing – (*He moves centre.*) but with no legal training, I think you've put your finger on a fatal weakness in our defence.

FOWLE: I was afraid it might be so.

MORGENHALL: It is so.

FOWLE: (*Moving to the downstage end of the bed.*) Then we'd better just give in.

MORGENHALL: Give in? (*He crosses to FOWLE.*) We do not give in. When my life depends on this case.

FOWLE: I forgot. Then we must try.

MORGENHALL: Yes. Brain. Brain (*He moves up centre.*) Go to work. It'll come to me, you know, in an illuminating flash. Hard, relentless brainwork. This is the way I go at the crosswords and I never give up. I have it. (*He moves down centre.*) Bateson.

FOWLE: The lodger?

MORGENHALL: Bateson, the lodger. I never liked him. Under a ruthless cross-examination, you know, he might confess that it was he. Do you see a flash?

FOWLE: You look much happier.

MORGENHALL: I am much happier. And when I begin my ruthless cross-examination…

FOWLE: Would you care to try it?

MORGENHALL: Mr Fowle, you and I are learning to muck in splendidly together over this. (*He moves behind the chair and puts on his wig.*)

(*FOWLE goes on to the doorstep and leans against the right wall of the doorway-arch, with his hands in his pockets.*)

Mr Bateson.

FOWLE: (*As Bateson.*) Yes, sir?

MORGENHALL: Perhaps you'd be good enough to take your hands out of your pockets when you address the Court. Not you, Mr Fowle, of course. You became on very friendly terms with the prisoner's wife?

FOWLE: We had one or two good old laughs together. Ha, ha, ha!

MORGENHALL: The association was entirely innocent?

FOWLE: Innocent laughs. Jokes without offence. The cracker or Christmas card variety. No jokes that would have shamed a postcard.

MORGENHALL: And to tell those jokes, did you have to sit very close to Mrs Fowle?

FOWLE: How do you mean?

MORGENHALL: Did you have to sit beneath her?

FOWLE: I don't understand.

MORGENHALL: Did she perch upon your knee?
(*FOWLE gives a horrified intake of breath.*)
What was that?

FOWLE: Shocked breathing from the jury, sir.

MORGENHALL: Having its effect, eh? Bateson, will you kindly answer my question.

FOWLE: You're trying to trap me.

MORGENHALL: Not trying Bateson, succeeding.

FOWLE: Well, she may have rested on my knee. Once or twice.

MORGENHALL: And you loved her, guiltily?

FOWLE: I may have done.

MORGENHALL: And planned to take her away with you?

FOWLE: I did ask her.

MORGENHALL: And when she refused...

FOWLE: Just a moment. (*He moves to the table, sits and puts on the towel. As the judge.*) Where's all this leading?

MORGENHALL: Your Lordship asks me. My Lord, it is our case that it was this man, Bateson, enraged by the refusal of the prisoner's wife to go away with him, who struck... (*He crosses to centre.*) You see where we've go to?

FOWLE: (*Removing the towel.*) I do.

MORGENHALL: Masterly. I think you'll have to agree with me?

FOWLE: Of course.

MORGENHALL: No flaws in this one?

FOWLE: Not really a flaw, sir. Perhaps a little hitch.

MORGENHALL: A hitch. Go on. Break it down.

FOWLE: No, sir, really. (*He rises and moves up left.*) Not after you've been so kind.

MORGENHALL: Never mind. All my life I've stood against the winds of criticism and neglect. I am used to hardship. Speak on, Mr Fowle.

FOWLE: Soon as he left my house. Bateson was stopped by an officer. He'd lifted an alarm clock off of me, and the remains of a bottle of port. They booked him in straight away.

MORGENHALL: You mean – (*He faces front.*) there wasn't time?

FOWLE: Hardly. Two hours later the next door observed Mrs Fowle at the washing. Then I came home.

MORGENHALL: (*Turning to FOWLE.*) Fowle, do you want to help me?

FOWLE: Of course. Haven't I shown it?

MORGENHALL: But you will go on putting all these difficulties in my way.

FOWLE: I knew you'd be upset. (*He sits on the bed.*)

MORGENHALL: Not really. After all, I'm a grown-up, even an old man. At my age one expects little gratitude. Oh, I'm not bitter. But a little help, just a very little encouragement..

FOWLE: But you'll win this case. A brilliant mind like yours.

MORGENHALL: (*Moving right centre.*) Yes. Thank God. It's very brilliant.

FOWLE: And all that training.

MORGENHALL: Years of it. (*He moves to the chair.*) Hard, hard training.

FOWLE: You'll solve it, sir.

(*There is a pause. MORGENHALL crosses to the upstage end of the bed, puts a foot up on it and leans over to FOWLE.*)

MORGENHALL: Fowle. Do you know what I've heard Tuppy Morgan say? After all, he's sat here in court year in, year out, waiting for the Dock Brief himself. 'Wilfred,' he's frequently told me, 'if they ever give you a brief, old fellow, attack the medical evidence. Remember, the jury's full of rheumatism and arthritis and shocking gastric troubles. They love to see a medical man put through it. Always go for a doctor.'

FOWLE: (*Eagerly.*) You'd like to try?

MORGENHALL: (*Straightening up.*) Shall we?

FOWLE: I'd enjoy it. (*He rises and goes on to the step.*)
(*MORGENHALL crosses to the chair right and leans over the back of it, with one foot on the chair.*)

MORGENHALL: Doctor, did you say the lady died of heart failure?

FOWLE: (*As the doctor.*) No.

MORGENHALL: Come, Doctor, don't fence with me. Her heart wasn't normal when you examined her, was it?

FOWLE: She was dead.

MORGENHALL: So it had stopped.

FOWLE: Yes.

MORGENHALL: Then her heart had failed. (*He takes his foot off the chair.*)

FOWLE: Well...

MORGENHALL: So she died of heart failure?

FOWLE: But...

MORGENHALL: And heart failure might have been brought on by a fit. I say a fit of laughter at a curiously rich joke on the wireless?
(*FOWLE claps his hands, then comes off the step.*)

FOWLE: Whew!

MORGENHALL: (*After a pause.*) Thank you, Fowle. (*He takes off his wig.*) It was kind, but, I thought, hollow. (*He crosses to the stool.*) I don't believe my attack on the doctor was convincing. (*He picks up his brief-case, puts it on the table, then sits on the stool.*)

FOWLE: Perhaps a bit unlikely. But clever.

MORGENHALL: Too clever. No. We're not going to win this on science, Fowle. Science must be thrown away. As I asked those questions, I saw I wasn't even convincing you of your own innocence. But you respond to emotion, Fowle, as I do, the magic of oratory, the wonderful power of words.

FOWLE: Now you're talking.

MORGENHALL: And I shall talk.

FOWLE: I wish I could hear some of it. Words as grand as print.

MORGENHALL: A golden tongue. A voice like a lyre to charm you out of hell.

FOWLE: Now you've commenced to wander away from all I've understood.

MORGENHALL: I was drawing on the riches of my classical education, which comforts me on buses, waiting at surgeries, or in prison cells. (*He rises.*) But I shall speak to the jury simply, without classical allusions. I shall say...

FOWLE: Yes?

MORGENHALL: I shall say...

FOWLE: What?

MORGENHALL: I had it on the tip of my tongue.

FOWLE: Oh.

MORGENHALL: I shan't disappoint you. I shall speak for a day, perhaps two days. At the end I shall say...

FOWLE: Yes. Just the closing words.

MORGENHALL: The closing words.

FOWLE: To clinch the argument.

MORGENHALL: Yes. The final, irrefutable argument.

FOWLE: If I could only hear.

MORGENHALL: You shall, Fowle. You shall hear it. (*He sits on the stool and takes out his handkerchief.*) In court. It'll come out in court, and when I sink back in my seat, exhausted, and wipe the real tears off my glasses... (*He replaces his handkerchief in his pocket.*)

FOWLE: The judge's summing-up.

MORGENHALL: What will Tommy say?

FOWLE: (*As the judge.*) Members of the jury...

MORGENHALL: Struggling with emotion, as well.

FOWLE: Members of the jury, I can't add anything to the words of the barrister. Go out and consider your verdict.

MORGENHALL: Have they left the box?

FOWLE: Just a formality.

MORGENHALL: I see. I wonder how long they'll be out. (*He pauses.*) They're out a long time.

FOWLE: Of course, it must seem long to you. The suspense.

MORGENHALL: I hope they won't disagree.

FOWLE: I don't see how they can. Look, they're coming back, sir.

(*There is a pause. FOWLE moves above the table.*)

MORGENHALL: (*As clerk of the court.*) Members of the jury, have you considered your verdict?

FOWLE: We have.

MORGENHALL: And you find the prisoner guilty or not guilty?

FOWLE: Not guilty, my Lord. (*He rushes to the table, sits on it and puts the towel on his head.*)

MORGENHALL: (*Rising and waving his wig.*) Hooray!

FOWLE: (*As the judge.*) Now, if there's any sort of Mafeking around, I'll have the court closed.

MORGENHALL: So I'm surrounded, mobbed. Tuppy Morgan wrings my hand and says it was lucky he left the seat. The judge sends me a letter of congratulation. The journalists dart off to their little telephones. And what now? 'Of course, they'd make you a judge but you're probably too busy...' There's a queue of solicitors on the stairs. My old clerk writes on my next brief, 'A thousand guineas to divorce a duchess'. There are questions of new clothes, laying down the port. Oh, Mr Fowle, the change in life you've brought me.

FOWLE: (*Rising.*) It will be your greatest day. (*He removes the towel and crosses to centre.*)

MORGENHALL: Yes, Mr Fowle. (*He crosses to FOWLE.*) My greatest day.

(*The bolts shoot back and the door slowly opens.*)

(*He moves up centre.*) What's that? I said we weren't to be interrupted. It's draughty in here with that door open. (*He calls.*) Close it, there's a good chap, do. (*He moves down centre to left of FOWLE.*)

FOWLE: I think, you know, they must want us for the trial. (*He moves up right centre, takes his jacket off the peg, goes to the chair, and sits and puts on his jacket.*)

(*MORGENHALL puts on his wig, puts the papers, medicine bottle, etc. in his brief-case, leaves the brief-case on the table, moves to the bed, picks up his gown and struggles to put it on. FOWLE rises, crosses to MORGENHALL and assists him.*)

MORGENHALL goes to the door, remembers his brief-case,
returns and picks it up. FOWLE does a 'thumbs-up' sign.
MORGENHALL nods, and with a dramatic sweep of his
gown, exits. FOWLE follows him off, and the lights dim to
black-out as the curtain falls.)

Scene 2

Scene: the same.

When the curtain rises, the sky through the window shows that it is
late afternoon. The table has been replaced under the window and
the stool is left centre. The cell is empty. The door opens.
MORGENHALL enters. He is without his wig and gown and is
more agitated than ever. He stands by the open door and speaks to an
unseen warder off.

MORGENHALL: He's not here at the moment – he's
not...? Oh, I'm glad. Just out temporarily? With the
Governor? Then, I'll wait for him. Poor soul. How's he
taking it? Well, I'll just sit down here and wait for Mr
Fowle.

(*The door closes.*)

(*He whistles for a few moments.*) 'May it please you, my
Lord – *members* of the jury...' I should have said, 'May it
please you, my *Lord* – members of the jury...' (*He moves*
to the stool and sits.) I should have said – 'Members of the
jury. Is there one of you who doesn't crave for peace –
crave for peace. The silence of an undisturbed life, the
dignity of an existence without dependants – without
jokes. Have you never been tempted?' I should have
said, 'Members of the *jury*. You and I are men
of the world...' 'If your Lordship would kindly not
interrupt my speech to the jury.' 'I'm obliged.' 'Members
of the jury, before I was so rudely interrupted...' I might
have said, 'Look at the prisoner, members of the jury.
Has he hurt you, done you the slightest harm? Is he not
the mildest of men? He merely took it upon himself to
regulate his domestic affairs. An Englishman's home is
his castle. Do any of you feel a primitive urge, members

of the jury, to be revenged on this gentle bird-fancier? Members of the jury, I see I'm affecting your emotions, but let us consider the weight of the evidence.' Might have said that. (*He rises and paces left and right.*) I might have said – (*With distress.*) I might have said something… (*The door opens.*

FOWLE enters. He is smiling to himself, but as soon as he sees MORGENHALL he looks serious and solicitous. The door closes.)

FOWLE: I was hoping you'd find time to drop in, sir. I'm afraid you're upset.

MORGENHALL: No, no, my dear chap. (*He moves down left.*) Not at all upset.

FOWLE: The result of the trial's upset you.

MORGENHALL: I feel a little dashed. A little out of sorts.

FOWLE: It was disappointing for you.

MORGENHALL: A touch of disappointment. But there'll be other cases. There may be other cases.

FOWLE: But you'd built such high hopes on this particular one.

MORGENHALL: Well, there it is, Fowle. (*He moves to the stool and sits.*)

FOWLE: It doesn't do to expect too much of a particular thing.

MORGENHALL: You're right, of course.

FOWLE: (*Crossing below MORGENHALL to the bed.*) Year after year, I used to look forward keenly to the Feathered Friends Fanciers' annual do. (*He sits on the downstage end of the bed.*) Invariably it took the form of a dinner.

MORGENHALL: Your yearly treat?

FOWLE: Exactly. All I had in the enjoyment line. Each year I built high hopes on it. 'June thirteenth,' I'd say, 'now there's an evening to look forward to.'

MORGENHALL: Something to live for?

FOWLE: In a way. But when it came, you know, it was never up to it. Your collar was always too tight, or the food was inadequate, or someone had a nasty scene with the fancier in the chair. So, on June fourteenth, I always said to myself: 'Thank God for a night at home.'

MORGENHALL: It came and went and your life didn't change?

FOWLE: No, quite frankly.

MORGENHALL: And this case has left me just as I was before.

FOWLE: Don't say that.

MORGENHALL: Tuppy Morgan's back in his old seat under the window. The judge never congratulated me. No-one's rung up to offer me a brief. I thought my old clerk looked coldly at me, and there was a titter in the luncheon-room when I ordered my usual roll and tomato soup.

FOWLE: But, I...

MORGENHALL: (*Rising and moving up right.*) And you're not left in a very favourable position.

FOWLE: Well, it's not so bad for me. After all, I had no education.

MORGENHALL: (*Turning to face FOWLE.*) So many years before I could master the Roman Law relating to the ownership of chariots...

FOWLE: Wasted, you think?

MORGENHALL: I feel so.

FOWLE: But without that rich background, would an individual have been able to sway the Court as you did?

MORGENHALL: Sway?

FOWLE: The Court?

MORGENHALL: Did I do that?

FOWLE: It struck me you did.

MORGENHALL: Indeed...

FOWLE: It's turned out masterly.

MORGENHALL: Mr Fowle, you're trying to be kind. (*He moves down left centre.*) When I was a child, I played French cricket with an uncle who deliberately allowed the ball to strike his legs. At the age of seven that irked me. At my age I can face the difficulties of accurate batting...

FOWLE: But, no, sir. (*He rises and moves to left of MORGENHALL.*) I owe it all to you. Where I am.

MORGENHALL: I'm afraid near the end.

FOWLE: Just commencing.

MORGENHALL: I lost, Mr Fowle. You may not be aware of it. It may not have been hammered home to you, yet. (*He crosses below FOWLE to the bed.*) But your case is lost. (*He sits on the downstage end of the bed.*)

FOWLE: But there are ways and ways of losing.

MORGENHALL: That's true, of course.

FOWLE: (*Moving to the bed and sitting beside MORGENHALL.*) I noticed your artfulness right at the start, when the policeman gave evidence. You pulled out that red handkerchief, slowly and deliberately, like a conjuring trick.

MORGENHALL: And blew?

FOWLE: A sad, terrible trumpet.

MORGENHALL: Unnerved him, I thought.

FOWLE: He never recovered. There was no call to ask questions after that.

MORGENHALL: And then they called that doctor.

FOWLE: You were right not to bother with him.

MORGENHALL: Tactics, you see. We'd decided not to trouble with science.

FOWLE: So we had. And with Bateson...

MORGENHALL: No, Fowle. I must beware of your flattery. I think I might have asked Bateson...

FOWLE: It wouldn't have made a farthing's difference. A glance told them he was a demon.

MORGENHALL: He stood there, so big and red, with his no tie and dirty collar. I rose up to question him and suddenly it seemed as if there were no reason for us to converse. I remembered what you said about his jokes, his familiarity with your wife. I turned from him in disgust. I think that jury guessed the reason for my silence with friend Bateson.

FOWLE: I think they did.

MORGENHALL: But when it came to the speech...

FOWLE: The best stroke of all.

MORGENHALL: I can't agree. You no longer carry me with you.

FOWLE: Said from the heart.

MORGENHALL: I'm sure of it. But not, dare I say, altogether justified. We can't pretend, can we, Mr Fowle, that the speech was a success?

FOWLE: It won the day.

MORGENHALL: I beg you not to be under any illusions. They found you guilty.

FOWLE: But that masterly speech...

MORGENHALL: I can't be hoodwinked.

FOWLE: (*Rising.*) I stood up, Mr Fowle, and it was the moment I'd waited for. Ambition had driven me to it, the moment when I was alone with what I wanted. Everyone turned to me, twelve blank faces in the jury box, eager to have the grumpy looks wiped off them. The judge was silent. The prosecutor courteously pretended to be asleep. I only had to open my mouth and pour words out. What stopped me?

FOWLE: What?

MORGENHALL: Fear. That's what's suggested. That's what the clerks tittered to the waitresses in the luncheon-room. Old Wilf Morgenhall was in a funk.

FOWLE: More shame on them.

MORGENHALL: But it wasn't so. (*He crosses to centre.*) Nor did my mind go blank. When I stood up I knew exactly what I was going to say.

FOWLE: Then, why...?

MORGENHALL: 'Not say it' – you were going to ask?

FOWLE: (*Turning to face MORGENHALL.*) It had struck me...

MORGENHALL: It must have, Fowle. It must have struck many people. (*He moves up centre.*) You'll forgive a reminiscence?

FOWLE: (*Sitting on the downstage end of the bed.*) Glad of one.

MORGENHALL: The lady I happened to mention yesterday. I don't, of course, often speak of her...

FOWLE: She, who, in the nineteen-fourteen...?

MORGENHALL: Exactly. But I lost her long before that. For years, you know, Mr Fowle, this particular lady and I met at tea-parties, tennis, and so on. Then, one evening, I walked home with her. We stood on Vauxhall Bridge.

It was a warm summer night, and silence fell. It was the moment when I should have spoken, the obvious moment. Then, something overcame me, it wasn't shyness or fear, then, but a tremendous exhaustion. I was tired out by the long wait, and when the opportunity came – all I could think of was sleep.

FOWLE: It's a relief...

MORGENHALL: To go home alone. To undress, clean your teeth, knock out your pipe, not to bother with failure or success.

FOWLE: So yesterday...

MORGENHALL: I had lived through that moment so many times. It happened every day in my mind, daydreaming on buses, or in the doctor's surgery. When it came, I was tired of it. The exhaustion came over me. I wanted it to be all over. I wanted to be alone in my room, in the darkness, with a soft pillow round my ears. So I failed.

FOWLE: Don't say that, sir.

MORGENHALL: Being too tired to make my daydream public. (*He moves up right centre.*) It's a nice day. (*He moves right and glances at the window.*) Summer's coming. (*He faces front.*) I think I shall retire from the Bar.

FOWLE: Don't say it, sir. After that rigorous training.

MORGENHALL: Well, there it is. I think I shall retire.

FOWLE: But, cheer up, sir. (*He rises and moves centre.*) As you said, other cases, other days. Let's take this calmly, sir. (*He crosses to MORGENHALL and seats him on the chair.*) Let's be very lucid, as you put it in your own statement.

MORGENHALL: Other cases? I'm getting on, you know. Tuppy Morgan's back in his place. I doubt if the Dock Brief will come round again.

FOWLE: But there'll be something.

MORGENHALL: What can there be? Unless...

FOWLE: Yes, sir?

MORGENHALL: There would be another brief if...

FOWLE: Yes?

MORGENHALL: I advised you to appeal.

FOWLE: Ah, now that, misfortunately... (*He turns away left.*)

MORGENHALL: (*Rising.*) There's a different atmosphere there, up in the Appeal Court, Fowle. It's far from the rough and tumble, question and answer – (*He crosses down left.*) swear on the Bible and lie your way out of it. It's quiet up there, pure law, of course. Yes. I believe I'm cut out for the Court of Appeal. (*He moves up centre.*)

FOWLE: But, you see...

MORGENHALL: A big, quiet Court in the early summer afternoon. Piles of books, and when you put one down the dust and powdered leather rises and makes the ushers sneeze. The clock ticks. Three old judges in scarlet take snuff with trembling hands. You'll sit in the dock and not follow a legal word. And I'll give them all my Law and get you off on a technicality.

FOWLE: But, today...

MORGENHALL: Now, if I may remind your Lordships of Prickle against the Haverfordwest Justices *ex parte* Anger, reported in ninety-six *Moor's Ecclesiastical* at page a thousand and three.

(*FOWLE sits on the chair.*)

Have your Lordships the report? Lord Bradwell, C.J., says, at the foot of the page, 'The guilty intention is a deep foundation-stone in the wall of our jurisprudence. So if it be that Prickle did run the bailiff through with his *poignard* taking him for a stray dog or cat, it seems there would be well raised the plea of *autrefois* mistake. But contra if he thought him to be his neighbour's cat, then, as my Brother Broadwinkle has well said in Lord Roche and Anderson, there might fall out a constructive larceny and *felo in rem.*' (*He moves to FOWLE.*) Oh, Mr Fowle, I have some of these fine cases by heart.

FOWLE: Above me, I'm afraid, you're going now.

MORGENHALL: Of course I am. These cases always bore the prisoner until they're upheld or overruled and he comes out dead or alive at the end of it all. Thank God, I kept my books. I shall open them up and say – I shall say...

FOWLE: (*Rising and crossing to left centre.*) It's no good.

MORGENHALL: What's no good?

FOWLE: It's no good appealing.

MORGENHALL: No good?

FOWLE: (*Sitting on the stool.*) No good at all.

MORGENHALL: (*Moving down centre.*) Mr Fowle. I've worked hard for you.

FOWLE: That's true, sir.

MORGENHALL: And I mean to go on working.

FOWLE: It's a great comfort...

MORGENHALL: In the course of our close, and may I say it – yes, our happy collaboration on this little crime of yours, I've become almost fond of you.

FOWLE: Thank you, sir, but I...

MORGENHALL: At first, I have to admit it, I was put off by your somewhat furtive and repulsive appearance. I saw in you a man marked by all the physical signs of confirmed criminality.

FOWLE: No oil painting?

MORGENHALL: Let's agree on that at once.

FOWLE: The wife thought so, too.

MORGENHALL: Enough of her, poor woman.

FOWLE: Oh, agreed.

MORGENHALL: My first solicitude for your well-being, let's face this, as well, had a selfish element. You were my very own case, and I didn't want to lose you.

FOWLE: Natural feelings. But still.

MORGENHALL: I haven't wounded you?

FOWLE: Nothing fatal, sir.

MORGENHALL: I'm glad. Because, you know, as we worked on this case, together, an affection sprang up...

FOWLE: Mutual.

MORGENHALL: You seemed to have a real desire to help, and, if I may say so, an instinctive taste for the law.

FOWLE: A man can't go through this sort of thing without getting legal interests.

MORGENHALL: Quite so. But I did notice, just at the start, some flaws in you as a client.

FOWLE: Flaws?

MORGENHALL: You may not care to admit it. But let's be honest. After all, we don't want to look on the dreary side! but you may not be with us for very long...

FOWLE: (*Rising.*) That's what I was trying to say...

MORGENHALL: Please, Mr Fowle, don't interrupt, not until we've –

(*FOWLE sits on the stool.*)

– cleared this out of the way. Now, didn't you, just at the beginning, put unnecessary difficulties before us?

FOWLE: Did I?

MORGENHALL: I well remember, before I got a bit of keenness into you, that you seemed about to admit your guilt.

FOWLE: Oh...

MORGENHALL: Just a little obstinate, wasn't it?

FOWLE: I dare say...

MORGENHALL: And now, when I've worked for fifty years to get the law at my fingertips, I hear you mutter, 'No appeal'.

FOWLE: (*Turning to MORGENHALL.*) No appeal!

MORGENHALL: Mr Fowle...

FOWLE: (*Rising.*) Yesterday, you asked me to spare you pain, sir. This is going to be very hard for me.

MORGENHALL: What?

FOWLE: (*Moving right.*) As you say, we've worked together, and I've had the pleasure of watching the ticking over of a legal mind. If you'd call any afternoon I'd be pleased to repay the compliment by showing you my birds.

MORGENHALL: Not in this world, you must realize, unless we appeal.

FOWLE: You see – this morning I saw the governor.

MORGENHALL: You had some complaint?

FOWLE: I don't want to boast, but the truth is – he sent for me.

MORGENHALL: You went in fear...

FOWLE: And trembling.

MORGENHALL: And trembling.

FOWLE: (*Moving up right.*) But he turned out a very gentlemanly sort of individual. Ex-army, I should imagine. All the ornaments of a gentleman. (*He moves down centre.*) Wife and children in a tinted photo framed on the desk, handsome oil painting of a prize pig over the mantelpiece. Healthy red face. Strong smell of scented soap...

MORGENHALL: (*Sitting on the stool.*) But grow to the point...

FOWLE: I'm telling you. 'Well, Fowle,' he says. 'Sit down, do. I'm just finishing this letter.' (*He sits on the chair.*) So I sat and looked out of his windows. Big wide windows in the governor's office, and the view...

MORGENHALL: Fowle. If this anecdote has any point, be a good chap – reach it.

FOWLE: Of course it has – where was I?

MORGENHALL: Admiring the view.

FOWLE: Panoramic, it was. Well, this governor individual, finishing his letter, lit up one of those flat type of Egyptian cigarettes. 'Well, Fowle,' he said...

MORGENHALL: Yes, yes. It's not necessary, Fowle, to reproduce every word of this conversation. Give us the gist, just the meat, you understand. Leave out the trimmings.

FOWLE: Trimmings there weren't. He put it quite bluntly.

MORGENHALL: What did he put?

FOWLE: 'Well, Fowle, this may surprise you.' (*He rises and crosses to MORGENHALL.*) 'But the Home Office was on the phone about you this morning, and...' Isn't that a government department?

MORGENHALL: Yes, yes. And well...

FOWLE: It seems they do, in his words, come through from time to time, and just on business, of course, on that blower. And quite frankly, he admitted he was as shocked as I was. But the drill is, as he phrased it, a reprieve.

MORGENHALL: A...

FOWLE: It's all over. I'm free.

MORGENHALL: Free?

FOWLE: It seems that trial was no good at all.

MORGENHALL: No good. But why?

FOWLE: (*Crossing to right.*) Oh, no particular reason.

MORGENHALL: (*Rising and crossing to FOWLE.*) There must be a reason. Nothing happens in the law without a reason.

FOWLE: You won't care to know.

MORGENHALL: Tell me.

FOWLE: You're too busy to wait.

MORGENHALL: Tell me, Mr Fowle, why this governor, who knows nothing of the law; should have called our one and only trial together 'no good'.

FOWLE: You yourself taught me not to scatter information like bombs.

MORGENHALL: Mr Fowle, you must answer my question. My legal career may depend on it. If I'm not to have wasted my life on useless trials.

FOWLE: You want to hear?

MORGENHALL: Certainly.

FOWLE: He may not have been serious. (*He moves above the chair.*) There was a twinkle, most likely, in his eye.

MORGENHALL: But he said...

FOWLE: That the barrister they chose for me was no good. 'An old crock,' in his words. No good at all. That he never said a word in my defence. So my case never got to the jury. He said the whole business was ever so null and void, but I'd better be careful in the future. (*He moves to MORGENHALL.*) Don't you see? If I'd had a barrister who asked questions and made clever speeches I'd be as dead as mutton. Your artfulness saved me.

MORGENHALL: My...

FOWLE: The artful way you handled it. The dumb tactics. They paid off! I'm alive!

MORGENHALL: There is that...

FOWLE: And so are you.

MORGENHALL: We both are...?

FOWLE: I'm free.

MORGENHALL: To go back to your birds. (*He moves up left centre, then returns to left of FOWLE.*) I suppose...

FOWLE: Yes, Mr Morgenhall?

MORGENHALL: It's unlikely you'll marry again?

FOWLE: Unlikely.

(*There is a pause. MORGENHALL crosses above FOWLE to the chair and moves it down right.*)

MORGENHALL: But you have the clear appearance of a criminal. I suppose it's not impossible, that you might commit some rather more trivial offence.

FOWLE: A man can't live, Mr Morgenhall, without committing some trivial offences. Almost daily.

MORGENHALL: Then we may meet again. You may need my services...

FOWLE: Constantly.

MORGENHALL: The future may not be so black...

FOWLE: The sun's shining.

(*MORGENHALL turns to the window, then turns again to FOWLE.*)

MORGENHALL: Can we go?

FOWLE: (*Moving to the door.*) I think the door's been open some time.

(*MORGENHALL follows FOWLE to the door. FOWLE tries the door. It is unbolted and swings open.*)

After you, Mr Morgenhall, please.

MORGENHALL: No, no.

FOWLE: A man of your education should go first.

MORGENHALL: I think you should lead the way, Mr Fowle, and as your legal adviser I will follow, at a discreet distance, to iron out such little angles as you may hope to leave in your wake. Let's go.

(*MORGENHALL whistles his fragment of tune. FOWLE joins in. Whistling, they leave the cell. MORGENHALL executing, as he leaves, the steps of a small, delighted dance. Slow curtain.*)

The End.

WHAT SHALL WE TELL CAROLINE?

Characters

LILY LOUDON ('BIN')

ARTHUR LOUDON

TONY PETERS

CAROLINE

What Shall We Tell Caroline? was first presented by Michael Codron with David Hall (for Talbot Productions Ltd.) in a double bill (with *The Dock Brief*) at the Lyric Opera House, Hammersmith, on 9 April, 1958, and on 20 May, 1958 at the Garrick Theatre, with the following cast:

LILY, Brenda Bruce

ARTHUR, Maurice Denham

TONY, Michael Hordern

CAROLINE, Marianne Benet

Director, Stuart Burge

Designer, Disley Jones

Scene 1

The Loudon's living room at 'Highland Close School', Coldsands. It is an extremely dilapidated room given as air of festivity, as the curtain rises, by the fact that a table is set for four and there are candles in odd candlesticks – one expensive silver, the other a china 'Present from Coldsands' on the table. Doors on each side of the room, one, left, is covered in green baize and has pinned on it a few yellowing curling notices and charts of lessons which haven't been read for years. The door is closed and leads to the boys' part of the house. The door on the right is open and light floods through it from a staircase which leads to the bedrooms. Another door backstage right leads to the kitchen. At the back of the room tall French windows, which have never shut properly and let in winds of icy severity, open on to a strip of grey asphalt, the white end of a flag pole and the gun-metal sky of an early evening in March.

Other furniture: a basket-work chair, a fireplace full of paper, a very small electric fan, a horse-hair sofa wounded and bleeding its stuffing; a roll top desk out of which bills, writs, exercise books and reports are perpetually being shaken by the draughts like the leaves of a dead tree. On top of the desk there is a ukelele and a globe. Among faded photographs of various towns an oar is hanging on the wall.

As the curtain rises LILY LOUDON has her back to the audience and is tugging at one of the drawers. As she tugs the drawer comes right out and the globe falls down with a sickening crash.

The crash is immediately followed by a roar from the lit door which leads to the bedrooms. It is the voice of a small man entirely consumed with rage.

ARTHUR: (*Off.*) Imbecile!
    (*LILY picks up the globe with great calmness and puts it back on the desk, thoughtfully spinning it to find England.*)
    (*Off.*) Lunatic! Fool! Whatever have you ruined now! What's broken! Go on. Don't keep it from me! Confess!
    (*LILY picks up the drawer and carries it towards the table. She is an untidy woman, once inconspicuously good looking,*

whose face now wears an expression of puzzled contentment.
She is wearing a lace evening dress of the late thirties, a
number of straps are showing on her pale shoulders and a
cigarette is dangling from a corner of her mouth. She shows
no reaction at all to the diatribe from off stage.)

(*Off.*) Just try and picture me. Stuck up here. Listening,
always listening while you systematically destroy...

(*LILY puts the drawer down on the table and knocks off a*
glass.)

(*Off.*) Aaah. What was that? The last of my dead
mother's crockery? Speak up. Put me out of my agony.
For pity's sake... The suspense... What was it you
imbecile? Side plate – dinner plate – not...? You're not
to be trusted on your own...

(*LILY takes out a number of presents wrapped in bright*
paper wad tied with ribbon and arranges them on the table.)

(*Off.*) Where are they? You've hidden them again?

(*LILY smiles to herself. Carefully puts out her cigarette.)*

(*Off.*) Do you realize what the time is?

(*LILY shakes her head.)*

Dusk. Have you done it? Answer me, can't you? The
loneliness – of getting dressed.

(*LILY puts a parcel by the place laid in the centre of the*
table. ARTHUR erupts into the room. He is a small, bristly,
furiously angry man. He is wearing the trousers only of a
merciless tweed suit, no collar and his braces are hanging
doom his back.)

(*His anger becoming plaintive.*) You can't imagine what a
fly you are in the ointment of any little ceremony like
this... How you take the edge off my pleasure in any
small moment of celebration. My own daughter's
birthday. A thing I've been keenly looking forward to
and you deliberately hide...my...clothes.

(*LILY puts the drawer, empty now, back in the desk and*
comes back to face her husband.)

Perhaps it's a mental kink in you. Is that the excuse
you'd make? Do you plead insanity? If I had a pound for
every time you've taken a collar stud and... I don't know
– eaten it...rolled it under the chest of drawers. Now, to

carefully conceal the club braces... The sort of kink that makes women pinch things in Woolworths. Itching, destructive fingers. Furtive little pickers.

(*LILY pulls his braces, which are hanging down the back of his trousers up across his shoulders, and fastens them. Then she kisses his forehead. This quietens him for a moment. Then he bursts out again.*)

That's hardly the point. It's dusk.

(*He runs to the windows and throws them open. A wind, howling in, makes the candles flicker. ARTHUR is hauling down the flag.*)

LILY: It's bitterly cold.

ARTHUR: Found your tongue at last?

LILY: I said, it's bitterly cold.

ARTHUR: (*Comes back into the room, the Union Jack bundled in his arms. He kicks the window shut behind him.*) Of course it's bitterly cold. That wind's come a long way. All the way from the Ural mountains. An uninterrupted journey.

LILY: Yes, I know.

ARTHUR: (*Folding up the flags – calm for the moment.*) Think of that. From Moscow and Vitebsk. The marshes of Poland. The flats of Prussia. The dykes of Belgium and Holland. All the way to Yarmouth. Just think of it. Flat as a playground. That's what I tell the boys.

LILY: I know you do.

ARTHUR: It's a geographical miracle. It makes this place so ideal for schooling boys. There's nothing like a wind from the Ural Mountains, Bin, for keeping boys pure in heart.

LILY: I suppose not.

ARTHUR: Added to which it kills bugs.

LILY: Yes, of course.

ARTHUR: Bugs and unsuitable thoughts. You know that, Bin. You're in charge of that side of it. Have we had a single epidemic this year?

LILY: They cough in the night time. (*She is arranges the presents on the table.*) Like sheep.

ARTHUR: Colds admitted. Infectious diseases not. I had a letter only the other day. A school in Torquay. Malaria. Decimated the boys. Brought on by the relaxing climate. Thank heavens, Bin, for our exposed position.

LILY: Yes, dear.

ARTHUR: For heaven's sake don't complain about the wind, then. It gets on the nerves of a saint. To have you always carping at the wind. Think of it – one little mountain range between here and Moscow and the boys might all go down with malaria.

LILY: I wonder if Caroline's going to like her presents?

ARTHUR: Like her presents? Of course she's going to like her presents. Doesn't she always like her presents?

LILY: I only wondered...

ARTHUR: If you set out to make her dissatisfied. If you sow the seeds of doubt in her young mind... If you deliberately undertake to puzzle and bewilder a young girl with your extraordinary ideas of what a present *ought* to be. If you carp and criticize...

LILY: I only wondered...if she wasn't getting on a bit for Halma...

ARTHUR: You wondered? Caroline takes it for granted. Every year she'll get her Halma and every year you'll lose three or four of her men... Swallow them up like collar studs. Of course she likes Halma, you've seen her in the evenings playing it with...

(*He puts the folded flag on top of the desk. Than shouts as he picks up the ukelele.*)

He was here again last night

LILY: Who?

ARTHUR: Tony Peters.

LILY: He's been here for eighteen years.

ARTHUR: But this wasn't here yesterday. He's been lurking about when I didn't know. *Singing* to you.

(*LILY smiles complacently downwards. ARTHUR shouts and holds out the ukulele. She takes it and holds it as if to play it. She stands still in the attitude of someone about to play the ukelele during the ensuing dialogue. The French windows open and TONY PETERS enters. He is tall, debonair, and gay, although balding, with the cuffs of his blazer slightly fraying, his suede shoes shiny and his grey flannel trousers faded. He is carrying a string bag full of screw top bottles of light ale.)*

TONY: It's bloody cold.

ARTHUR: It's you.

TONY: Of course it's me. Look here, old man. Aren't you going to dress? I mean it is Caroline's birthday.

ARTHUR: Oh my God. How far can I be goaded?

TONY: (*Unloads his bag, sets the bottles out on the table and then throws it on top of the Union Jack.*) I don't know. It's amusing to find out.

ARTHUR: You were here last night?

TONY: Certainly.

ARTHUR: Singing to Bin?

TONY: Keeping her company while you gave, to those few unlucky boys whose temperatures are still normal and who can still breathe through their noses, your usual Sunday evening sermon on 'Life as a stiff row from Putney to Mortlake'.

ARTHUR: So you chose that as a moment for singing...to a married woman.

TONY: She sat in your chair, Arthur. We turned out the lights. The room was softly lit by the one bar of the electric fire. I was cross-legged on the floor. In the half-light I appeared boyish and irresistible. Lily needs no concealed lighting to look perpetually young. From under all the doors and through the cracks of the windows the wind sneered at us from Moscow – but we didn't feel the cold. In the distance we heard you say that it is particularly under Hammersmith Bridge that God requires ten hard pulls on the oar. Above us the coughs crackled like distant gunfire. My fingers cramped by the cold, I struck at my instrument. (*He takes the ukulele from LILY and plays.*)
(*Singing.*) 'Oh the Captain's name
Was Captain Brown,
And he played his ukulele
As the ship went down...'

ARTHUR: That idiotic song.

TONY: (*Singing close to ARTHUR.*) 'Then he bought himself
A bar of soap,
And washed himself
Ashore.'
(*LILY puts her hand flat over her mouth like a child to stifle
her giggles.*)

ARTHUR: If either of you had the slightest idea of loyalty.
If you had a grain of respect for me, for Sunday evening,
for decent, wholesome living.

TONY: (*Singing.*) 'Oh we left her baby on the shore,
A thing that we've never done before.'

ARTHUR: It's obscene.

TONY: Obscene?

ARTHUR: Perhaps. Not the words. The dirty expression
you put into it. When I'm not looking.

TONY: (*Singing.*) 'If you see the mother
Tell her gently
That we left her baby on the shore.'
(*The giggles explode past LILY's hand.*)

ARTHUR: Bin!

LILY: I'm sorry. It just gets me every time. Poor baby! It's
so damned casual.

ARTHUR: It doesn't seem to me a subject for joking.

LILY: But the way Tony sings it. Just as if he'd forgotten a
baby.

ARTHUR: He probably has.

LILY: What can you be saying?

ARTHUR: I don't know. How can I know anything?
Everything goes on when I'm not there. Furniture falls to
the ground. This man sings. Crockery breaks. You pull
his ears, stroke his hair as he squats there in front of you.
Don't think I've no imagination. I've got a vivid
imagination. And my hearing is keen. Remember that
I warn you both. My hearing is exceptionally keen.

TONY: Hear that Lily? Stroke my hair more quietly in
future.
(*As ARTHUR seems about to hit him a clock groans and
strikes off stage.*)

LILY: Arthur. You must get dressed. It's nearly time. Caroline'll be down.

ARTHUR: Let her come down. It's time she found out something. Let her find out the lying and deceit and infidelity that all these years…let her find out that her mother spends musical evenings breathing down the neck of an ex-night club gigolo, lounge lizard, wallflower, sensitive plant, clinging vine, baby leaving, guitar twanging, Mayfair playboy, good-time Charlie, fly-by-night, moonlight flit, who can't even do quadratic equations. Let her find out all she is. Poor girl. Poor child. You're right Bin – you've brought it on us all. She's too old for Halma now.
(*He sits down exhausted. They look at him in horror. He, too, is a little horrified by what he has said.*)

TONY: Arthur. Look here, my dear old fellow. It's Caroline's party. You wouldn't spoil a party?

ARTHUR: I don't know that I feel particularly festive.

LILY: Come on, Arthur. You know how you enjoy Caroline's birthday.

ARTHUR: I always have. Up to now. Ever since she was born.

TONY: And look Arthur, my dear old Head, I bought these for us in the pub. A whiff each after dinner.
(*He takes two battered cigars out of his breast pocket.*)

ARTHUR: (*Crackles and smells the cigar.*) That was thoughtful of you Peters.

TONY: I know you don't smoke them as often as one might like. Only when something a little bit festive arises from time to time.

LILY: (*Ecstatic.*) Oh, Tony Peters! Beautifully managed.

ARTHUR: Perhaps my suspicions are unfounded.

LILY: You manage him so beautifully.

TONY: Why not finish dressing, my fine old headmaster? Let us both face the fact, you must be bitterly cold.

ARTHUR: (*Starts to work himself up again.*) I tell you I never feel cold. Anyway it's never cold here. Only occasionally a little brisk after sunset. Anyway who's old? Didn't you tell me, Tony Peters, that in your prep school the Third Eleven Match play was once stopped by a Zeppelin? You didn't mean to let that slide out did you? What does that make you? Pretty long in bottle for a junior assistant Ha! Ha!

TONY: I'm not a junior assistant

ARTHUR: What are you then?

TONY: A senior assistant.

ARTHUR: You're the only assistant. I think of you as junior.

TONY: (*Shrugging his shoulders.*) It's a fact. I give an impression of perpetual youth. (*He slaps his pocket, brings out a half-bottle of whisky.*) I thought this might slip down well with the whiffs.

ARTHUR: (*Mollified.*) It looks like good stuff.

TONY: I've always had an eye for a piece of good stuff. (*ARTHUR looks up suspiciously.*)
Arthur, Head, do believe me. That remark was in no way meant to be offensive.

ARTHUR: I'll take your word for it.

LILY: So hurry on Arthur do. We must be just so for when Caroline comes in.

TONY: Go on Head. Spick and span. That's the order of the day. Look, Lily's in her best. As always, on these occasions.
(*LILY and TONY pat him, steer him towards the door; he turns to them before he goes out.*)

ARTHUR: For God's sake, you two. Use your imaginations. Think what it's like being up there, wrestling with a collar in utter ignorance. Tormented...

TONY: Get a start on the collar now. You'll be back with us in five minutes.

ARTHUR: Five minutes? Haven't you ever thought, Peters, the whole course of a man's life can be changed in five minutes. Does it take five minutes to die? Or catch malaria? Or say the one word to unhinge another man's wife from him? All right, I'll trust you. But look here, both. No singing. Don't torture me with that.

TONY: If I do sing. I'll sing so quietly that no human ear could ever pick it up. I'll sing in notes only audible to a dog.

ARTHUR: That's worse.

LILY: Now go on, really. Caroline can't sit and gaze at a brass collar stud on her birthday.

ARTHUR: I'm going. For Caroline's sake, I'm going. Poor child. (*He stands in the doorway, the door open.*)

TONY: For Caroline's sake. Goodbye.

(*TONY shuts the door on him. Then walks over to the basketwork chair and drops into it.*)

He's not right.

LILY: About what?

TONY: About me.

LILY: What about you?

TONY: I *can* do quadratic equations.

LILY: Another year gone. Another birthday come again.

TONY: Gather all the Xs and Ys on to one side.

LILY: Eighteen years old. (*She fiddles with the presents.*)

TONY: Remove the brackets.

LILY: Oh Tony, can she possibly be happy?

TONY: Remember that minus times minus makes plus.

LILY: Tony can you hear me?

TONY: As an example. In the problem, if it takes ten barbers twenty minutes at double speed to shave 'y' tramps let 'x' equal the time taken to shave half a tramp. That's Arthur's problem. Arthur can *teach* quadratics all right. But can he *do* them. Isn't that rather the point?

LILY: Everyone here is so taken up with their own concerns.

TONY: I'm sorry.

LILY: I quite understand. You're naturally anxious for your algebra.

TONY: No, Lily. Not at all. Come and sit down.

LILY: Where?

TONY: Here. (*He slaps his knee.*)

LILY: I'd be taking a risk.

TONY: All we can take in this mean, tight-fisted world. (*She giggles and sits on the floor in front of him, her elbows on his knees, gazing up at him.*)

LILY: Now is Caroline...?

TONY: What?

LILY: Happy.

TONY: She shows no signs of being otherwise.

LILY: (*Looks down suddenly. Her eyes full of tears.*) How can she tell us?

TONY: Poor Arthur. It may not be so bad as he thinks.

LILY: When it's something we must have all noticed why don't we discuss…

TONY: At first perhaps, it was our headmaster's fault. When it happened at first I blamed him. But since last birthday I've begun to suspect…

LILY: Tony. You're talking about it. About Caroline…

TONY: (*Talking quickly as if to avoid an awkward moment.*) Caroline is now eighteen which must mean that she was born in 1940. Dark days with storm clouds hanging over Europe. Poor child she never knew the pre-war when you could week-end in Paris on a two-pound ten note and get a reasonable packet of cigarettes for elevenpence complete with card which could be collected towards a jolly acceptable free gift. She never borrowed a bus and took a couple of girls from Elstree Studio out dancing up the Great West Road and home with the milk and change left out of a pound. (*LILY begins to smile at him.*)

LILY: It's yourself you're discussing.

TONY: She missed the Big Apple and the Lambeth Walk and the Palais Glide. She couldn't even come to the party I gave for the Jubilee. Poor child, God knows I'd have invited her. Twenty-three of us in a line gliding down the Earls Court Road at three in the morning. Smooth a skaters. (*Takes up his ukelele and sings.*)
'She was sweet sixteen.
On the village green.
Poor little Angeline!'

ARTHUR: (*Off stage shouting.*) For pity's sake.
(*TONY shrugs his shoulders and puts his ukelele down, exasperated.*)

TONY: Really. He's like my old landlady in the Earls Court Road. Bump on the ceiling with a broom if you so much as lifted a girl from the floor to the sofa.

LILY: (*Elbows on his knees.*) Was it so carefree for you then, in Earls Court?

TONY: (*Modestly.*) Carefree? Look Lily, I knew ten clubs where the drummers were happy to allow me a whirl with their sticks. I knew twenty pubs in S.W. alone which were flattered to take my cheque, and as for the opposite sex...

(*LILY looks at him admiringly.*)

I had enough telephone numbers to fill a reasonably bulky pocket diary from January to Christmas. Even the little space for my weight and size of hat, Lily, was crammed with those available numbers.

LILY: What do you think took away all our happy days?

TONY: Are they gone?

LILY: Arthur says so. Driven away, he says, by the Russians and the Socialists and the shocking way they've put up the rates.

TONY: We can still have a good time.

LILY: But can Caroline? If she could only tell...

(*She gets up and wanders to the table, arranging the presents.*)

TONY: Well there...

LILY: And when she never knew...

TONY: Isn't that rather the point?

LILY: Deprived, Tony, of all the pre-war we ever had?

TONY: All that pre-war denied her.

LILY: What would become of us, do you suppose, if we hadn't go that pre-war to think about?

TONY: (*He gets up from the chair and stands with his arm round her shoulders.*) It's not all over. We don't just let it die out.

LILY: It mustn't.

TONY: We keep it going you see. And it keeps us going too.

(*Pause, as they stand side by side.*)

ARTHUR: (*Yelling from off stage.*) What have you two got to be so damned *quiet* about?

(*They smile at each other and TONY breaks away from her and walks round the room rubbing his hands and flapping his arms. He begins to talk in the clipped, stoical voice of an explorer reminiscing.*)

TONY: The glass stood at forty below when we unpacked our Christmas dinner in Camp A. (*He blows on his nails.*)

LILY: (*Thoughtfully, softly.*) I remember the day you arrived. It was summer and Arthur was out taking Cricket practice.

TONY: Frozen penguin and a mince pie which my dear sister had sent from Godalming, found, quite by chance, stuffed in a corner of my flea-bag.

LILY: I heard the sound of your two-seater on the gravel.

TONY: We broke the mince pie with our ice axes. Three dogs died in the night.

LILY: Why did you have to sell that two-seater?

TONY: ...Prayed to God before sharing our penguin. Now a thousand miles from base camp. Had a premonition we should never see England again...

LILY: I was alone in the middle of the afternoon. I heard you singing outside the window. It opened and you came in... When you saw me standing all alone...

TONY: Peters...

LILY: Yes?

TONY: With silent heroism...

LILY: What?

TONY: Walked out of the tent.

(*With a dramatic gesture he steps behind the curtain of the French windows and is lost to sight.*)

LILY: (*Standing alone centre stage, her arms extended. A slight wait.*) Tony! Why won't you ever be serious with me? (*ARTHUR enters, fully dressed, his hair brushed and shining.*)

ARTHUR: Where the hell's he got to now?

(*LILY makes a gesture of despair.*)

It's no use lying, Bin. I can see his filthy suede shoes under the curtain.

(*He pulls the curtain aside. TONY smiles at him, pats his shoulder and walks out into the room. TONY lights a cigarette with great finesse. ARTHUR sits down at the table, raises his hands as if to say something several times. The words don't exist for what he feels that he must say.*)

TONY: Now Arthur. Don't make a fool of yourself over this.

ARTHUR: I....make a fool?

TONY: It's quite reasonable.

LILY: Tony, it seems, was discovering the North Pole.

ARTHUR: The North Pole?

TONY: Shut your eyes, Headmaster, and what can you hear? The ice cracking like gun fire in the distance. The wind howling in the guy ropes. The fizz of the solid fuel as it melts a little snow for your evening cocoa.

ARTHUR: Oh my god! (*He buries his face in his hands.*)

LILY: (*Laughing.*) Give the poor man a little peace.

TONY: Peace? What does Arthur want with peace? He'd be as bored as a retired General with nothing to do but keep chickens and explore the possibility of life after death. As lonely as a bull without a bull fighter. As hard up for conversation as an invalid without his operation. Give him peace and you'd bury your husband. What can he listen to in this great frozen institution except the sound of his own eternal irritation? (*He claps him on the shoulder.*) Keep going, Headmaster, go off every minute. You're the dear old fog horn that lets us know we're still afloat.

LILY: Ssh. Caroline!

(*ARTHUR has raised his two clenched fists and now opens his hands and pushes himself up from the table.*)

ARTHUR: She's been out for a walk.

(*CAROLINE has come in through the French windows halfway through TONY's speech. Now she closes them and comes into the room, crosses it, and hangs her mackintosh on the back of the door that leads to the school.*)

(*Pulling out his watch and looking at it.*) She usually does at this time.

(*CAROLINE comes up to the three of them, and looks at them without expression. She sits down. The others stand. She is eighteen and extremely beautiful, her beauty being such that it is strange, composed and vaguely alarming. She has a look of complete innocence and wears, unexpectedly the sort of clothes worn by starlets on the covers of very cheap film magazines. These clothes have an appearance of being home made. She does not speak. While she is on the stage the other characters speak faster as if to conceal the fact of her silence from themselves.*)

TONY: I wonder where she's been?

LILY: Usually along the front.

TONY: She doesn't feel the cold?

ARTHUR: Brought up here, of course she doesn't notice it.

TONY: She always walks alone?

LILY: Hardly ever picks up a friend.

> (*Pause while they all think of something to say. CAROLINE it still expressionless.*)

ARTHUR: Well – she's back just in time.

TONY: Haven't you got something to say to her?

ARTHUR: You needn't remind me. Many happy returns of the day.

> (*He puts his hand out. CAROLINE shakes it. ARTHUR sits down at the table.*)

TONY: Many, many, happies, Caroline dear. (*He stoops to kiss the top of her head.*)

> (*CAROLINE lifts her face and kisses him on the mouth. She is still expressionless. He sits down, disconcerted, patting his lips with his handkerchief.*)

LILY: Caroline, my baby. Don't grow up any more.

> (*LILY hugs CAROLINE like a child and then sits down.*)

ARTHUR: She didn't like you saying that.

TONY: She didn't mind.

> (*Pause while LILY begins to cry.*)

ARTHUR: (*Suddenly loses his temper.*) Will you provoke me, Bin, with these bloody waterworks?

TONY: Look. She hasn't noticed her presents yet.

ARTHUR: She was upset.

TONY: No she wasn't.

> (*CAROLINE looks down at her place and lifts her hands in amazement. Her face is still without expression.*)

LILY: (*Recovering.*) She's seen them now.

ARTHUR: (*Eagerly.*) She may open mine first.

TONY: Well, of all the selfish...

ARTHUR: She's going to. I hope you didn't notice me buying it, Caroline, in the High Street yesterday. Creeping out of W H Smith's.

TONY: Now you've given the game away.

ARTHUR: What are you hinting?

TONY: The mention of W H Smith. Now she can rule out stockings or underwear or any nice toilet water.

(*CAROLINE shakes the parcel.*)

TONY: Now she's guessed what it is.

ARTHUR: I don't believe she has.

(*CAROLINE shakes her head.*)

No, she hasn't.

(*CAROLINE opens the parcel, it contains a Halma set and three boy's adventure books.*)

TONY: Same old things. She's bored with Halma.

ARTHUR: No she's not!

TONY: Yes she is.

ARTHUR: Anyway it's a wholesome game, Peters, unlike the indoor sports you're addicted to.

TONY: And these books! You only buy them to read them yourself. Three midshipmen stranded on a desert island. (*Picks up one and starts to read.*) 'Give over tickling, Harry, giggled his chum, little guessing it was the hairy baboon that had crept up behind the unsuspecting youngsters...'

ARTHUR: She appreciates it.

LILY: (*Soothingly.*) Of course she does, don't let's quarrel. Not on the birthday.

TONY: (*Putting down the book.*) I suppose it takes all tastes.

LILY: Perhaps now she'll open mine.

(*CAROLINE picks up a parcel.*)

I made it for you, dear. It took so long. I seem to have been making it all my life.

(*CAROLINE opens the parcel. A long sweater, white and endless with the school colours at the neck. She holds it in front of herself. It's far too long.*)

Oh Caroline. There's too much of it. I had far too much spare time.

TONY: (*Putting his hand on LILY's shoulder.*) She likes it. She thinks it'll keep her warm.

ARTHUR: Warm? Keep her warm did you say? I tell you its perfectly warm here, all the year round.

TONY: There now, Headmaster. Lily's right. We shouldn't quarrel on the birthday. And look. She's knitted in the school colours. That'll cheer you up, you know. When you see those colours always round your daughter.

ARTHUR: At least it shows some sense of loyalty.

TONY: Of course, not being, strictly speaking, a parent my present gets opened last.

ARTHUR: (*Resentfully.*) A treat saved up for you.

(*CAROLINE picks up TONY's present. Holds it against her cheek. Listens to it.*)

TONY: I believe... Yes. I think I am right in saying...
(*Radio commentator's voice.*) 'The ceremony is just about to begin. It's a wonderful spectacle here to-day. The lady Mayoress has released the pigeons. The massed bands are striking up. The Boy Scouts are fainting in unprecedented numbers and...'

(*CAROLINE undoes the parcel, produces a gilt powder compact.*)

ARTHUR: What can it be?

(*CAROLINE opens the compact and sprinkles powder on her nose.*)

LILY: My baby.

ARTHUR: Take that muck off your face. I forbid it. Go straight upstairs and wash.

TONY: Headmaster!

LILY: Surely Tony. She's still too young.

(*TONY goes behind CAROLINE, his hands on each side of her head he directs her face to one parent, then another.*)

TONY: Can you be such unobservant parents? Your daughter has now been using cosmetics in considerable quantities for many years.

ARTHUR: Is this true, Bin?

LILY: She's still a child.

TONY: Her table upstairs is covered with tubes, little brushes and the feet of rabbits. In an afternoon, with nothing better to do, she can turn from a pale, coal eyed, fourteenth wife of an oil sheik to a brash, healthy, dog-keeping, pony-riding, daddy-adoring virgin with a pillar box mouth. Her beauty spots come off on the face towels and when she cries she cries black tears.

ARTHUR: Your appalling influence.

TONY: The passage of time, Headmaster. What can you and I do to prevent it?

ARTHUR: I see her as a little girl.

TONY: Then you don't bother to look.

ARTHUR: Did *you* notice Bin?

LILY: When the sun falls straight on her I do have my suspicions. We've had so little sun lately.
(*The clock groans and strikes. CAROLINE puts down the powder compact and goes out of the room, through the door to the boy's department.*)
She's gone.

TONY: To collect her presents from the boys.

ARTHUR: Of course. I was forgetting.

TONY: She always does that next. Then she comes back to show us what they've given.

ARTHUR: Of...of course.
(*ARTHUR and LILY are staring thoughtfully in front of them. TONY walks about nervously, about to broach a difficult subject.*)

TONY: My old friends. (*He gets no reaction and starts again.*) Colleagues. Of course I'm not a parent.

ARTHUR: (*Angrily.*) If only I could be sure of that.

TONY: (*Smiling flattered.*) Not in any official sense. But I have at least been a child.

LILY: (*Looking at him affectionately.*) Yes, Tony, of course you have.

TONY: Now frankly speaking, isn't eighteen a bit of a cross roads? Isn't there something, can't you feel, that Caroline ought to be told?

ARTHUR: Told?

TONY: Yes.

LILY: What sort of thing, Tony, had you in mind?

TONY: (*Suddenly at a loss.*) We must have *something* to tell her. At least I should have thought so. Nothing to embarrass any one to tell, of course... But (*More positive.*) ...her *education*. Aren't there a few gaps there?

ARTHUR: You don't find everything in the covers of books, Peters. That's why I always lay the emphasis on organized games.

TONY: Yes. I noticed. (*He picks up his ukelele and begins to play odd notes, tuning it as he speaks, more vaguely and with less assurance.*)

(*LILY goes out and, during TONY's speech, comes back with a tray, including a dish of sausages and mash which she puts down to keep warm by the electric fire.*)

It's not that I'm all that keen on education myself. In fact I merely drifted into it. It was a thé dansant on the river, Maidenhead. The waiter was feeding the swans, he had an apron full of bread crumbs. I was dancing with a girl called Fay Knockbroker. She was so small and yellow and it was hot to touch her. Like a red hot buttercup.

(*ARTHUR makes an explosion of disgust. LILY looks up at him from the dishes and smiles and goes out again.*)

…'Tony', she said, 'Why don't you do something? Why don't you work?' It appeared her father Knockbroker, what did he deal in, taps? – I really forget, has said marriage was forbidden unless I worked. I had five shillings in my trousers that afternoon. I couldn't have covered the cucumber sandwiches.

ARTHUR: Grossly irresponsible.

TONY: In fact marriage, was far from my thoughts. I only wanted to get Fay launched in a punt and pushed out under the willows.

ARTHUR: Disgusting.

TONY: Probably. But it's that punt, those willows, that have kept me going in all our cold winters.

(*LILY comes in again wish the tomato ketchup.*)

That and…

ARTHUR: Don't say it! I can guess…

TONY: How do you live, Headmaster, without any of those old past moments to warm you up?

ARTHUR: I have my memories. A cry from the megaphone on the tow path. A cheer under Barnes Bridge.

TONY: But Miss Knockbroker wasn't stepping on board that afternoon. 'You get a job,' she said, 'or I stay on dry land and marry Humphrey Ewart. He works!'

ARTHUR: (*Interested grudgingly.*) Did he?

TONY: She met him at the Guards' Boat Club. Blowing safes turned out to be his profession. Knockbroker was very livid when it all came out after the marriage.

ARTHUR: And you?

TONY: I went up to London to get a job. I had to leave her to pay for tea. What could I do? I didn't know anything. I had to teach. I had no great enthusiasm for education. I might have come to love it. As tutor cramming a young millionaire in the South of Prance, with his widowed mother bringing us long pink drinks to wash dawn the logarithms...

ARTHUR: (*Suddenly roaring with laughter.*) And you ended out here!

TONY: I only came temporarily. Till something else offered.

ARTHUR: You are still temporary. As far as I'm concerned.

LILY: You don't regret it Tony?

TONY: (*Looking round at her, then brassily.*) Of course not. No regrets. I've no enthusiasm for education. But I can't help thinking. There are things Caroline should be *told.*

ARTHUR: What for instance?

TONY: We've had experience of life.

LILY: (*Lovingly.*) Ah yes. How very true. Great experience of life.

TONY: Now, shouldn't we be passing on that experience to her?

ARTHUR: I'm against passing on experience. Boys find it very embarrassing.

TONY: But Caroline, Headmaster, isn't this rather the point we have to face? Is not, and can never be, barring all accidents, a boy.

ARTHUR: The principle's the same. I have it so often in class. You start by telling them something unimportant like the date of the Spanish Armada, 1585.

TONY: 1582.

ARTHUR: 1585

TONY: 1582.

ARTHUR: Fifteen hundred and eighty five. The year of our Lord.

LILY: What can it matter after all these years?

ARTHUR: Imbecile. Don't interrupt me. Of course it matters. It's the mental discipline.

TONY: All right, Headmaster. Have it your own way. 1585.

ARTHUR: 1585. You start to tell them… The Battle of the Armada. When England's Virgin Queen… Then you've laid yourself open…

TONY: (*Imitating.*) Sir! What's a virgin?

ARTHUR: You see! It's most undesirable. The lesson may have half an hour to go, and if you start telling them about virgins where will you be when it's time to ring the bell? Know what I do Peters, if any questions of that type come up?

TONY: Yes. I do.

ARTHUR: I run straight out of the room and ring the bell myself. And that's my advice to you.

LILY: I suppose it's natural for them, to be curious.

TONY: They don't ask any questions unless they already know the answers.

(*ARTHUR gets up and walks about, gradually working himself into a rage again.*)

ARTHUR: That's purely cynical. Their minds are delightfully blank. That's how it's got to stay, it's the only way for Caroline. You start it, Peters. You feed her with bits of geography and history and mathematics. What comes next? Little scraps of information from you about Maidenhead and the Earls Court Road. Little tips from Bin on how to make love to another man while your husband's upstairs dressing. Little hints from both of you about face powder and silk stockings, free love and Queen Elizabeth and birth control and decimals and vulgar fractions and punts under the willow tree and she'll be down the slope – woosh! on the toboggan and you'll never stop her until she crashes into the great black iron railings of the answer which, please God, she mustn't ever know.

TONY: Which one is that?

ARTHUR: That ever since you came here and met Caroline's mother this decent school has been turned into a brothel! A corrupt...
(*He stops at the sound of a baby crying off stage.*)
What ever?
(*The baby cries again.*)
LILY: (*Delighted.*) A baby crying.
TONY: One of the boys has asked the right question at last.
(*CAROLINE wanders in from the bays' door, her arms full of jokes. She stops by ARTHUR and hands him the cardboard box which, when she turns it upside down, cries like a baby. ARTHUR turns it and it yells. He slowly relaxes.*)
LILY: It's just a joke...
TONY: One of her presents from the boys.
ARTHUR: How very, very amusing.
TONY: How strange these boys are.
(*CAROLINE hands TONY a bottle of beer. He tries to open it and finds it's made of rubber. LILY gets a squeaking banana. CAROLINE has a pair of glasses which include a nose and teeth which she puts on. They all sit down, CAROLINE quite motionless in her false nose, the others urgently talking.*)
Will you light the candles, Headmaster? Give a warm, shade, Café Royal touch to the proceedings.
ARTHUR: (*Lighting the candles.*) Sausages and mash I see.
LILY: (*Serving it out.*) And red jelly to follow.
ARTHUR: Always Caroline's favourite menu.
TONY: Since she was twelve.
ARTHUR: That's why we always put it on for the birthday.
LILY: It marks the occasion.
ARTHUR: When I was a boy my birthday always fell when I was away from home at Cadet camp. My old aunt gave me my cake to take in a tin. I had to keep it under my camp bed until the day came, then I'd get it out and eat it.
LILY: Let's be grateful. Caroline doesn't have to go to Cadet camp. She can birthday at home.
ARTHUR: As often as not when I came to open that tin the bird had flown.
TONY: Poor old Headmaster. I never knew that about you.

ARTHUR: Odd thing about it. I suspected that chaplain.

TONY: Not of scoffing your cake?

ARTHUR: It's a fact. I couldn't get it out of my head. An effeminate sort of fellow, the chaplain. Welsh. And he had a sweet tooth.

LILY: I'm giving Caroline some more because it's her favourite dinner.

TONY: Yes. I see.

ARTHUR: It was terribly upsetting for a young boy in my position.

TONY: Indeed yes.

ARTHUR: You can't put your heart into Church Parade when you suspect the padre of nibbling at your one and only birthday present.

TONY: Let's hope you misjudged him.

ARTHUR: I was a sound judge of character. He was a man who let the side down badly.

TONY: Suspicious of everyone. Even then.

ARTHUR: What are you trying to infer?

TONY: Nothing at all. Shall I do the honours again, Headmaster?

ARTHUR: Yes. And when you come to Caroline's glass.

TONY: What?

ARTHUR: Fill it up.

LILY: With alcohol? She won't like it.

(*TONY fills CAROLINE's glass. She drains it thirstily.*)

TONY: There, Lily. It appears you were wrong.

ARTHUR: Thinking it over, Peters, I have thought your earlier remarks weren't entirely senseless. Caroline *has* reached a turning point. The time has come when she can be invited to join her father and mother in a light stimulant. It's a privilege, and like all privileges it brings new responsibilities.

TONY: In my humble opinion there are very few responsibilities involved in a glass of beer.

ARTHUR: There are responsibilities in everything, running a school, getting married, living at all. That's what we've got to tell Caroline. She's got to have faith in something bigger than herself.

LILY: Caroline's a woman now. Isn't that right, Tony? Didn't you say that?

TONY: Almost a woman, I should say.

LILY: Then there are things only a woman can tell her.

ARTHUR: There are bigger things in life than knitting patterns and...bottling fruit. I mean there *are* things a person can sacrifice himself for. The side. The school. The right comrades, sweating at the oar.

TONY: There speaks the cox of the West Woolwich rowing club.

ARTHUR: Will you mock everything Peters?

TONY: The small man yelling through a paper megaphone while the comrades lug themselves to death at forty from fatty degeneration of the heart.

ARTHUR: Is nothing to be sacred?

TONY: There are better ways of getting heart failure.

ARTHUR: It all comes down to *that.*

TONY: Caroline's young. Every day she should collect some small pleasure, to keep her warm when the years begin to empty out. She should try everything, and not mind making mistakes. When she reaches our age it won't be her mistakes she'll regret...

ARTHUR: What are you telling her?

TONY: When I remember those girls at Maidenhead, their thumbs up, their faces smiling, doing the Lambeth Walk... It's not the ones I got away for the weekend I regret. It's the ones I never had the courage to ask.

ARTHUR: I was trying to give Caroline something to believe in, and you will everlastingly chip in with your unsavoury reminiscences...

TONY: Headmaster, are we attempting too much? Suppose we just give her some accurate information. Such as...where Gibraltar is.

ARTHUR: Gibraltar?

TONY: Yes. Go on. Tell her.

ARTHUR: At the bottom of Spain.

TONY: The bottom?

ARTHUR: Coming round the corner. Cadiz on the right.

TONY: You mean the right?

ARTHUR: The left then. Malaga on the right. Do I mean the left?

TONY: Headmaster. Are you sure you have any information to transfer?

ARTHUR: All right Peters. (*Getting up.*) You've managed it. You've cast a blight. You've had your mockery. You've sneered at the moot respected club on the river. You've spoiled the birthday for me now. I'm not staying. It's no use beseeching.

TONY: But Headmaster.

ARTHUR: You've rubbed the bloom off the birthday for me. I'm leaving you two together. Remember – a child is watching.

(*He goes out slamming the door to the bedrooms.*)

LILY: He's gone.

TONY: Yes.

(*CAROLINE sighs and sits down on the basket chair.*)

If only he wouldn't take it as such a personal matter. It's not my fault where they put Gibraltar. (*He picks up the ukulele and tunes it.*)

LILY: Ssh. Caroline's expecting a song.

TONY: An old one...

LILY: That Turk and the extraordinary Russian?

TONY: (*Singing.*) 'Oh the sons of the prophet are hardy and bold
And quite unaccustomed to fear,
But the greatest by far
In the courts of the Shah –
Was Abdul the Bul Bul Emir.'

LILY: Of course Caroline adores this one...

TONY: 'If they wanted a man to encourage the van or shout...'

LILY: (*Shouts.*) 'Atta boy.'

TONY: 'In the rear
Without any doubt
They always sent out...'
Damn. I almost forgot I owe the pub for those whiffs.
I'm duty bound to slip back.

LILY: Oh Tony.

TONY: They were an expensive gesture…

LILY: Have a look in that box. The egg money…

(*TONY finds five shillings in a box on the mantelpiece. Pockets it in triumph.*)

LILY: Must you go tonight?

TONY: (*Dramatic voice stifling sobs, tough American accent.*) 'I'm only a small guy, not very brave. I guess this is just one of the things that comes to a small guy and well, he's just got to go through with it if he ever wants to be able to shake his own hand again this side of the Great River. Maybe if I go through with this Lily, hundreds of little guys all over the world are going to be safe to shake their own hands and look themselves in the whites of their eyes. Maybe if I don't they won't. Kinda hard to tell. (*Looks out of the French windows.*) It's just about sun up time. Guess Arthur Loudon's boys are sawing off their shot guns 'bout now down there in the alfafa. So long folks. If ma sobers up tell her Goodbye. Let's hit the trail now. Don't forget the empties. (*He hitches up his trousers, picks up the string bag of empties and lurches out of the French windows.*)

(*LILY is laughing hard. CAROLINE is quite impassive.*)

(*Off stage.*) Bang, bang, bang.

LILY: Tony, you'll kill me.

TONY: (*Staggering in backwards, his hand on his heart.*) They killed me too, honey. Tell ma I'm feeling just fine, can't hardly notice the difference. (*Looks religiously upwards.*) O.K. Mr Gabriel Archangel. I heard you. I'm a coming. Maybe take a little time on account of this old webbed foot of mine.'

(*Limps out of French windows.*)

LILY: Oh Tony Peters. What should I do without you? (*Pause.*)

Caroline, they try to tell you things – but what can they tell you? We're not men you see, we're something different. Lots of men don't realize that. All men except, except Tony.

(*CAROLINE still sits impassively. LILY kneels on the floor in front of her.*)

LILY: I'm a woman, Caroline. And you're going to be one as well. Nothing can stop you. I'm a woman and what does Arthur call me? He calls me Bin. Bin, when my name is Lily. Now does Bin sound like a woman's name to you? You know why he calls me Bin? Because he wants me to be his friend, his assistant, his colleague, his thoroughly good chap. To rough it with him on a walking tour through life. He's said that to me, Caroline. How can I be a good chap, I wasn't born a chap. *My sex gets in the way.* That's why he gets so angry. (*She gets up and moves about the room.*) Look Caroline, do you know why he calls me Bin? Because my father did and my uncle did and so did my five brothers who all married soft hearted tittering girls in fluffy pullovers which came off on them like falling hair and white peep toe shoes and had pet names for their hot water bottles. Those brothers called me Bin. Good old Bin, you can put her on the back of the motor bike. Bin's marvellous, she can go in the dicky because her hair's always in a tangle and her cheeks are like bricks and the wind can't do her any harm, but Babs or Topsy or Melanie has to sit in front because she's such a fuss pot and so I can change gear next to her baby pink and artificial silk and get her angora all tied up in my Harris tweed. If you take Bin out it's for great slopping pints and the other one about the honeymoon couple in the French hotel, and then you can be sick in the hedge on the way because Bin's a good chap. We're women Caroline. They buy us beer when we long to order protection and flattery and excitement and crème de menthe and little bottles of sparkling wine with silver paper tops and oh God, we long to be kept warm. Aren't I right? Isn't that how we feel? Mothers and daughters and wives... (*Kneeling again.*) Oh Caroline tell me I'm right. Caroline. Speak to us. What have we done wrong?
(*CAROLINE says nothing, but, for the first time she smiles slowly and puts her hands on her mothers shoulder. LILY gets up, gets the tray which she has left leaning against the wall and begins to stack the plates.*)

Anyway all my friends got married and there was only Arthur. He was small and violent and believed in everything. Life wasn't much fun at home, my brothers got married and their wives refused to take on their pets. After the youngest left I was walking out with five Alsatian dogs. Father economized on the wedding. 'We needn't hire a car for Bin,' he said. My brother Tommy took me to the church on the back of his motor bike. My first long dress and I was rushed up to my wedding wearing goggles and waving in the wind like a flag. We're women, Caroline. There's supposed to be a mystery about us. We should be sprung on our men like a small surprise in the warmth and darkness of the night – not delivered by a boy on a motor bike like a parcel that's come undone in the post. It shouldn't be like that for you Caroline. The day after the marriage I told Arthur I loved him. 'There are more important things than love,' he said. 'What more important things? 'Companionship,' be said, 'helping one another. Now we're dedicated, our lives are dedicated.' 'What to?' I asked him. 'The boys.' Can you believe it? Those dreadful children coughing like old sheep upstairs. I was dedicated to *them*. I went to look at them. They were in striped pyjamas, they looked like little old convicts with cropped heads and match-stick arms and legs. They had hard, sexless voices and the faint, cold smell of lead pencils. And you know what? Arthur said it would make them think of me as more of a sport. He told them to call me Bin. I ask you. Is that a name for a woman?

ARTHUR: (*Shouts offstage.*) What are you doing, Bin?

LILY: (*Suddenly shouts back.*) Clearing away. (*Then quietly.*) That day was so empty. It seemed I'd been born a woman for nothing at all. Yet I couldn't be a man. Arthur wanted me to play cricket with the boys – can you imagine that Caroline? My legs were still young, and his idea was to see them buckled up in cricketing pads. My soft hands in the gloves of a wicket-keeper…

ARTHUR: (*Off stage shouts.*) I heard singing. Then the singing stopped. What's he got round to now?

LILY: I was a woman and there was no time for me.

ARTHUR: (*Off stage.*) Don't you realize? I went to bed because of the way you all treated me. I can't get out again. It'd be ridiculous!

LILY: (*Shouts.*) I'll be up in a minute. (*Quiet.*) Just a succession of days. Saints' Days with no lessons before breakfast. Sundays when the boys hit each other in the evening. Mondays when Arthur loses his temper. Nothing. Like a party when no one's remembered to send out the invitation... Then Tony came...

(*She leaves the dishes stacked on the tray and sits near CAROLINE.*)

ARTHUR: Bin! Come here, Bin! Don't leave me alone.

LILY: You know Tony can never be serious. Perhaps he's not very honest. Does he speak the truth all the time? I don't care. He treats me as if I was born to be a woman. Lily, Lily, all the time and never a nickname. And he's made Arthur jealous. (*Triumphant.*) *They quarrel over me Caroline. They've been fighting over me for years.* Imagine that! Good old Bin. She won't mind going home alone now we've met you girls...

(*LILY gets up. Turns to the middle of the room.*)

But now it's Lily Loudon and Arthur's developed jealousy.

ARTHUR: (*Shouting off stage.*) Are you going to rob me of my sleep? It's the semi-finals tomorrow.

LILY: (*Shouting.*) What semi-finals?

ARTHUR: (*Shouting back.*) Squash. Masters v Boys.

LILY: (*Contemptuously.*) Squash! What did Tony say today? 'Lily,' always Lily you see, 'needs no half light to look perpetually beautiful.' He said that. A man with all those available telephone numbers.

ARTHUR: (*Plaintively off.*) The boys'll make a fool of me if I don't get some sleep.

LILY: It'll come to you Caroline. If you're a woman it's bound to come. In the middle of the afternoon, perhaps. During cricket practice. You'll hear a sound in the gravel, someone singing outside the window. You stand quite still holding your breath in case they should go away. And then, when the windows open... Caroline, I'm telling you. It's the only thing that matters...

ARTHUR: (*Shouts.*) Am I never to see you again?

LILY: One day he'll do his insides mischief; shouting like that. Just put the tray in the kitchen would you. We'll wash up in the morning. I shouldn't have told you all that. I've enjoyed it though, telling myself. Don't remember it all. Only remember you're Caroline – make them call you that. Don't let them call you a funny name.

ARTHUR: (*Offstage.*) Bin!

LILY: Coming Arthur. I'm coming now.

(*She looks at CAROLINE and then goes out of the door. CAROLINE sighs, stretches and then gets up and carries the tray out of the room. The stage is empty. CAROLINE comes back and looks round the room. She takes out her powder compact. Standing over by the mantelpiece, powders her nose. She puts out the light. The stage is dark, only the electric fire glowing. She draws the curtains in front of the French windows showing a square of grey moonlight. She goes and sits down to wait. She waits. There's a footstep. She stands, her arms outstretched.*)

TONY: (*Off stage, singing.*) '..."Do you hold life so dull.
That you're seeking to end your career?"
Vile infidel know
You have trod on the toe...'

(*TONY comes in at the French window. Stumbles in the darkness.*)

What's up? Everyone gone to bed?

(*CAROLINE makes a slight sound and falls on him, her arms round his neck, her mouth pressed on his. In the square of moonlit French windows he is struggling to release his neck from her hands. When he frees himself he dashes to the door and switches on the light.*)

Caroline. What have they been telling you now?

(*She moves towards him.*)

Whatever it was – you can't have understood. You must have got it wrong.

(*He opens the door behind him. He disappears rapidly through the door. CAROLINE faces the audience. She is not unduly upset. Her hands turn palm outwards, she heaves a small sigh, her eyes turn upwards in mock despair. On her, the curtain slowly falls.*)

Scene 2

Early evening, the next day. The table is laid with an assortment of tea cups and plates. CAROLINE is alone, reading a letter propped up on the tea pot in front of her. She looks very pleased, as she folds up the letter and puts it in pocket of her skirt.

She gets up and goes over to the roll top desk. In wrestling to get a suitcase from behind it she knocks over the globe.

ARTHUR: (*Shouting off stage, from the right.*) What's that for mercy's sake?
(*CAROLINE brings out the battered suitcase and takes it over to the hearth rug where she opens it and begins to drop in the presents which she has arranged on the mantelpiece.*)
(*Shouts.*) Bin. Is that you?
(*CAROLINE drops in the baby crier which screams in the case.*)
What are you playing at you imbecile?
(*CAROLINE shuts the case. TONY appears outside the French windows and starts to haul down the flag. CAROLINE crosses the room, and, as he comes in hastily puts her suitcase outside the door that leads to the boys' department.*)
(*Off.*) Who is it, burglars? Answer me, Bin.
TONY: (*Folding up the Union Jack.*) It may be a silly business but it pleases the headmaster. Caroline. I wanted to talk. Couldn't we talk. I promise you... I haven't slept.
I believe, I feel sure...we could...both...talk.
(*CAROLINE exits through the boys' door. ARTHUR bursts into the room putting on his coat.*)
ARTHUR: I heard you Peters. Make no mistake about that...
(*TONY hold up the Union Jack, puts it on the desk and goes over to the table, sits down and pours himself out a cup of tea. He looks very tired.*)

TONY: I've never felt it before, Headmaster. It never really took hold of me till now.

ARTHUR: Not to speak can be just as deceptive as lying, Peters. There's an awful, deceptive silence about people in this house, a goading, tormenting, blank silence. Every question I shout is like sending a soldier into the dark night of a silent, enemy country.

TONY: Have a cup of tea?

ARTHUR: Were you in here with her?

TONY: They sat in front of me, rows of boys. Usually I feel quite indifferent about them, as if they were rows of strangers sitting opposite me in a train. I merely want to avoid conversation with them until the bell rings and we can all get out at the station.

ARTHUR: What were you two doing, banging about in here? Shall I never know the truth?

TONY: Sit down and have some tea. All that shouting must leave you parched.

ARTHUR: How can I spare my voice? Leading this sort of life, I mean.

(*He sits down. TONY pours him tea.*)

TONY: It's hard for you, I do appreciate.

ARTHUR: But you're the one reason for my shouting...

TONY: Let me try and explain. There they sat, these children, with the pale look of old age hanging around them – of course they're much older than us, Headmaster, you do realize that don't you?

ARTHUR: Older?

TONY: And before they are finally taken away, done up in blankets, muffled in scarves, tweed caps balanced on their ancient heads, to institutions, I felt there was something I ought to tell them. Only...

ARTHUR: Yes?

TONY: I couldn't for the life of me remember what it was. But if you don't tell children anything...

ARTHUR: Well?

TONY: They get some extraordinary ideas.

ARTHUR: What do you mean?

TONY: I'm not sure if I'm in a position to tell you. All I can say is that I've had a shock, a pretty severe shock as it so happens, in the last twenty-four hours. I tell you, I don't often get a jolt like that these days. Last night, I say this quite frankly, sleep eluded me.

ARTHUR: Well, of course.

TONY: What do you mean, 'Well of course'?

ARTHUR: Missing Bin, weren't you?

TONY: Not at the time.

ARTHUR: I winkled her away from you.

TONY: Did you now?

ARTHUR: Brought her up to bed when you least expected it.

TONY: Oh, I see.

ARTHUR: My God, I'd liked to have seen the bewildered expression on your face when you found your beautiful bird – caged for the night.

TONY: Look, Headmaster, this shock I was referring to, it's made me think – well, I feel we shall have to face things as they are at very long last. Now I know this business has been a source of considerable interest and excitement to us all over a long period of years. It's kept us going, as you might say, when the results of the squash rackets competition and the state of the weather and the suspicion about who pinched the nail brush off the chain in the downstairs loo have been powerless to quicken the pulse. But it's gone too far, you know – we should never have started it.

ARTHUR: Of course you shouldn't. Now there's a twinge of conscience.

TONY: You know as much as I do. There's never been a breath of anything amiss.

ARTHUR: (*Singing bitterly.*) 'Tell me the old, old, story…'

TONY: It started as an occupation. Like Halma or sardines. It's kept us from growing old.

ARTHUR: Bluff your way out of it, like when the waiter comes with the bill and 'Most unfortunately my cheque book caught fire in my overcoat pocket'.

TONY: Must we go on pretending? I don't even fancy Lily. Hardly my type.

ARTHUR: (*Aghast.*) What are you saying?

TONY: That I don't love your wife...

ARTHUR: You don't?

TONY: And never have.

ARTHUR: (*With quiet fury.*) You unspeakable hound! (*Beginning to shout.*) You don't love her? My God, I ought to strike you Peters.

TONY: That young Fay Knockbroker remains my ideal. Small and yellow and red hot. The girl you have to keep on protecting from the wicked results of her own innocence.

ARTHUR: But Bin...

TONY: Not my sort at all. A very decent, understanding sort, naturally: but the sort you'd always cram into the dicky if you had a girl like Fay to ride with in front.

ARTHUR: You don't love Bin?

TONY: I'm afraid not...

ARTHUR: She's given you the best years of her life...

TONY: Really, Headmaster... I feel we ought to face these facts squarely...otherwise...well it may have, perhaps it's already had...results we didn't foresee.

ARTHUR: Bin. Poor girl. She mustn't ever guess.

TONY: (*Gently.*) You are...fond of your wife, Headmaster?

ARTHUR: Fond of her. I *love* her, Peters. When I married I expected it would be for companionship – I'd known friendship before, Peters, genuine friendship. Someone to tramp around Wales with, to give a fill from your pouch, to share a hunk of cold Christmas pudding on a Boxing Day morning by Beachy Head – marriage is different, Peters. It takes place with a *woman*.

TONY: So I've been led to believe.

ARTHUR: And with a woman as attractive, soft, yielding, feminine as my Bin.

TONY: You take that view of her?

ARTHUR: Who mustn't ever be hurt... Oh it's hard. I tell you that at once, Peters, to live with such a feminine person as a woman in your life.

TONY: Problems arise of course.

237

ARTHUR: We had our work to do. We had the school to serve. Our lives aren't ours I told her. We're dedicated to the boys. And all the time all I wanted was to stay in bed with her all day only occasionally getting up for bread and marmalade.

TONY: Really.

(*A long, embarrassed pause.*)

ARTHUR: Women are sensitive creatures, Peters. Lily mustn't be allowed to guess at what you've just told me.

TONY: (*Gestures resignedly.*) But it's led to this...

ARTHUR: She mustn't be *hurt*. Lily must never be *hurt*. (*Pause.*)

TONY: You'll perhaps resent my saying this Arthur, and that's the risk I'm bound to take. But if you don't want Lily hurt...sometimes I'm bound to notice...

ARTHUR: (*Proudly.*) I shout at her you mean?

TONY: Well, not exactly coo.

ARTHUR: That's love...

TONY: Oh yes?

ARTHUR: It takes people in different ways. Now when *you* want to make love to her I've noticed...

TONY: But really!

ARTHUR: You make a joke. You pretend to be at the North Pole. You sing a song.

TONY: My weakness: I'm not serious.

ARTHUR: But when I see all that I love about my wife. The way she twists the hair over her ears when the time comes to make out a list. The soft smile she gives when no one's looking. How she shuts in laughter with the palm of her hand... Then, I feel so small and angry. I see myself so powerless, so drawn into her that once I let myself go, all I believe in, all I'm dedicated to would be spent on afternoons of bread and marmalade. Then I shout I don't know why it is. The terms of endearment I'm meaning to say just come out screaming. Is it a natural reaction?

TONY: I hardly know.

ARTHUR: And the agony of being in a room without her. The doubt and the anxiety that she'll be taken from me by the time I get back.

TONY: Really. We've got to stop it. This performance of ours has had its influence on Caroline...

ARTHUR: Caroline? She's innocent of it all. She doesn't enter...

TONY: It has to stop, Headmaster.

ARTHUR: Who's going to stop it?

TONY: I am.

ARTHUR: You couldn't stop a catch.

TONY: I'm in duty bound... (*Standing up.*)

ARTHUR: To tell Bin you don't love her...

TONY: To tell the truth. For Caroline.

ARTHUR: (*Standing up, facing him.*) Tony Peters. I need you. I know I have a sense of dedication which my wife doesn't altogether understand. In a way I'm a hard row for a woman like Bin to furrow. I shout. I'm a prey to irritation. I can't imitate snowstorms. I've forgotten all the jokes I've ever heard. She needs the bright lights, Peters, the music. The interest of another man. I knew that soon after I married her. I can't tell you how relieved I was the day you walked through those French windows. Then I knew my married life was safe at last.

TONY: (*Sitting down, bewildered.*) Headmaster. This is a thought I would have put well beyond you.

ARTHUR: (*Solicitous.*) I've shocked you?

TONY: Deeply. Deeply shocked.

ARTHUR: Together, all these years, we've kept Lily so happy.

TONY: You seem, Headmaster, to have the most tenuous grasp of morality.

ARTHUR: My temper and your songs – what a crowded, eventful time we've given her. And you must confess, Peters, it's been an interest for you. I mean there can't still be so many irons in your fire these days, whatever your part in Earls Court may have been.

TONY: Oh, Headmaster. I don't know what you're trying to find, but you're getting dangerously warm.

ARTHUR: We depend on each other, Peters. You mustn't tell her. We all depend on each other...

TONY: But the younger generation? What are we doing for it?

ARTHUR: Our best, Peters. Let's allow ourselves that...

TONY: But when I walked through these French windows...

ARTHUR: You took on a job, Peters. You can't get out of it now.

TONY: I shouldn't have been singing. That was when I made my great mistake...

(*The kitchen door opens. LILY enters smoking a cigarette, carrying a plate of bread and butter.*)

LILY: Has Caroline had her tea? I've been cutting all this bread and butter. The trouble with living here, the butter gets as hard as the rock of Gibraltar. It blasts great holes in your sliced bread.

TONY: Don't mention Gibraltar, Lily.

ARTHUR: There you go. Trying to pretend it's cold.

(*LILY drops cigarette ash on the bread, blows it off and sits down.*)

LILY: Out in the kitchen I heard men's voices rising and falling, rising and falling. What've you two been talking about now?

TONY: About you.

LILY: How nice.

ARTHUR: Tony's confessed.

LILY: Confessed?

ARTHUR: What he feels about you.

LILY: What he feels. (*She looks delightedly at TONY.*) Have you Tony? (*She's biting bread and butter and smoking at the same time.*) What did you say?

ARTHUR: Do you want to tell my wife, Peters? Do you want to put a stop to this whole business, once and for all?

(*They both look at him. TONY gasps, smiles, and then gets up and walks up and down talking in clipped naval accents.*)

TONY: 'Ladies and gentlemen. It is my duty to inform you that we have struck an iceberg. At nine-o-hundred hours, fish were noticed swimming in the first-class bath water. All ports have been alerted and in approximately ten-o-o hours they will start looking for us by helicopter. If the

ship has already sunk we will rendezvous at latitude
9.700 and bob about in the water together as long as
possible...'

(*He comes to rest behind LILY's chair.*)

Oh Lily. I can't tell you how complicated it's all become.

ARTHUR: No. You can't.

(*CAROLINE enters from the boy's side, left. She is carrying
her suitcase which she puts down on the floor.*)

LILY: Caroline!

(*CAROLINE unhooks her mackintosh from the back of the
door and slowly puts it on. ARTHUR and LILY watch her
fearfully. She picks up the suitcase and stands in front of the
French windows.*)

ARTHUR: She's going for a walk.

LILY: Probably that's it.

TONY: Haven't you noticed the suitcase? Does she usually
go for a walk with a suitcase?

LILY: Caroline. Put it down.

(*She gets up and goes towards CAROLINE. TONY puts out
his arm and stops her.*)

TONY: Better to let her do what she wants.

LILY: What does she want? How can she tell us?

(*CAROLINE opens her mouth. Long silence in which she is
making an enormous effort until she says –*)

CAROLINE: I want to go to London.

(*They look at her in amazement. In dead silence CAROLINE
puts down her suitcase.*)

I've got a job with the Threadneedle Street Branch of the
Chesterfield and National Bank. I start at a salary of
seven pounds ten shillings a week.

(*She takes the letter and hands it to LILY. LILY crying looks
at it and hands it to ARTHUR. ARTHUR reads it and gives
it to TONY.*)

TONY: There seems to be some truth in what she says.

LILY: Stop her. Stop her leaving us, Arthur.

ARTHUR: She spoke. Our daughter spoke.

(*TONY gives CAROLINE back the letter.*)

CAROLINE: I have a third floor room at 109 Great
Bidford Street which costs four pounds ten shillings a

week, with board. I shall therefore have three pounds
fifteen shillings a week leftover…

TONY: Caroline… I hate to disillusion you.

ARTHUR: She's talking. She's talking to me.

CAROLINE: Goodbye. (*She shakes ARTHUR's hand.*)

ARTHUR: Forgive me.

CAROLINE: Goodbye. (*She shakes LILY's hand.*)

LILY: What have we done wrong?

CAROLINE: Good-bye. (*She shakes TONY's hand.*)

TONY: Good-bye.

LILY: It's too late to go now…

CAROLINE: The train leaves at 7.15 from Coldsands
Station. Platform One. Change at Norwich. (*She goes out
and closes the French windows. For a moment she stands
looking in at them through the glass. Then she disappears.*)

TONY: Let's hope she's right about that.

LILY: Why didn't you stop her?

ARTHUR: (*Sitting down.*) She spoke to me. She said good-bye.

TONY: Well, that's right, she did.

LILY: (*Standing distractedly in the middle of the room.*) What
shall I do?

TONY: Clear away the tea.

ARTHUR: Lily. There's something you ought to know
about Caroline. She hasn't said anything for a long time.
(*Silence. Then TONY says.*)

TONY: We'd noticed that.

ARTHUR: You didn't comment?

(*TONY shrugs his shoulders.*)

You didn't like to?

TONY: It seemed unnecessary.

ARTHUR: Kindness held you back?

LILY: We must stop her going.

TONY: She won't meet any harm.

ARTHUR: But you don't know why she didn't speak? I told
you, Peters, all the terms of endearment start shouting
and screaming when I utter them. When I love someone
all my love turns to irritation. I lost my temper with
Caroline! I hit her! I actually hit her!

LILY: (*Crossing towards him.*) No dear. You didn't.

ARTHUR: How do you know?

TONY: We were here in the room. You didn't hit her, Headmaster.

ARTHUR: (*Deflated.*) I did. I wanted to hit her. After that, I thought she didn't speak. The nervous shock. Was it the nervous shock do you think, either of you?

LILY: Perhaps she didn't want to.

TONY: Or she had nothing to say to us. Although we had enough to say to her...

LILY: Who shall we talk to now?

TONY: Each other, Lily. Always to each other.

LILY: Caroline! Why should she have to go, Tony?

TONY: She has to go sometime.

ARTHUR: I made her go. I hit her. I must have hit her. There's no other explanation.

TONY: (*Sits down in the basket-chair and picks up his ukelele.*) How shall we ever know?

ARTHUR: What do you mean? For God's sake explain what you mean.

TONY: Was it your temper or her temper that stopped her speaking? Was it just the complete lack of interest that overcomes all children at the thought of the parents who gave them birth?

ARTHUR: I wasn't responsible?

TONY: What's responsible for Caroline as she is? What you told her? What you didn't tell her? The fact we told her a lie? The fact we told her the truth? Look back, Arthur. Look back, Lily do. What made us what we are? Anything our fathers and mothers said? More likely something that happened when we were all alone. Something we thought of for ourselves, looking for a passable disguise in a dusty attic, or for a path that didn't exist in the hot summer in the middle of a wood that smelt of nettles.

ARTHUR: Is that how you found things out?

TONY: My dear old headmaster. I've never found out anything. I'm not a parent, but in my weak moments, like this afternoon, I've wanted to tell things to the young. Why do we do it? Not to give them information, but to make them repeat our lives. That's all. It's finished with us and we don't want it to be finished. We'd like them to do it for us – all over again. It'll be better for Caroline to work in the bank. If only her *adding* weren't quite so shaky. Let's hope she errs, Headmaster, on the side of generosity.

(*LILY gets up and begins to put things on a tray.*)

ARTHUR: What are you doing, Bin?

LILY: Clearing away the tea. (*She goes out with the tray.*)

TONY: (*Looking at his watch.*) Just ten minutes and the boys have to stop their so called 'free time' and be hoarded into prep. I shall sit with them in silence. I'm not tempted to communicate with them any more.

ARTHUR: I'd better start to get the history corrected. Then I must take the roll-call Let's hope the boys are...still with us.

(*He goes over to the roll top desk. Starts marking exercise book.*)

TONY: (*Singing softly.*) 'Here we sit like birds in the wilderness, Birds in the wilderness.

Birds in the wilderness.

Here we sit like birds in the wilderness...'

ARTHUR: Peters.

TONY: (*Singing.*) 'Down in Demerara...'

ARTHUR: Was Henry the Third the *son* of Henry the Second?

TONY: He certainly wasn't his daughter.

ARTHUR: It doesn't *look* right somehow.

TONY: I suspect him of having been the son of King John.

ARTHUR: This boy misled me!

TONY: You can't rely on *them*. Not for accurate information.

ARTHUR: Peters.

TONY: Yes, Headmaster?

ARTHUR: Bin hasn't taken it too well, Caroline going off like that.

TONY: A loss for us all, of course.

ARTHUR: It's taken, a great deal from her.

TONY: Yes.

ARTHUR: It's more important than ever...

TONY: What is?

ARTHUR: That we should keep going. Like we always have. If we stopped quarrelling over her now...

TONY: Yes Headmaster?

ARTHUR: Think how empty her poor life would be.

TONY: And our lives?

ARTHUR: Empty too, perhaps.

TONY: You know, it must be almost twenty years ago that I came in through that window and made a joke. And now, it seems, I've got to live on that joke for ever.

(*LILY comes in. She shivers, rubs her hands and crouches by the electric fire to warm them.*)

LILY: It's cold.

ARTHUR: Nonsense.

LILY: It seems strange. Just the three of us. Shall we always be alone now?

ARTHUR: There it is.

TONY: You never know. Just when you felt most lonely in Earls Court I always noticed this, it was always the same when you met a bit of new. I remember feeling damned lonely one spring evening, about this time, walking down the Earls Court Road, and there was this beautiful girl, about eighteen, no older than Caroline in fact, her gloved finger pressed to a bell.

ARTHUR: I hope there's nothing disgusting about this reminiscence Peters.

TONY: So I said nothing. I went and stood beside her. She gave me a glance. It wasn't exactly marching orders. Then the door was opened by another girl, slightly older. 'Come in darling,' she said. 'I'm so glad you could bring your husband.' So we sat us down to four courses and later as it came on to fog, it was carte blanche of the spare bedroom for the night. You see the hostess, it all turned out, had never seen the husband.

LILY: And that poor husband?

TONY: Unexpectedly lamed that very afternoon. A taxi had run over his foot, so she explained it in the spare room.

LILY: And you walked straight up to her?

TONY: Quick work wasn't it?

LILY: A quick worker, Tony.

TONY: No grass grows under Tony Peters, thank God.

ARTHUR: I made sure that story would end up as disgusting.

LILY: Oh Tony! What adventures you've had!

TONY: Adventures, thank goodness, still come to me.

(*He looks at LILY. She puts an elbow on his knee and gazes into the electric fire.*)

ARTHUR: Isn't the room big enough? Do you have to sit on top of one another?

TONY: Now Headmaster. It'll soon be time for roll-call.

LILY: (*Thoughtfully.*) I haven't really had many adventures. Have you, Arthur?

ARTHUR: What?

LILY: Had many adventures?

ARTHUR: (*Reading.*) Was that Henry II?

TONY: Was what Henry II?

ARTHUR: The chap whose son was drowned?

TONY: Drowned?

ARTHUR: In the White Ship.

(*TONY picks up his ukelele and sings to LILY.*)

TONY: (*Singing.*) 'Here we sit like birds in the wilderness, Birds in the wilderness.'

ARTHUR: (*Closing the exercise book and beginning to shout.*) Peters. Bin. Stop goading me both of you. Don't you even wait now until I'm decently out of the room?

TONY: (*Singing.*) 'Here we sit like birds in the wilderness, Down in Demerara.

As the ship went down.'

ARTHUR: (*Standing up and hitting his desk with a tremendous crash with his fist.*) Stop singing to my wife! Take your greedy eyes off her!

(*ARTHUR and LILY look at each other with deep affection. TONY plays a note on his ukulele. ARTHUR exits. Curtain.*)

The End.

LUNCH HOUR

Characters

THE MAN

THE GIRL

THE MANAGERESS

Lunch Hour was first performed at The Playhouse, Salisbury, on 20 June 1960. Later produced at the Arts Theatre Club, London, on 18 January 1961, and subsequently transferred to the Criterion Theatre, with the following cast:

MAN,   Emlyn Williams

GIRL,   Wendy Craig

MANAGERESS,   Alison Leggatt

Director,   Donald McWhinnie

Set designer,   Brian Currah

The action of the Play passes in a bedroom
in a small hotel near King's Cross

Time – the present

Scene: a small hotel room near King's Cross. 1 p.m. exactly of a winter's day.

There is a double bed centre, set diagonally with the foot pointing down right. The door is right of the bed in the back wall, and there is a window right looking out over railway signals and the tops of houses. Left of the bed is a shilling-in-the-slot gas-fire with a mantelpiece. On the mantelpiece are a Bible, an A.B.C. train time-table and a chiming clock. A wooden chair stands down left of the fire.

When the curtain rises, the room is empty and the gas-fire unlit. There is a sound of trains off. The clock chimes one. The GIRL enters and looks cautiously round the room. She is twenty-three, a textile designer. She wears an overcoat. The MAN follows her. He is in his early forties, and is Policy Director of a department in the firm for which the girl works. He wears an overcoat, a hat and horn-rimmed spectacles. The GIRL crosses to the fireplace and picks up the A.B.C. She begins to laugh gently. The MAN puts his spectacles in his pocket and takes off his hat.

MAN: Why're you laughing?
GIRL: I don't know. (*She puts the A.B.C. back on the mantelpiece.*)
MAN: You're happy?
GIRL: I laugh when I'm hungry too.
MAN: (*Disappointed.*) If you'd rather eat...
GIRL: Not at all.
  (*The MAN throws his hat on the bed. They meet centre.*)
  (*She takes his hands.*) You look so big in that overcoat –
  like a house.
MAN: I'll take it off. (*He unbuttons the overcoat.*)
GIRL: Not yet. (*She crosses to the window.*) What's this place?
MAN: (*Crossing to the fireplace.*) Just a hotel...
GIRL: A hotel?
MAN: By the station. It's convenient...
GIRL: (*Turning.*) What for?
MAN: The North of England.
GIRL: (*Dreamily.*) You say the most ridiculous things...
  (*They meet centre and hug.*)
  And no-one knows we're here?
  (*They come out of the hug.*)

251

MAN: I'm having a long business lunch with the textile
   buyers in the Tudor room.

GIRL: And I'm alone with an open continental sandwich in
   a dark corner of the coffee-bar with the rubber plants
   brushing my cheek.

MAN: And I'm saying: 'Well, gentlemen, have a large plate
   of smoked salmon on the Commissioners of Inland
   Revenue.'

GIRL: But if they looked for us in those places...

MAN: They wouldn't find us.

GIRL: No, we're nowhere...

MAN: We're here.

GIRL: We've disappeared... We don't exist.

MAN: For an hour – or longer. (*He tries to kiss her.*)
   (*The GIRL steps back a pace.*)

GIRL: No.

MAN: Business lunches go on for ever.

GIRL: (*Moving away right.*) You can't spend much time on an
   open continental sandwich.
   (*There is a pause.*)

MAN: (*Taking a step back.*) You look so small in that overcoat.

GIRL: What do I look like?

MAN: A child in the park on a snowy morning. A woman
   who's disguised herself to run away to sea.

GIRL: Go on talking...

MAN: The inexperienced wife of an arctic explorer... (*He
   pauses.*)

GIRL: Go on.

MAN: I've run out.

GIRL: What of?

MAN: Words.

   (*The GIRL laughs. The MAN looks at his watch. The GIRL
   sees this and her laugh dies. There is a pause.*)

GIRL: As a matter of fact they're quite good, those
   sandwiches.

MAN: Are they?

GIRL: And they have other things, too – hamburgers, hot
   franks in soft floury rolls, great tubes of mustard...

MAN: You don't say.

GIRL: Such up-to-date and convenient foods.

MAN: Would you rather be in a coffee-bar?

GIRL: This is much more…

MAN: What?

GIRL: Exciting.

MAN: You mean that? (*He steps forward.*)

GIRL: (*Stepping back.*) Because I love you.

MAN: And me!

GIRL: How long?

MAN: Since the day you walked into my office…

GIRL: With the new design for bedspreads.

MAN: Spanish ivy!

GIRL: You remember!

MAN: And said, 'Is this the way to the duplicating department?'

GIRL: And you said…

MAN/GIRL: (*Together.*) 'No, but I'll show you…'

GIRL: And you rose up with the light from the window behind you so you appeared all silver –

MAN: Did I?

GIRL: – like a shining statue…

MAN: And I took you to Mr Jevons…

GIRL: Down the long dark corridors, past the rude and elderly stares of the typing pool…

MAN: In the lift.

GIRL: You didn't say a word!

MAN: We certainly established sympathy…

GIRL: Oh, love, how it attacks you!

(*The MAN steps forward. The GIRL steps back.*)

You being so quiet in the lift was what I appreciated. Not saying any vulgar remark such as 'Where have you been all my life?', or 'Is there another one at home like you?' Not even looking…

MAN: I was genuinely impressed!

GIRL: Yes.

MAN: (*Moving to the bed.*) And you seemed so lost and uncertain. Like I sometimes feel in that great organization.

GIRL: Such words – from the head of the textile buying department!

MAN: You mean the policy director. (*Thinking of his work.*) I'm only the Number Two in that slow-moving setup. Blast Harris! (*He sits on the bed.*)

GIRL: (*Moving up to his right.*) You don't think I'm the sort of girl who comes to a place like this?

MAN: (*Giving her all his attention again.*) No!

GIRL: Then why'm I here?

MAN: My fault.

GIRL: (*Shaking her head thoughtfully.*) I'm the sort to come here. (*The sounds of a train come through the window.*) What's that?

MAN: The station.

(*There is a pause.*)

GIRL: (*Struck by a thought.*) And what about you? Is this how all your lunch hours are spent with some girl or other, and you have to creep out of the office at four o'clock every day for an enormous high tea?

MAN: I've never been here before.

GIRL: Honestly?

MAN: Yes.

GIRL: I'm sorry.

MAN: I love you.

GIRL: Say it again.

MAN: I love you.

GIRL: Mmm. (*She kneels right of him.*)

MAN: For six months...

GIRL: All through the summer.

MAN: With nowhere to go.

GIRL: In spite of the office and your – home life.

MAN: It kept us alive.

GIRL: When we had only a few moments; standing by the tea trolley in the corridor...

MAN: Holding hands in the lift...

GIRL: You waiting for me in the Embankment Gardens always first out of the office being on the executive planning side...

MAN: Always the same bench.

GIRL: With the flowers standing straight as soldiers and the one-stringed fiddle playing in front of the Tube and tramps asleep under their sheets of newspaper. We had ten minutes a day, now we've got...
(*The clock chimes a quarter. They rise. The MAN moves away left.*)

MAN: Three-quarters of an hour.

GIRL: In this room.

MAN: You don't like it?

GIRL: (*Brushing dust from her knees.*) It's not all that sordid really...

MAN: We could make ourself more at home – take off our coats. (*He opens his coat.*)

GIRL: It's cold.

MAN: I'll light the gas. (*He moves to the fireplace, strikes a match and tries to light the fire.*) It needs a shilling. (*He searches his pockets unsuccessfully for a shilling.*) Damn!

GIRL: I'll look. (*She burrows in her handbag.*) Only sixpences. Would it take two sixpences? (*She goes to the fire, left of the man, and puts in her sixpences. But the fire still fails to work.*)

MAN: Now you've lost your money.

GIRL: It really doesn't matter.

MAN: Let me give it back to you.

GIRL: It couldn't matter less.

MAN: By the end of the week you'll be short of a coffee.

GIRL: No, really.

MAN: Here. (*Counting money to give her.*) Sixpence – sevenpence – ninepence...
(*There is a quick knock at the door. The MANAGERESS enters.*)

GIRL: (*As the MANAGERESS enters; almost shouting.*) I don't want your money!

MANAGERESS: (*Coming to the foot of the bed.*) Do you want something?

MAN: Ah, yes, a shilling for the gas.

MANAGERESS: (*To the GIRL, moving a little towards her.*) You're cold. A journey does make you cold. Much snow up there?

GIRL: Up where?

MANAGERESS: The North of England.

(*There is a slight pause.*)

MAN: (*Hastily.*) Just a powdering of snow, didn't you say, dear?

GIRL: (*Bewildered.*) I've no idea...

MAN: The train was going too fast to take a good look.

MANAGERESS: An express?

MAN: That's it.

MANAGERESS: They *can* be fast. Was it the Scotsman?

GIRL: Was what?

MANAGERESS: The Flying Scotsman. (*She moves closer.*) My little boy collects engine numbers. Many a time he's seen the Scotsman, waiting at the end of the platform. Puffing and blowing. Would you like a cup of tea?

MAN: Not at all.

MANAGERESS: (*To the GIRL.*) Wouldn't you?

GIRL: Well...

MANAGERESS: Isn't that husbands for you? Never appreciate the plain and simple fact that what we wives need after a long cold train journey is a home-made cup of tea. Much snow, did you say?

MAN: She had lunch on the train...

MANAGERESS: That doesn't take the place, dear, does it?

GIRL: What of?

MANAGERESS: (*Moving towards the door.*) A cup of tea.

GIRL: Just a...

MAN: Very short cup.

(*The MANAGERESS exits.*)

GIRL: (*Turning to the MAN for an explanation, lost and puzzled.*) Where've I come from?

MAN: Scarborough.

GIRL: (*Moving to him.*) Why?

MAN: I told her that's where you live.

GIRL: Why should I live in Scarborough?

MAN: Because you're married to me. (*He moves away to right centre.*)

GIRL: (*Following him; accusingly.*) Then why don't you live in Scarborough, too? What's the matter with you? Can't you stand the climate? You delicate or something?

MAN: I've got digs in London.

GIRL: Thank you very much!

MAN: (*Patiently.*) It's the housing shortage, you see. I've simply got to be near the office. So you're living with your mother in the North.

GIRL: (*Moving down stage.*) Charming!

MAN: Naturally it's a long journey and you don't get up to London very often...

(*There is a knock at the door.*

The MANAGERESS enters with a cup of tea. The GIRL crosses to the MANAGERESS. The MAN moves to the fireplace.)

MANAGERESS: Now drink that down and you'll feel the benefit. You must be worn out.

MAN: She's not very tired...

MANAGERESS: But they *are* a strain. On a long journey...

GIRL: What are?

(*The MAN picks up the A.B.C. from the mantelpiece.*)

MANAGERESS: Running up and down the corridors. Poking their noses into the first class. Playing with the chickens in the guard's van and locking themselves in the toilets.

(*The MAN puts the A.B.C. back on the mantelpiece.*)

GIRL: (*Lost and confused.*) It's like a sort of dream.

MANAGERESS: Never seen London before? This is their first glimpse of the smoke?

GIRL: What's she saying?

MANAGERESS: Their first Tube and double-decker? If I know anything that'll mean the Chamber of Horrors for you this afternoon. (*She sits on the bed.*)

GIRL: Is she out of her mind?

MANAGERESS: You know what mine does on a long journey?

GIRL: How can I possibly tell?

MAN: Well, I think you've finished your tea.

GIRL: It's hot.

MAN: You don't want it?

GIRL: Might as well...

MANAGERESS: On a long journey mine always takes out his box of crayons and chalks the marks of an infectious disease on his face before the journey commences.

GIRL: What for?

MANAGERESS: To ensure privacy in the compartment.

GIRL: (*Interested.*) Does it work?

MANAGERESS: Nine times out of ten. And if not...

GIRL: What?

MANAGERESS: He can make it pretty sticky for those that do venture in.

(*The MAN tries to speak.*)

But why I mentioned the Chamber of Horrors was this. When his cousins come on a visit from the North, it's always downstairs at the Tussaud's they make their first port of call.

MAN: Ours doesn't like that sort of thing. (*He moves towards the GIRL.*) Finished your tea, dear?

MANAGERESS: They don't like the Tussaud's? (*She rises and moves back a little.*)

MAN: Gentle, nervous kiddies, weak on history... (*He takes the cup from the GIRL and crosses to the MANAGERESS.*) You'll want to wash the cup up.

GIRL: (*Following him.*) Who are we talking about now?

MAN: Our children.

GIRL: (*Breathless.*) How many?

MANAGERESS: (*Accusingly.*) Three.

(*The MAN takes a quick drink of tea.*)

GIRL: Three?

MANAGERESS: Two boys and then your husband got his girl.

GIRL: Congratulations!

MAN: The time's getting on.

MANAGERESS: (*Taking the cup and saucer.*) I've got things to do, too. They'll be excited though, seeing auntie after all this time...

(*The MANAGERESS exits.*)

GIRL: Who's auntie?

(*The MAN tries to kiss her, but she turns her face away. She repeats insistently.*)

Who's auntie?

MAN: (*Moving down left.*) My married sister. She lives near the heath.

GIRL: Is that a good thing?

MAN: It's a godsend, as I told the Manageress. She can look after the kiddies.

GIRL: They're with her now...

MAN: She's quite capable – a trained nurse, that's what she used to be.

GIRL: (*Moving away down stage.*) Well, I should think they must be totally confused in their small minds.

MAN: Confused?

GIRL: Bewildered.

MAN: But why...

GIRL: For heaven's sake! What's it all about? Those quiet, gentle, little children with no sense of history are woken out of their warm beds at what must have been a cruelly early hour in Scarborough and dragged all the way to London only to be dumped with some ex-matron of an aunt while we scurry off to a small private hotel in King's Cross!

(*The MAN tries to speak.*)

And another thing about those children – where are they going to spend the night?

MAN: (*Guiltily.*) I thought...

GIRL: (*Challengingly.*) Well?

(*There is no reply.*)

(*Incredulously.*) You can't mean...

MAN: You'll all want to get back.

GIRL: To *Scarborough?*

MAN: Well, it is home. Only temporary, of course.

(*The GIRL rushes to the mantelpiece and seizing the A.B.C. turns the pages with bitter determination. The MAN moves centre to the foot of the bed.*)

GIRL: Scarborough. Saxmundham. Scably... Scarborough! Pop. forty-three thousand, nine hundred and eighty-five. Early closing Wed. London two hundred and three miles! Four hundred and six miles a day you would laughingly see me travel with three young children who can't be all

that grown up and responsible, bearing in mind the fact,
which you very well know, that I am not a day over
twenty-three.

MAN: (*Moving down right; miserably.*) The boys were twins.

GIRL: You know what.

MAN: What?

GIRL: *I don't think you're fit to have children!* I can't think
why you went on breeding for the selfish reason of
wanting a girl after the twins, and, when I've given birth
to them and all that, you can only think of sending them
on pointless and exhausting train journeys practically the
whole length of the British Isles...

MAN: (*Moving towards her to left centre.*) Listen!

GIRL: (*Moving down to him.*) They'll be dropping asleep by
the time we get home, and suppose we can't find a taxi...

MAN: Please, let me explain...

GIRL: Four lives you've got in your hands.

MAN: I was desperate!

GIRL: *Then why couldn't you come up to Scarborough for the
week-end?*

(*The clock chimes the half hour.*)

MAN: There's so little time...

GIRL: (*Moving away down left.*) Such inconsiderate
behaviour!

MAN: (*Following her a little way.*) Do we have to talk?

GIRL: I certainly think you owe me an explanation.

MAN: I'm in love with you.

GIRL: You have odd ways of showing it. If that's the way
you treat all your wives!

MAN: (*Moving towards her.*) You're not my wife!

GIRL: That's one consolation.

MAN: We love each other!

GIRL: What about it?

MAN: Let's be thankful. Let's celebrate the revolution. Our
victory against the dull rulers of our lives! Look at this
room! Look, what we've achieved!

GIRL: What?

(*They look round at the room.*)

MAN: A beach-head in a dark grey enemy country! A small clearing in the jungle behind our own impermanent and wobbling stockade. A place on our own! Does it matter what I had to say to win it for us? (*He moves centre.*)

GIRL: Sometimes it matters.

MAN: (*Turning to her.*) What?

GIRL: What you have to say.

MAN: (*Moving to the foot of the bed.*) It doesn't matter.

GIRL: Anyway I'm curious to know.

MAN: What?

GIRL: How you got us here.

MAN: Later on…

GIRL: No, now! (*She moves up stage.*) I want to know exactly who I am. I puzzle myself at the moment.
(*The MAN takes a quick look at his watch, and then sits on the bed.*)

MAN: Well, I was walking along the street and I happened to catch sight of this hotel. It seemed small and…

GIRL: Unostentatious?

MAN: So I was faced with a problem. How could a man and a…

GIRL: Woman?

MAN: Exactly. Without any kind of luggage…

GIRL: We've got no luggage!

MAN: Take a room for an hour, in the middle of the day…

GIRL: Your only time for adventure.

MAN: That was the problem. I solved it!

GIRL: (*Moving towards him.*) You did?

MAN: After a little thought. I said we wanted somewhere to talk…

GIRL: (*After a slight pause.*) To what?

MAN: To talk.

GIRL: (*After another slight pause.*) It's incredible…

MAN: The Manageress understood.

GIRL: She hadn't got to face the endless journey back with three uncontrollable children.
(*The MAN rises and moves right centre. The GIRL follows.*)
Anyway, we could have done that in the lounge.

MAN: What?

GIRL: Talked.

MAN: No privacy.

GIRL: Or at our married sister's – the one who lives up by the heath.

MAN: (*After a moment's hesitation.*) Well, no – we went into that. It wasn't at all a practicable idea.

GIRL: Why not?

MAN: (*Turning down stage.*) Well, there's no point in digging up that old buried hatchet.

GIRL: What?

MAN: (*Turning to her.*) You see, you've never got on with my married sister.

GIRL: Never?

MAN: She stayed away from the wedding.

GIRL: (*Moving down left centre.*) Oh, did she?

MAN: Since then there's been a bit of an east wind between us.

GIRL: I should think so.

MAN: Just one of those little failures of understanding that happen in all families. It wasn't at all your fault. You certainly did your best, I told the Manageress that, but, well there it is.

GIRL: What a lot you told that Manageress!

MAN: (*Moving towards her.*) To get the room.

GIRL: Yes.

MAN: All for that.

GIRL: I suppose so.

MAN: (*Moving to her.*) Because I honestly loved you. (*He tries to kiss her.*)

GIRL: (*Breaking away from him down right centre.*) What's she got against me?

MAN: Who?

GIRL: Aunty.

MAN: Nothing.

GIRL: What kept her away from the wedding then?

MAN: Well, you know how people are, old-fashioned ideas.

GIRL: (*Turning to face him.*) You mean you *told* her?

MAN: What?

GIRL: (*Pointing at the bed.*) About this afternoon.

MAN: Now where have you got me? (*He looks at her in confusion and then moves away to the fireplace.*)

GIRL: Where've you got yourself? Do you ever stop to ask yourself that? I mean, whose side are you on, anyway?

MAN: Yours, of course.

GIRL: Well, it doesn't look so very much like it! Keeping up such friendly relations with a woman who wouldn't even condescend to turn up at the reception my father can ill afford, leaving our children to the tender mercy of this starched and creaking old matron with her grey moustache and celluloid cuffs, who treats me (*Crying.*) like a nasty mess in the out-patients. (*She moves centre.*) I should have thought you might show a little more honesty and integrity and act more like the bright shining husband in glittering armour that you let me think you were when you tricked me...

MAN: I tricked you?

GIRL: You let me believe I was the only thing that mattered in your life.

MAN: You are!

GIRL: Now it seems any old aunt gets more consideration...

MAN: *It's not true!*

(*There is a pause. Then she moves over to him, and they break down in each other's arms.*)

GIRL: (*Sobbing.*) I'm sorry.

MAN: I'm sorry, too.

GIRL: You are?

MAN: I'm sorry we had to have all these complications.

GIRL: I didn't mean you tricked me.

MAN: I know you didn't.

GIRL: I just thought you might write to her, that's all.

(*The MAN takes a step back.*)

Nothing abusive, of course, nothing to bring us down to her level. Just 'in view of your attitude, it would no doubt be more convenient if you let at least twenty years elapse before paying your first call'. You never wrote her a line like that?

MAN: Of course I didn't. Because...

GIRL: You never came out in the open in support of me?

MAN: Because...

GIRL: (*Advancing on him, her anger returning.*) And who is she, anyway? Trained nurse? What's that? Florence Nightingale? Madam Curie? What's her great achievement? Rolling up some royalty in a blanket bath? (*The MAN sits in the chair down left of the fireplace.*) Being present at the removal of a so-called appendix from a so-called film star in a nameless nursing home in Hammersmith? I know those trained nurses! Heartless! (*She moves away centre.*) Knit and gossip all night and drink cocoa in the face of death! (*She comes back to him.*) Just let her try and hold down my job which isn't just automatic and calls for some creative imagination! We do two hundred versions of the Spanish ivy pattern now – and not one of them a repeat.

MAN: I know.

GIRL: Well, you should appreciate that.

MAN: Don't worry about her.

GIRL: Why not?

MAN: She's not real.

GIRL: She's real to me! (*She moves to the side of the bed.*) (*The MAN follows her.*) (*She turns.*) Snobs! That's one thing we don't tolerate in our family, thank God. That's one type of person that just seems to me so low that I couldn't get any lower if I got down on my stomach and wriggled under that door! My father's been an ordinary printer for the best part of thirty years, but there's only one type of person that he wouldn't give house-room to in any circumstances and that's a *snob*. Also he can't put up with the Irish. But he's never been the sort to go poking and prying into someone's past history and drawing aside his skirts and refusing to attend the ceremony of marriage and turning young children against their mother when her back is turned.

MAN: Look at me. (*He sits her on the bed and himself sits beside her.*)

GIRL: Well?

MAN: We're alone.

GIRL: Yes?

MAN: Remember. Nothing else exists. Everyone else in the world has faded away. All our friends and families –
(*The GIRL tries to interrupt.*)
– and relations. We're alone here together. Fixed and solitary in this moment of time. No-one can come near us. (*He moves close, about to kiss her.*)
(*There is a quick knock at the door. The MANAGERESS enters.*)

MANAGERESS: I've found a shilling for you! (*She goes to the gas-fire and puts in the shilling.*) Now. Who's got a match?
(*The MAN and the GIRL rise. The GIRL moves down right. The MAN moves to right of the fireplace and silently hands the MANAGERESS a box of matches.*)
Of course you'll hardly be needing all that shilling's worth now, will you?
(*There is a pause.*)
You'll be good Samaritans to the next occupants. (*She lights the gas.*) There now! That makes it more cosy and home-like, doesn't it?
(*There is a pause.*)
I always say, after a nice coal fire I like a nice gas-fire. (*There is another pause. The MAN holds out his hand for his matches. The MANAGERESS puts them in her pocket.*)
A nice fire is nice to talk by, and you'll want to get on with your discussion.

MAN: Yes.

MANAGERESS: If you give me that change then.

MAN: We had two sixpences.

GIRL: (*After searching her bag.*) We put them down the slot.

MAN: I've only got ninepence after the taxi.

MANAGERESS: (*Stonily.*) Well, you asked me to get the shilling. I distinctly heard you.

MAN: Yes, we did.

MANAGERESS: Naturally I assumed you had change to give me for it.

MAN: (*Taking out his wallet.*) I've got a pound. (*He takes out a pound note.*)

MANAGERESS: That's hardly very convenient. How can I change a pound at short notice?

MAN: I don't know.

MANAGERESS: I had to *send out* for the shilling!

GIRL: We've given you a shilling already.

MANAGERESS: What?

GIRL: My two sixpences straight down the slot with no result at all!

MANAGERESS: Really.

GIRL: You can't expect to get any more out of us.

MANAGERESS: Me? I'm not making a penny! That goes straight to the North Thames Gas Board.

GIRL: With the price of the room add on two shillings for gas...

MANAGERESS: I've never had any complaints before.

GIRL: How much was the room?

MAN: Well...

GIRL: Tell me, how much?

MAN: (*Turning up stage.*) Two guineas.

GIRL: For an hour!

MANAGERESS: It's no concern of mine if you leave after an hour.

GIRL: Two guineas an hour! Forty-eight guineas a day –
(*The MAN looks at the MANAGERESS.*)
– for a broken-down old bed and peeling wallpaper and a gas-fire that's daylight robbery and the use of a chiming clock and the A.B.C. of trains! We're in the wrong business! (*She moves a towards the MANAGERESS.*) I knew it didn't pay to be creative!
(*The MANAGERESS moves centre to meet the GIRL. The MAN tries to part them during the following speech, and failing, moves up right to the window.*)

MANAGERESS: I've had twenty-five years in the King's Cross area as Manageress of this private hotel and I've never heard words like that spoken to me before.

GIRL: Well, it's about time you did. And what about that little boy of yours?

266

MANAGERESS: What about him!

GIRL: Playing round the station. Going round all the telephones and pressing the button B's, I should think most likely.

(*The clock chimes three-quarters of an hour.*)

MANAGERESS: I've a very good mind...

GIRL: I'm perfectly sure there's some law...

MANAGERESS: I put myself out to get you a little warmth...

GIRL: Some people work for their living!

MANAGERESS: Because you've had a long day!

MAN: (*Coming down to the MANAGERESS in despair and forcing the pound note on her.*) Take this.

(*The MANAGERESS takes the note and crosses to the door. The MAN moves to the side of the bed. The GIRL crosses left.*)

Don't come back with the change.

MANAGERESS: Peeling wallpaper! I tell you, I've had government officials sleep in this very room. Indian gentlemen. And very nicely spoken. Only I was sorry for the fix you and your husband was in I agreed to take you for the hour. He wanted to talk to you, you see. On a serious matter! *Well he might!*

(*The MANAGERESS exits. There is a pause. The MAN crosses to the door.*)

MAN: I thought we'd never get rid of her. (*He locks the door.*)

GIRL: (*After a pause.*) Well, she's gone now.

(*The MAN returns to centre. Another pause.*)

MAN: We've only got fifteen minutes left...

GIRL: Now it's coming.

MAN: Darling, won't you take your coat off?

GIRL: I dread it.

MAN: (*Moving to her.*) No, come on...

GIRL: I'm sorry. (*She goes to him and takes his hands.*) I know it's silly and stupid and weak of me perhaps. But ever since I was a child, quite a young girl, you understand, this has been something I have dreaded and I knew it was coming the moment I stepped into this roam. I know that was why you brought me here. But whatever the good reason you may very well have had, I don't want it to happen.

MAN: But we discussed...

GIRL: (*Stepping back from him.*) It's just a horrible feeling I get in the pit of my stomach. I've felt it coming on and perhaps that was why I was a bit sharp with that old girl, although heaven knows when you have to count every penny, and sometimes travel on the Tube with nothing but a hopeful wink at the ticket collector, it makes you sick to see money demanded on that exorbitant scale! However. If anyone says to me, 'Could I have a word with you?' it's always and quite certainly the one word I don't want to hear.

MAN: What do you mean?

GIRL: The head designer may say: 'I'd like a word with you in the office,' or my father says: 'We'd like to talk to you if you can arrange to be home early next Wednesday,' or they say: 'This Underground ticket looks a bit exhausted, could we talk to you about it?' and whatever it is they have to say I don't want them to say it, so please forgive me if all I can think of at this moment is *I don't want you to talk to me.*
(*There is a pause.*)

MAN: I'm not going to talk.

GIRL: (*After a pause.*) What do you mean?

MAN: You've got nothing to worry about.

GIRL: Why did she say that then?

MAN: Say what?

GIRL: That you wanted me – for a serious talk?

MAN: Please listen. (*He takes her hands and tries to get her to sit on the bed.*)

GIRL: No!

MAN: (*Sitting on the bed himself.*) We've got so little time, and if this goes wrong...

GIRL: What?

MAN: What've we got left?

GIRL: It seems I've always got the children...

MAN: (*Pulling her gently down to sit on his left.*) Don't you see, you're the one oasis in the desert of my days and nights. The one person that's saved me from suddenly growing old and spent among the business lunches, and the Scandinavian lamp-shades, and the bright red hang-it-yourself wallpaper. So if we've got a few minutes, don't let's waste them.

GIRL: (*After a pause.*) No. (*She pauses again.*) I did love you. When you stood up so silver against the light – and when I got out of the lift and a draught of air from the print-room blew up my skirt I saw you turn away your eyes and spare me the look of curiosity – and I thought – here's someone quite exceptional in this building riddled with intrigue and romance...

(*They kiss. The MAN tries to take her into his arms.*)

What were you going to say?

MAN: When?

GIRL: I mean it must have been something of great importance.

MAN: It was nothing.

GIRL: To bring a person all that way on the train to hear it.

MAN: Nothing.

(*The GIRL rises and stands back from him, looking at him carefully, as if for the first time.*)

GIRL: I mean you're not the sort of man that wants a woman to travel all that way just to discuss the weather, are you! It must have been something serious and terrible you had to disclose.

MAN: I never thought.

GIRL: And that journey! What about it? Hour after hour, watching the frozen lines, trying to keep the children quiet. All the time the thought going round in my head – he's got something to tell you. What's it going to be? What's so bad it can't be stuck in an envelope or said out over the telephone? Are you the sort of man that would keep a woman in suspense like that?

MAN: Of course I'm not.

GIRL: But it must be days ago you asked me to come up. How do you think I've been feeling since then. *Do you think I've had much sleep? Do you care?*

MAN: Don't you understand?

GIRL: No. You haven't told me yet. (*She faces out front.*) Let's face it now. Let's get it out of the way at last!

MAN: There's nothing to say.

(*There is a pause. Then they look at each other.*)

GIRL: Or are you the sort of man that would bring his wife all this way to tell her something of great importance which might affect their whole lives and then shut up as tight as an oyster the moment he was in her presence!

MAN: No.

(*There is a pause. The GIRL rises and crosses to his right.*)

GIRL: Coming to look at you clearly with the light in front of you I think that's the sort of man you might be.

MAN: I'm not. Listen…

GIRL: Because it can only be one thing, can't it? For me to have come all this way to hear it, it can only be one logical thing.

MAN: (*Interested in spite of himself.*) What?

GIRL: That it's over. Finished. (*She sits on the foot of the bed.*) You don't care about the children and me any more. Oh, it was very convenient for you, having me tucked away at the end of a long cold railway line! It gave you plenty of scope to cultivate your friendships in the office. To take girls down in the lift and lure them into strange hotels during the lunch hour. You were able to take full advantage of the two hundred and three miles you so carefully put between us. So now you'll write a letter starting 'No doubt this will come as a terrible shock to you…' which you want me to hand in to give you your so-called freedom. Isn't that what it all comes to, if you had the courage to put it into words?

MAN: I never thought of that!

GIRL: Yes, you did. When you started to talk to the Manageress! When you told her the story. The story had to end, didn't it? Can you think of a different ending?

MAN: (*After thought.*) There must be one, somewhere.

(*The clock begins to chime two o'clock. The GIRL rises first – then the MAN rises.*)

GIRL: It's over. (*She looks at him with tenderness and pity.*)
You should never have explained our presence.
(*The GIRL exits.*)

MAN: Wait. Wait a minute.
(*But the GIRL has gone. The MAN looks round the empty room. He puts on his hat and stoops to the gas-fire. He hesitates, puts on his spectacles, and then turns off the gas. He crosses to the downstage corner of the bed, and there notices that his overcoat is undone – the overcoat that he never took off. He turns towards the door, braces himself to face the world outside, and exits as the curtain falls.*)

The End.